KT-173-493

Pete Hill, MIC, FRGS

Pete has been walking and climbing for many years, and runs his own company, Highlander Mountaineering, in the Highlands of Scotland, delivering rock- and mountain- sports' courses at the highest level for a number of years. An associate instructor with Glenmore Lodge, Scotland's National Outdoor Training Centre, he holds the top UK qualification, the Mountain Instructor Certificate, and is a full member of the Association of Mountaineering Instructors. He is also a Fellow of the Royal Geographical Society.

Pete has climbed extensively all over the world, and has led expeditions to the Nepalese and Indian Himalayas, including three first ascents in Kashmir. Closer to home, he has climbed the Matterhorn and Eiger north faces in winter, and has also done a lot of eminently more sensible things!

As far as other interests are concerned, Pete is a member of the International Association of Egyptologists, as well as a life member of the United Kingdom Tae Kwon-do Association. He shares his home in the Scottish Highlands with his wife Ravelle and daughters Rebecca and Samantha.

If you are interested in gaining experience in rock climbing or mountaineering by attending a course, Pete can be contacted through his web site at: **www. highlandermountaineering.co.uk**

Stuart Johnston, MIC

Stuart has been delivering mountaineering instruction and guiding at the highest level since 1991, and is an associate member of staff at Glenmore Lodge, Scotland's National Outdoor Training Centre. He holds full membership of the Association of Mountaineering Instructors (AMI) and possesses a Mountaineering Instructor Certificate (MIC).

An active mountaineer, Stuart provides training and assessment programmes for a wide range of National Governing Body awards/qualifications, to aspiring mountain leaders and instructors.

Stuart has an extensive background in the field of training and development, designing and delivering training programmes at national levels for corporate organisations. He also thrives on designing and managing corporate team-challenge events embracing many industries and products.

His main objective is to provide his clients with knowledge which will enhance their experience, and to help them to live lives that are more fulfilling. This, together with his integrity and knowledge of his subject, gains trust and confidence from all.

Today Stuart continues to provide an all-season event-management consultancy and professional mountaineering instruction/guiding business based in Scotland. To find out more about any of these services contact: **www.climbmts.co.uk**

The Association of Mountaineering Instructors

The Association of Mountaineering Instructors (AMI) is the representative body of professionally qualified mountaineering instructors in the British Isles. AMI is committed to guaranteeing quality and promoting good practice in all mountaineering instruction.

AMI members are highly experienced mountaineers who have undergone rigorous training and assessment to qualify under the United Kingdom Mountain Training Board (UKMTB) Mountain Instructor Scheme. They are trained not only in technical mountaineering skills but also in the personal skills of teaching and mountain leadership. Only instructors holding the MIA (Mountain Instructor Award) or the MIC (Mountain Instructor Certificate) qualifications are permitted to become full members and display the AMI logo.

The AMI ensures the continuing development of instructors through a series of workshops and training courses, which means that members remain at the forefront of technical and coaching developments.

Further information about the AMI can be found on its web site at **www.ami.org.uk**

The
MOUNTAIN SKILLS
Training Handbook

Pete Hill & Stuart Johnston

Foreword by Nigel Williams

David & Charles

Photograph, page 2: Beinn Alligin, Scotland

A DAVID & CHARLES BOOK

David & Charles is a subsidiary of F+W (UK) Ltd., an F+W Publications Inc. company

First published in the UK in 2000
Reprinted 2002, 2003
First paperback edition 2004
Reprinted 2006

Copyright © Pete Hill and Stuart Johnston 2000, 2004

Distributed in North America
by F+W Publications, Inc.
4700 East Galbraith Road
Cincinnati, OH 45236
1-800-289-0963

Pete Hill and Stuart Johnson have asserted their rights to be identified as authors of this work in accordance with the Copyright, Designs and Patents Act, 1988.

A catalogue record for this book is available from the British Library.

ISBN 0 7153 1848 9

All photographs by Derek Croucher except pp8, 40, 104 & 116 by Pete Hill, Stuart Johnston and Steve Blagbrough

Artwork by Ethan Danielson

Printed in Singapore by KHL Printing Co Pte Ltd for David & Charles
Brunel House Newton Abbot Devon

Visit our website at www.davidandcharles.co.uk

ACKNOWLEDGMENTS

We are very grateful to a number of people who helped in the production of this book.

Eric Pirie, Steve Blagbrough and Shaun Roberts have been invaluable in shaping its outcome. They are all mountain instructors, qualified to the highest level, and have burnt a large amount of midnight oil proof-reading the text for us, for which we are eternally grateful.

Nigel Williams, as well as writing the Foreword, provided us with much-needed inspiration throughout the writing process, and without his guidance our task would have been far more difficult.

Our thanks must go to Rab Carrington Ltd, who provided the clothing that we used in the photographs, and which was also used during our technical work-shopping sessions for the diagrams. Our days out with a camera and note book were made far more comfortable due to them, and their excellent kit stood up to the worst weather that a Scottish winter (and summer!) could throw at us. Details of Rab products can be found on their web site at www.rab.uk.com.

Thanks must also go to our long-suffering families, who have put up with months of neglect while we both giggled and grinned our way through the text, in shadowy computer-screen-lit rooms across the country.

PETE HILL & STUART JOHNSTON

PUBLISHERS' NOTE

Throughout this book 'he' has been used to avoid awkward constructions such as 'he/she', 'his/hers' and so on. All the techniques covered are equally applicable to men and women.

Contents

KARABINERS

Screwgate karabiners have been referred to at a variety of places throughout this work. It is assumed that, as soon as they have been clipped, they will be screwed in to the locked position. Also, as HMS or 'pear shaped' karabiners are essential for the smooth running of certain systems, these have been highlighted in the text. If 'HMS' is not mentioned, then a standard 'D' shape will suffice. Please note that the authors do not encourage the use of karabiners using an automatic security system for the gate locking procedure.

Foreword

Mountaineering is about enjoyment and recreation, meeting physical and often mental challenges in the extremes of our rich and varied landscape. Learning the skills of mountaineering has often been done through trial and error somewhere on the knife-edge between adventure and misadventure.

Guiding others in the mountains is an old and honourable profession, and man's ingenuity, modern equipment, accurate maps and related paraphernalia have made it into a sophisticated business. The UK has one of the most developed systems of instructor/leader awards and the number of qualified instructors is increasing rapidly. It is therefore very appropriate that this book should be published pulling together the themes of each of the awards into one book. It is worth having a look at some of the older books on mountaineering techniques to see how far safety and training has moved on. It should also be a reminder that we never stop learning as we operate in an ever-changing environment. It should also be noted that, although these awards are UK based, the skills contained within are universal.

The Mountain Skills Training Handbook provides a wealth of up-to-date material that reflects current thinking and practice around the world. When 'playing' in the outdoors there is often not a clearly defined way of doing things. The skills clearly illustrated and explained in these pages have to be practised and require sound judgement applied appropriately. Good judgement is born out of experience usually combined with a good handful of epics. Successful professional instructors like Pete and Stuart have an added talent, and that is the ability to communicate and make learning an enjoyable experience, even in the worst of conditions.

The Mountain Skills Training Handbook is an excellent, practical and entertaining guide for the recreational and professional mountaineer alike.

Nigel Williams, Glenmore Lodge

Introduction

The incentive for this book has come from mountaineers, both active and aspiring. We are frequently asked where the skills that we teach can be found in printed form; that is, presented in a practical, down-to-earth manner and easy to relate to. Although many instructional books exist on the market, we have found none that fitted these criteria, as all too often publications rely on the quantity rather than the quality of the information, making it difficult to extract the relevant techniques.

We believe that this book fills that gap. It presents skills in an easy-to-read manner, and we have phrased it in the same way as we might teach; thus it is practical, informative and completely up to date.

The contents are aimed at both the beginner and active mountaineer. We decided to start at a level that assumes a little walking or climbing experience, and have not dwelt on the practicalities of the softer skills such as choosing a rucksack or buying a compass – there are plenty of other books to perform that task. Instead, those technical skills relevant to modern-day mountaineering are introduced straight away, and a logical progression is made.

We hope that you enjoy studying the book, and would encourage you to take it out in the hills to be used as a reference when learning techniques, for it is only after repeated practice that skills can become second nature.

PETE HILL & STUART JOHNSTON
Scotland, 2000

*The Committee of the Association of Mountaineering Instructors
recommends this book as a relevant and up-to-date work, valuable to
both aspirant and experienced mountaineers.*

PART ONE: SUMMER

Mountain Leadership Skills

This section covers a number of the essential skills needed by anyone taking walking groups out into the hills. Some of the techniques are relevant to both summer and winter conditions.

Mountain Weather

In this chapter we highlight important aspects of mountain weather for people who use the mountains for recreational purposes. It is also important to point out that while there are many first-class mountain-weather publications available, this book differs as it illustrates a practical approach to weather forecasting prior to and during your planned trip. We offer you a guide to the varied conditions one would expect to experience in either summer or winter.

Our aim is to provide you with a basic understanding of how the weather works and to enable you to interpret weather charts and understand the prevailing conditions, as well as to start recognising meteorological hazards in the mountains.

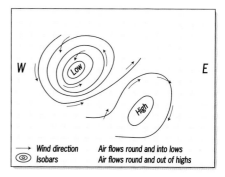

| → Wind direction | Air flows round and into lows |
| ◎ Isobars | Air flows round and out of highs |

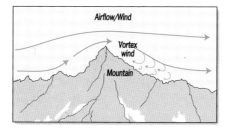

Airflow across a mountain range

Pressure Fuels the Weather

To understand how the weather works, we should first consider what weather actually is: it is elements of the atmosphere reacting with each other. Atmospheric pressure will vary in different places at different times. For example, mountaineers generally know that pressure falls with altitude; the higher up the mountain the lower the pressure. The Earth's surface is patterned with areas of pressure, or, as the weathermen say, high or low pressure.

■ Heavy and descending air will flow outwards; this movement of air pressure is known as the wind.

■ The greater the contrast between high pressure and low the stronger the wind.

Weather charts indicate the centres of high pressure and of low. We can also forecast the

pressure from the isobars, as well as the force and direction of the wind.

■ The closer the isobars the stronger the wind.

■ Observe the isobars on the weather maps for several days before your trip. Should the isobars remain widely spaced then high pressure is dominant and the weather should remain settled.

When your back is to the wind, the centre of the low pressure will be to your left. This helps you to know your position in relation to a low pressure system.

WEATHER FRONTS

Basic Rules

For the following sections, it is important to understand that cold air is heavier than warm air. It is also important to realise that warm air can hold a great deal more moisture than cold air but as air rises it expands and cools, lessening the amount of moisture that it can retain.

Warm and Cold Fronts

In addition to isobars, the weather charts will illustrate the position of warm and cold fronts. These mark the boundaries between the air masses with varied characteristics.

Warm Air

When warm air spirals round the centre of a low pressure, it will rise over the cooler air and develop into a warm front.

As the warm-front air is rising it will soon cool and begin to condense its water vapour, causing clouds and possible precipitation. On the weather map, the warm front is indicated by

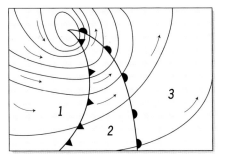

Fronts advancing
Section 1: It will be cold, showery and sunny.
Section 2: It will be warm and wet, overcast and the wind will be rising.
Section 3: It will be cold, dry and cloudy.

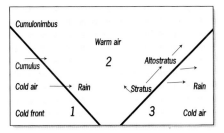

Section through front

small semicircles along the interface of the advancing front.

Cold Air

The warm, wet and windy weather behind the warm front will soon be displaced by cooler, heavier air. This cooler air will undercut the warm air forcing it to rise. The cold front is marked on the weather map by small triangles along the interface of the advancing front. The weather map below highlights a warm and a cold front advancing and explains what the weather will be doing at elevation.

Temperature Inversion

This is when cold air is trapped between the mountain tops and the ground, often seen in valleys. Warmer air will sit on top of the colder, causing the cold air to contain a lot of moisture in the form of thick fog. This condition often leads to superb weather on the mountain tops.

Wind Strength

The strength of the wind is generally controlled by the pressure gradient: the greater the difference the faster the airflow.

We know that the more packed are the isobars the stronger the wind, so a tightly packed isobar weather chart means a strong and serious wind hazard. The higher you go, the lower and less dense the air pressure becomes, and wind can travel faster in less dense air.

In the event that your intended route takes you over ridges, then you may wish to consider an alternative, as wind gust may also be present.

- Winds up to 40mph, are classed as gale force, but can generally be tolerable for most people.
- Winds up to 60mph are gale force going on hurricane force, with the most experienced considering getting well out of there!
- Winds gusting over 60mph become unmanageable for most, with an increased risk of being blown over and receiving an injury.

Wind Language

- Gust: a sudden increase of wind speed lasting for a few seconds.
- Squall: an expected increase of wind speed lasting up to a couple of minutes.
- Gale: a very strong wind.
- Lull: a decrease in wind speed.

Cloud Formation:
Warm Front Advancing

When in the mountains, look out for the advance of a front by watching the cloud increasing and spreading across the sky. The sequence of clouds when a warm front passes over are:

- Mares' tails: cirrus cloud.
- Mackerel sky: cirrocumulus cloud.

These clouds will form at the highest level, around 30,000ft, and are the first signs of condensation occurring. The interface between the cool air and rising warm air is not vertical but inclined, so the first signs of the approaching front is high above the ground.

Cirrus clouds will give us several hours of warning of the approaching disturbance, but the cloud must be spreading and increasing. If the cloud is dissolving and the sky is clearing then the weather should turn out fine.

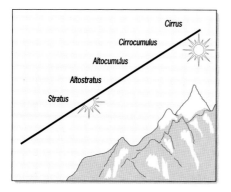

Cirrus

Cirrocumulus

Altocumulus

Altostratus

Stratus

Inclined front

OBSERVATION

Observe the patterns in the sky, especially to the west from where most of the weather will arrive. Altocumulus and altostratus are the clouds at middle height, with the altocumulus appearing before the altostratus, soon after which the sky will become overcast.

By now the inclined front is much lower than before and the weather will soon be changing at ground level. Stratus, the next phase, is a grey sheet of cloud obscuring the sun, and rain may soon follow.

Cloud Formation: Cold Front Advancing

Cumulus cloud will appear, and as the cold front approaches the weather will change dramatically. First there will be heavy rain as the cold air undercuts the warmer air and forces it to rise. The temperature will fall and the sky will clear. The sun will appear with the heavy clouds having been blown away leaving fair-weather cumulus cloud. Some showers may appear.

High Pressure

High pressure often means fine settled weather, because the descending air is generally stable with no tendency to rise. (Low pressure usually means that unstable air is associated with wind and rain.)

With the earth rotating in a spiralling motion, the airflow circulates round and out of high-pressure systems and round and into low-pressure systems. In the Northern hemisphere

the flows around the highs are clockwise and around the lows anti-clockwise, while in the Southern hemisphere the reverse takes place.

CLOUD IDENTIFICATION

Orographic Uplift

Clouds form by air being lifted away from the surface which is its heat source, causing it to expand and cool. It will then reach dew point at condensation level and above this level the cloud will form. There are a number of ways in which the air will lift. Here are the two most common:

■ Orographic lift: air rising over the hills and mountain tops.

■ Turbulence: air currents formed by wind blown across rough ground.

Altitude	Stability Cloud	Instability Cloud
Low	Stratus	Cumulus
	Stratocumulus	Cumulonimbus
	Nimbostratus	
Medium	Altostratus	Altocumulus
High	Cirrus	Cirrocumulus
	Cirrostratus	

Altitude: Low

Stratus and Stratocumulus: These are the type of clouds that obscure the mountain tops and will generally produce a light drizzle; visibility is often poor within these clouds, especially in winter. Gale-force winds are again associated with this formation, driving them across the tops.

Nimbostratus: This cloud type is associated with rain; it is a thick layer of stratus which supports larger water droplets.

Cumulus and Cumulonimbus: These cloud types are associated with showery weather often in short bursts not lasting more than an hour. Bright sunny intervals will also occur between these showers.

Cumulus clouds will form first often overland in the warm sunshine. Cumulus clouds are easily recognised by their flat bottoms and tall turret-like columns. A few hours on, the cumulus cloud has now grown into cumulonimbus. As they grow, their shape will expand into huge towers with flat bottoms and turret, anvil shapes swelling and dominating the skyline.

This weather pattern is often associated with high altitudes around a large low.

Altitude: Medium

Altostratus: This type will have little influence upon the weather. However, it is the next cloud in line prior to the arrival of a warm front. This cloud will easily block out the sun, with a brighter spot showing through the clouds. The sky will have a grey appearance and the wind speed will be increasing.

Altocumulus: This cloud has an unusual appearance to it, as it looks streaky and broken banded. The cloud will then thicken and lower in altitude. This often indicates that the atmosphere is becoming unstable, and rain with the possibility of thunderstorms is possible.

Altitude: High

Cirrus, Cirrocumulus and Cirrostratus: These types have no direct influence on the weather as you observe them. Cirrus is a thin wispy cloud, often known as 'mares' tails'. Cirrocumulus is also known as 'mackerel sky' or 'streets', as it has a uniform line appearance. It is then replaced by cirrostratus; this is a high layer of cloud giving you an indication that a warm front is approaching. Should you be high on a mountain you should be thinking of getting down within the next six hours as gale-force winds are frequently associated with it.

THE LAPSE RATE

The 'lapse rate' is the difference in temperature between sea level and altitude. This means that when the weather forecast provides you with temperature information, which is normally taken to be at sea level, you can then work out what the temperature should be at various altitudes when ascending or descending.

This information is really important when planning your route, particularly when winter climbing or when leading parties in the mountains.

Temp(Degrees)	Metres Above Sea Level	Air Type
Less 1	Per 100	Dry Air
Less 1	Per 200	Wet Air
Less 1	Per 150	Average

WEATHER-REPORT SOURCES

It is worthwhile noting that a forecast is only good for up to six hours in advance; this is why learning to interpret a weather forecast is a good skill to master. Ideally you need to know what's going to happen on the high mountain tops during your trip. However, you also need the practical skills to be able to identify the warning signs of gale-force winds and poor visibility, and those of generally unstable weather fronts advancing.

Today we have a wide variety of weather-reporting sources from which we can gain an up-to-date and reasonably accurate forecast. Ideally, it is good practice to check the forecast several days prior to your trip, particularly in winter. This information will provide you with valuable information on what the weather conditions have been like, and whether it may affect route planning. Weather forecasts can be obtained from the following sources:

■ Telephone and fax weather lines.
■ Weather and avalanche reports from local avalanche-information centres
■ The internet
■ Radio
■ Television
■ National and local press
■ Observation

It is also worthwhile remembering that weather forecasts are updated at various times of the day as well as evening forecasts for the following daylight hours.

Weather

WEATHER QUIZ

1 What fuels the weather engine ?

2 Facing into the wind, in which direction is the low pressure ?

3 When isobars remain close together, what does this mean ?

4 When a warm front is advancing, what is the cloud sequence ?

5 From a warm front, is the weather likely to be dry or wet ?

6 When a cold front is advancing, what is the cloud sequence ?

7 From a cold front will the weather be wet or dry ?

8 Wind language: what does 'gale' mean ?

9 If the wind blows at 25mph at 1,000ft what is the likely wind speed at 3,000ft ?

10 What do small semicircles on a weather map denote?

11 What is the orographic-uplift effect ?

12 At what altitude would you observe the following clouds ?

Cirrus, Cirrocumulus, Cirrostratus.

Altostratus, Altocumulus.

Stratus, Stratocumulus, Nimbostratus.

13 What is the average lapse rate ?

14 In a high camp, you wake up to find that the air pressure has fallen. Do you climb or retreat?

15 When forecasting, approximately how many hours in advance can we accurately predict the weather?

16 What is the purpose of isobars ?

17 Name six weather-forecast sources.

Answers

1. Air pressure
2. Right
3. Strong winds
4. Cirrus & cirrocumulus, cirrostratus
5. Dry then wet
6. Cumulus cloud will appear
7. Heavy rain at first
8. Strong and hazardous wind
9. 50 to 60 mph
10. Warm-front interface
11. Air rising over the mountain tops
12. High, medium, low altitude
13. 1 degree per 150 metres
14. Retreat
15. 6 hours
16. Identifies air pressure and wind direction
17. Newspapers, internet, radio, weather lines, television, avalanche-information centres etc

River Crossing

t may happen that, having enjoyed a day out in the hills, you find your return route blocked by a river whose waters are swollen by a cloudburst in the hills many miles away. That river stands between you and your objective. It is tempting to include just one word in this chapter that sums up river crossing in its entirety – **DON'T!**

It cannot be emphasised enough that river crossing should be avoided as far as possible. If it means a huge detour to find a bridge, then that must be the first choice. If there is no chance of finding a dry crossing point, then sitting out the night should also be considered, allowing the river a chance to abate. River water levels subside almost as fast as they rise, so the wait might not have to be that long.

The following procedures are for when no other option is available, the river *must* be crossed, and the decision to do so has been taken.

■

CROSSING POINTS

Consideration should be given to the suitability of any given crossing point. There will be less flow above a junction, where the river is split into two, rather than below. Bends are best avoided, as the outside bank will tend to be undercut, and the water will be deeper on the outside than the inside. A widening is a better place to cross than a narrowing, as the same volume of water will be spread over a larger area.

Easier gradients are worth looking for, as there is a good chance that the water will be moving slower across flatter areas of terrain. Areas of trees are best avoided, as there is a chance of fallen branches lying unseen under the water, and to slip and be caught by one of these would certainly mean being dragged under. An area with small islands can help, as can individual boulders. These will often create a back-wash, creating an area of slack water which can be used as a rest point. Consider also the bed of the river. Sandy chippings are easier to maintain footing on than rounded greasy boulders.

The consequences of a slip must be considered. Would this result in being gently washed to the bank somewhat further downstream, or is there a waterfall, log jam or waterchute nearby downstream? And what is happening upstream? Is it still raining hard, and

does this mean that there is a risk of half of your party crossing and the other half being stranded by the ever-rising water level?

EQUIPMENT CONSIDERATIONS

One of the most useful pieces of equipment for river crossing, apart from a boat, is a straight 2.5m-length of timber pole, and one is often supplied during formal instructional sessions. It may be useful to cast your mind back to the last time that you saw one of these lying next to a river in the mountains, and thus to try to work out some other way of obtaining a similar piece of kit. The closest that we can get using standard mountaineering equipment is by using ski poles, either singly or strapped together with tape from the first-aid kit. Taping them together will make them less flexible, offering more support when leant upon, and removing the baskets will make them easier to handle in the water.

Crossing points

PREPARATION

Rucksacks are surprisingly buoyant for a time, so they should be prepared by rolling up and securing the top enclosure. Waist belts should be left undone and shoulder straps kept loose – there is an argument for just having one shoulder strap on, but this may add to instability when in the water. Chest straps should not be used. Boots should be worn on all but the sandiest of river beds, but socks should be removed in order to keep the worst of the water off them and, more importantly, to provide a quick way of warming up feet when on the other side. It makes sense to wear waterproofs, both top and bottom, do them up and make sure that pockets are fastened.

Remember to brief all party members as to what is needed from them, as communication is often difficult from one bank to another when water is travelling fast. An important point to remember when crossing a river, using any of the techniques described, is to lessen the chance of the water knocking you over by facing upstream where possible. If facing downstream, the force of the water would push at the back of the knees and cause them to bend, throwing you off balance.

One Person Crossing

Face upstream, holding the pole vertically in front of you so that you create a strong triangle. Move each foot, one at a time, and resist the temptation to place it too close to the other. Then move the pole back to the apex of the triangle. Ensure that you have a secure footing and pole placement before moving on.

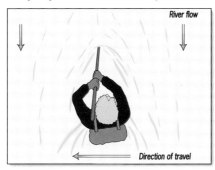

One crossing with pole

Two People Crossing

The most secure method is a variation of the single-person system.

- One person takes up position as above, the second stands behind him, also facing upstream, securely taking hold of the shoulder straps of the first's rucksack and leaning into give support. Progress is made by shuffling as above.
- A second method, when no poles are available, is for both people to stand at right angles to the flow facing each other, taking a firm grasp of each other's shoulder straps. Feet are kept

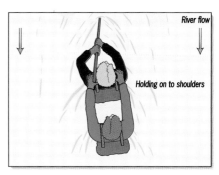

Two crossing with pole

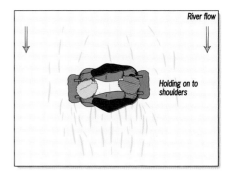

Two crossing without pole

wide, allowing a four-point stable base to be maintained. It is important to ensure that both stay sideways on to the flow – if one turns to face into it, the other will have a good chance of his knees being bent forwards by the flow.

Three People Crossing

Once again, the best method is to stand one behind another and shuffle across in a line, the front person using a pole for support.

- The three should firmly grasp each other's shoulder straps, keep their legs wide, and shuffle across, the person on the downstream side co-ordinating movement and keeping the group in line.
- If there are no poles to hand, a huddle can be made. The strongest person will be on the downstream side facing the flow. The second strongest will be positioned with his back to the direction of travel, the third will face across the river. It is unavoidable at this point having two people with their knees a little vulnerable to the flow, but good measured movements and support from each other will help counter this.

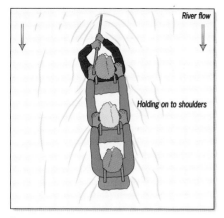

Three crossing with pole

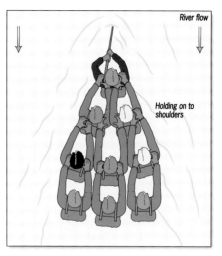

Arrowhead with nine people

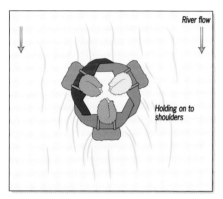

Three crossing without pole

Crossing with a Group

Depending upon your group's abilities, you may wish to cross as one large team, rather than split down into individual sections. There are two ways to organise this.

■ Firstly, the simplest method is, as before, to stand in a long braced line behind the leader with a pole. However, if more than four or five people are trying to cross, it becomes very difficult to co-ordinate the movements of each person. Inevitably the line will get out of true and present a larger surface area to the flow, with the subsequent chance of someone being knocked over.

■ A better method is to construct an arrowhead formation. The strongest person goes at the front, with extra support from a pole if possible. Two people go behind him, then three, then another three, and so on, not having more than three abreast. The weaker members, in this instance, will go in the middle of the pack, receiving support from the others. Shoulder straps are grasped, and the movement of the group is once again controlled from the front.

Roped Crossing

This should only be considered when all other possibilities have been exhausted. However, it must be accepted that there is a chance that a roped crossing will have to be organised.

■ Remembering that ropes and water DO NOT mix, the system given overleaf is the simplest to learn and set up. The positioning of the crossing must be carefully considered, taking into account all of the above points, as well as having a section of bank on either side of the crossing point that will allow unrestricted movement up and down it for some distance. Other important points must be remembered:

■ NEVER tie off the rope on either bank.

■ NEVER field the rope from a sitting position – it is important to be mobile at all times.

■ NEVER try to pull a fallen person upstream – he will immediately be pulled underwater.

■ NEVER tightly tie the person crossing into the loop.

■ NEVER let the rope fall into the water.

■ NEVER have any knots in the rope, apart from the central loop.

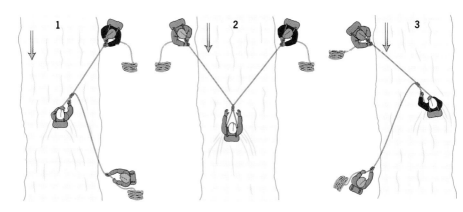

The 'V' System

Locate the centre of the rope, and tie an overhand knot on the bight into it, creating a large loop. The first to cross, usually not the leader but a well-briefed and reliable person, puts the loop round himself. It is not tightened up, but left loose. It may be decided to have the loop running under one arm and over the opposite shoulder, in order that it may be shrugged off if required.

■ One person takes station upstream of the crossing point, another positions himself downstream (1). The upstream person braces himself and provides support to the person crossing by means of the rope. The first may then cross, facing upstream. Should he lose his footing, the upstream belayer immediately runs downstream along the bank, the second belayer taking in the rope as he also moves downstream, and the fallen person is washed towards them. It is important that at no time is the rope held tight on the upstream side, as anyone fallen will be pulled under by the flow.

■ Assuming the first person crosses successfully, he takes off the loop and shuffles it back over to the first side, taking the rope in from the second belayer. The rope is best held high above the heads when doing this, as there is less chance of it catching in the water. The downstream person on the original bank can throw any spare rope across at the relevant moment when doing this, and the person on the far bank takes up position opposite the first belayer.

■ The second person to cross now steps into the loop, and receives support from either bank as he crosses, one belayer giving support until he reaches the centre, then the belayer on the far bank takes over (2). Should this person fall in, the

belayer giving support at that moment immediately runs downstream past him, pulling in on the rope as he goes, in order to bring him in to the side. The other belayer must allow sufficient slack on his rope to let this happen unhindered, but not to the extent that his rope either enters the water or is let go. Once the crossing has been successfully made, the loop is then pulled back across for subsequent group members.

■ When only one person is left on the original bank, he pulls the loop across, steps into it, throws his end of the rope across to a person on the opposite bank who takes up position downstream as for the first crossing, and the final member joins the rest (3).

OBSERVATIONS

1 There is a great reluctance by many people to knot the rope at any point, and quite rightly so. A knotted rope has a chance of catching on any submerged obstruction, causing either the rope to be lost or, more seriously, the dragging down of the person attached, with him being unable to escape the loop. For this reason, it may be decided to do without the loop altogether. If there is any concern that a dragged rope could catch, such as on a boulder-strewn river bed, it will be much better to keep the system clean and simply have the person crossing holding on to the rope for support. He should be positioned on the downstream side of it, to avoid being caught and pulled under should he stumble.

2 Following the crossing, chances are that your group will be wet and cold, and possibly quite tired. You should take time to ensure that all members are fit before moving on: getting inside a group shelter and having a food-and-drink break is a very sensible idea, and it does wonders for morale.

Security on Steep Ground

This chapter introduces the techniques necessary to provide a group with safe passage over an unexpected rocky hazard, either in ascent or descent.

■

GROUP MANAGEMENT ON AWKWARD TERRAIN

Emergency Techniques prior to Rope Deployment: Steep-ground Management

It is worthwhile exploring various options when managing the security of people on steep ground prior to deploying a rope. The leader of a group should always have this at the forefront of his thinking when faced with a situation:

■ Consider a safe route alternative.
■ Look for a line of least resistance through the steep ground, safe from falling debris.
■ Check out the route prior to committing your group to it.
■ Ensure that the leader can easily cross the ground to be negotiated.
■ Keep the least able group member near to the leader.
■ Explain to the group what you are doing.
■ Keep close together.
■ Brief the group on relevant terrain-crossing skills.
■ The leader can use his downhill arm to secure the weak group member by holding snugly on to his rucksack strap, thus providing support and reassurance.
■ The leader may consider tying an overhand knot in a large tape sling, creating a loop for the group member to slip round his waist, and continue to lead him under a tensioned line. The leader should be positioned up-slope of the member, as before.
■ Should more than one group member require assistance, then only one person should be led at any one time, while the others wait in a safe area.
■ It is vital that the leader instructs the group members on how to balance and scramble on awkward terrain. Should the ground be steep, wet and grassy, then the leader must consider an alternative route as this sort of terrain is extremely hazardous.

In any situation in which the group leader needs to think about safer alternative options, this can save much time. When a rope is deployed a leader must work very fast, and only experience, skill and knowledge can ensure a smooth transaction of rope management and group safety.

CONFIDENCE ROPING

What is confidence roping ?

A method used to secure one nervous, tired or injured person while descending, ascending or traversing a short section of ground. This type of roping is unplanned and is classed as an emergency procedure only.

Where would I use it ?

It can be used on any type of terrain, from scree slopes to short sections of snowy ground. There are two extremely important considerations when confidence roping. Firstly, the leader must be entirely confident in his own ability to cross safely the terrain that is proving a problem; and, secondly, as confidence roping only looks after one party member at a time, the rest of the group must also be completely happy and able to continue unaided. It must be emphasised that any danger perceived by the person being roped – such as the feeling of walking on angled wet grass and the assumption that a slip will turn into a catastrophic fall – should be imaginary and not real. If there is any objective danger to the leader or any group member, different tactics or route choice should be employed.

Method

■ This can be readied before it is needed. The rope is fed into the top of a rucksack, ideally inside a stuff bag, with a few inches of the rope tail protruding. To deploy the rope, pull

on the tail end. You will require around 3m.

■ Tie the end securely round the person's waist. No more than 1m from the waist attachment, tie an overhand knot on the bight, creating a small loop.

■ Hold below this knot with your downhill hand, with the rope to the person emerging from the little-finger side of your hand. The overhand knot becomes an effective stopper, preventing your hand from slipping along the rope. DO NOT put your hand through the loop created by the overhand knot. An alternative knot is the disappearing overhand knot (see below). This has the advantage that it is solid when held below, but when the rope is pulled from above the knot it undoes itself, useful if a direct belay needs to be quickly taken.

■ Should there be any excess rope between hand and rucksack, some butterfly coils can be positioned through the rucksack waist belt.

■ The arm holding the rope is positioned so that it is at a right angle with the elbow bent, so it can now act as a shock-loading mechanism, as it moves forwards and backwards maintaining tension at all times.

■ The body position of the leader is important, leaning slightly into the slope to counter any outwards pull, the edges of the boots being used to create extra purchase on slippery ground.

OBSERVATIONS

1 The leader must be uphill of the person at all times.

2 It is important that the waist tie is snug so that the loop cannot slip down over the client's hips, and he feels as though he is receiving support.

3 The leader must never take hand coils; this is only appropriate for short-roping terrain.

4 It is important that if the client slips, the leader must be able to hold him without compromising his own balance and safety.

Method: Moving Together

Once you decide on which direction you wish to travel, you need to think about the direction of pull from the knot tying off at the client.

■ The knot tying off the client should always be on the uphill side of the client. This is important to assist with the tensioning of the rope between client and leader.

■ To change direction the leader provides clear instruction to the client to stop, the leader swaps hands and then turns into the new position.

■ Knots pp42–6

- The client now turns into new position, facing uphill when making a turn, and sliding his waist-loop knot round to the uphill side.
- This process should be repeated when changing direction; with practice this technique is very quick to adjust.
- The uphill arm of the person is often best positioned behind the rope to the leader. This allows him to comfortably use his arm to support himself, particularly if he should take a small slip or stumble.

Winter Considerations

In winter conditions the transfer of hands requires some care as you will have your ice axe positioned in your uphill hand. To change direction and transfer smoothly, both leader and client stop.

The leader informs the client to take a good firm stance. Then, while maintaining tension on the rope, he places his ice axe under the arm holding the rope, changes direction by turning to face downhill, then retrieves the axe from under what is now the uphill arm with the uphill hand. This transfer is very quick when practised.

The client now turns round facing up-slope, using the ice axe to support the turn, and slides the waist loop knot round to new uphill position.

Another method on easy terrain is simply to place your ice axe into the snow, make the hand transfer as for summer then simply pick up the axe with the uphill arm.

OBSERVATION

While managing a party on steep ground the leader should be coaching the correct methods for use of feet and balance (and ice axe if appropriate) while travelling, and not be tempted to march blindly along pulling the person with him. Reassurance will go a long way in helping someone's confidence grow.

When managing a party on steep icy slopes or steep wet-grass terrain, always consider the consequences should someone slip: are there rocks at the bottom, are there hidden outcrops, how far will someone travel before stopping?

Should the leader be in any doubt as to the safety of the entire party, then he should be looking for an alternative descent or ascent. Good judgement is based on experience.

EMERGENCY GROUP ROPEWORK ON STEEP GROUND

This is a section dedicated to the solving of problems that may occur when crossing mountainous terrain with a group of friends or clients. The classic example is, when descending, finding your way blocked by a very short but greasy slab of rock, with an unpleasant landing at the bottom. Rather than spend a lot of time in re-ascent or searching for a way through, you may elect to lower your group with the security of a rope, then follow by abseil. Another reason may be finding your way barred by a short section of steep ground while ascending, with little option but to cross it.

It must be said that the descent scenario is the more likely, as this could well be encountered on a concave section of slope, at the end of the day when the group is tired, the light is fading and the possibility of motivating your group to go uphill again almost non-existent. In ascent, however, you are far more likely to see the steeper section from a distance, and be able to make an alternative route choice.

When leading groups in the hills under normal summer conditions, carrying a rope is a very sensible thing to do. For the sake of most trips, a 35m length of 9mm- or 10mm- diameter dynamic rope is ideal. It is important, though, to treat the rope as part of the first-aid kit – that is, there is *no intention* of deploying it. If you *are intending* to use the rope, that will mean that you are aware of the hazards that exist on your route and have either made a bad choice for the day, or are entering scrambling terrain which is another discipline entirely.

Finally, remember that the safety of your group is paramount. Never lower your group in darkness when you are not sure if they will reach safety, always be 100 per cent happy about the security of your anchors, and, if your abilities and the situation dictates, be prepared to sit out the night.

Anchors

It goes without saying that the security of your anchors must be beyond question. Having selected a likely-looking anchor, maybe a large boulder, and after considering such factors as

Security on Steep Ground

direction of pull and a suitable stance, start with a visual inspection. Is it part of the mountainside, or is it simply perched on other rock or turf? Progress then to tapping the boulder, and progress to kicking it. If you do this with one hand on the rock, you will be able to feel any vibration and movement transmitted through it. Try to move the boulder with a rocking action. When testing an anchor, ensure that you are trying to move it in the direction of loading – for instance, it is useless kicking into the hillside if the boulder is loose in an outward direction.

Group Safety

Although your attention will be taken up with organising the lower or scramble, do not neglect the well-being of your group. As soon as the rope is deployed, your group will be feeling somewhat uneasy, so reassurance is important. Make sure that people are positioned in an area that is safe for them to be in, and get them to sit down. Stopping your group halfway up a steep, black, dripping slab is not the mark of a good and attentive leader. Consider also members' safety when you or others are overhead. Having them huddled at the bottom of a gully, at the top of which you are trying to shift a 7-ton granite boulder, is completely unacceptable.

Attaching to an Anchor

There are many ways to attach yourself to an anchor point; the most relevant are given below. Overhand knots are extremely useful and quite acceptable; the bowline may also be considered for some applications.

If using a thread (such as two boulders securely butted together):

■ Pass the end of the rope through and tie a re-threaded overhand knot (in a similar fashion to the re-threaded figure of eight). Then tie an overhand knot further down the rope to create a loop to step into (1).

■ If tied on to the end of the

rope, a bight can be passed through the thread and back to the waist tie-in loop, and then connected (2).

If using a spike:

■ If not tied on to the rope, a large loop can be tied in the end of the rope using an overhand knot on the bight, it then being placed over the spike. A second overhand knot can then be tied further down the rope to create a loop to step into (3).

■ If attached round the waist, either loop the rope around the spike and attach it to yourself by using an overhand knot or figure of eight on the bight, or tie a loop in the rope and drop it over the rock (4).

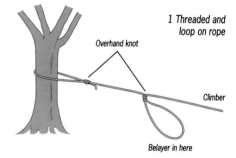

1 Threaded and loop on rope

Overhand knot

Climber

Belayer in here

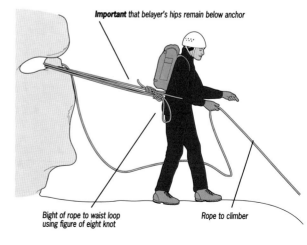

Important that belayer's hips remain below anchor

Bight of rope to waist loop using figure of eight knot

Rope to climber

2 Threaded bight to waist tie in

Knots pp42–6 • Tying in pp54–7

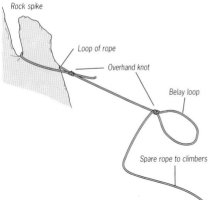

Rock spike
Loop of rope
Overhand knot
Belay loop
Spare rope to climbers

3 Spike with loop over and belay loop further down

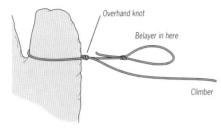

Overhand knot
Belayer in here
Climber

4 Spike with loop dropped over from waist tie

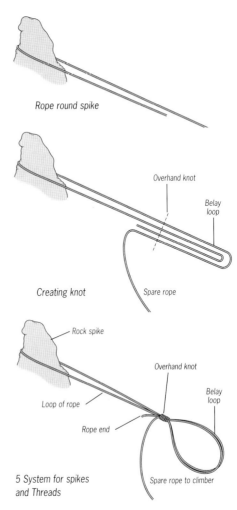

Rope round spike
Overhand knot
Belay loop
Creating knot
Spare rope

Rock spike
Overhand knot
Belay loop
Loop of rope
Rope end
Spare rope to climber

5 System for spikes and Threads

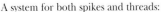

A system for both spikes and threads:

■ This last system is extremely quick and efficient if practised. Holding about 3ft from the end of the rope, loop the rope around the spike (or through the thread), and grasp the two lengths at the point from which you wish to belay. Fold the ropes back on themselves, so that you are now holding four pieces of rope in your hand. Tie an overhand knot in them to create a loop to belay from. Step into it, and, with a little practice, you will be able to tie it the right size first time. You have now created both an anchor attachment and belay point by tying just one overhand knot (5).

Lowering

This is the safest means of getting your group down an awkward step. The anchor selected in this case is a solid spike with a smooth back to it. While organising the lower, continuously consider the safety of the rest of your group, keeping them well away from the edge.

■ Tie yourself on to one end of the rope. Tie a Thompson knot in the other end (see diagrams overleaf) and fit it on to a group member. Attach yourself to the anchor in a suitable position, and prepare to lower.

■ In a less-than-perfect situation, you will need to directly lower the person by facing out and using a classic waist belay (1). It can be imagined how painful this would be for the belayer when lowering an adult, and it is rather hard to control. However, with an anchor such as we have selected, the spike can take a lot of the weight for us.

■ Face into the anchor, with the rope round your body for a classic belay (2). The rope leads up, round the anchor, and down to the person to be lowered. Take up a braced position, leaning out on the anchor with a foot braced uphill to stop any chance of being pulled in. You can now start to lower, keeping it steady, and make sure that the person adopts the correct posture of leaning back with straight legs and his heels on the rock.

■ Once he is down and in a safe area, he can take off the Thompson knot and remain there until the rest of the group joins him.

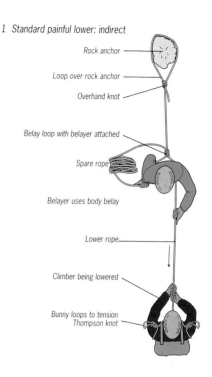

Rock anchor
Loop over rock anchor
Overhand knot

Belay loop with belayer attached

Spare rope

Belayer uses body belay

Lower rope

Climber being lowered

Bunny loops to tension Thompson knot

THOMPSON KNOT

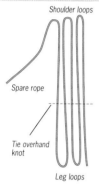

Shoulder loops

Spare rope

Tie overhand knot

Leg loops

This a very useful knot for lowering, but it should not be used for climbing, either up or down, as the leg loops drop down and catch behind the knees. Ensure that the knot is adjusted to be by the sternum for each person, and the rope to the lowering system is coming out of the top of the knot. To avoid having to retie the knot for each person, make the first one over-generous and take up the

slack by tying 'bunny's ears' at the shoulders. Ensure that they are tied just in front of the shoulder, where the person lowered can reach to untie them again.

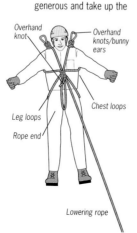

Overhand knot

Overhand knots/bunny ears

Chest loops

Leg loops

Rope end

Lowering rope

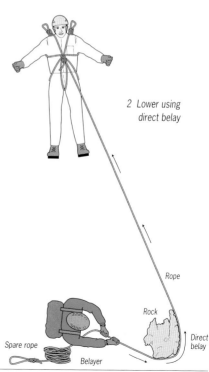

2 Lower using direct belay

Rope

Rock

Direct belay

Spare rope

Belayer

Abseiling

Abseiling, in this situation, is ONLY for the leader – you cannot expect other members of your group to do so. They should be lowered over the obstruction, then you follow by abseil descent. For many years, the 'classic' abseil has been the standard way of approaching a descent. However, another method has recently been introduced that is eminently more user-friendly, being less painful, easier to control and having less chance of being fallen out of. Introduced as the South African abseil, it can now be referred to as the 'new classic', as it is surely destined to become.

Its only disadvantage is that it requires the rope to be doubled, whereas the older version can be performed on a single thickness. However, as abseiling on a single thickness means that you will be abandoning the rope, the chances of needing to abseil like this are hopefully few and far between. We would encourage you to find out about the original classic. However, here we are only going to describe the new-classic method, that ensures that your most sensitive areas do not have smoke rising from them during the descent.

Method

■ Having selected the anchor and thrown the ends, equally, down the cliff, stand between the ropes. Take one in each hand, cross them behind your back and bring them to your sides in front of you. You now have a loop of rope on either side, running from each hand down behind you (1).
■ Step your left leg over the left loop, your right leg over the right (2), grasp the ropes together behind you between your legs, and bring them up together to be held in the right hand for

right-handed folk, and in the left hand for left-handed people (3).
■ This hand is your controlling hand: feeding the rope through controls your speed of descent. The other hand can hold one of the lengths of rope in front of you, but as it does not contribute to the descent, do not hold too tight. The further you go down from your anchor, the higher up under your arms the rope will support you, which also creates a supporting-harness shape behind you.
■ Try to keep a stable position while descending, sitting back out with your heels touching the rock.
■ Retrieval of the rope after an abseil can be awkward, due to the amount of friction present. It may be prudent to tie a sling around the anchor, made from a length cut from the rope for this purpose. The abseil rope can then be threaded through this, making it far easier to pull down (see page 51).

OBSERVATION

It should be noted that, within the sphere of mountaineering, anything called 'classic' hurts! A 'classic' abseil hurts, a 'classic' belay hurts, and a 'classic' route will tend to be a dank, dripping-green terrifying chimney with no runners, first climbed in the 1800s. Just thought you'd like to know!

Ascent of a Rock Step with a Group

The simplest way to solve this, once a stance has been taken, is to throw down the end of the rope with a loop tied in it, either an overhand knot on the bight, or a triple fisherman's sliding up to a stopper knot (see diagram overleaf). The problem with this method, however, is the

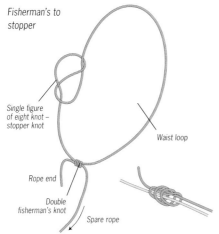

Fisherman's to stopper

Single figure of eight knot – stopper knot

Waist loop

Rope end

Double fisherman's knot

Spare rope

- Get him to sit down and slip off the loop. This is then pulled back down by the helper, and another group member placed into it.
- Continue like this until all members but one are up, and finally bring up the last person, the helper, who is already attached.

difficulty in high winds of delivering the end of the rope to where it needs to go. This also might present another problem in that the knotted end of the rope could jam out of reach in an awkward position. The following is a way of organising the ropework in a manner that should help negate nearly all problems.

- Organise your group in an area away from any danger of falling debris.
- Tie the rope around the waist of a reliable person, ensure that it is flaked out tidily on the ground, and either tuck the other end through your rucksack waist belt, or tie it round you.
- Scramble up a short distance to a suitable ledge or stance and anchor yourself.
- Identify an area near to you that you consider to be completely safe for your group to be on when they untie from the rope, and mark it with your rucksack. Pull up all of the slack rope between yourself and the person tied on.
- Allowing enough rope for people to reach the safe area, tie an overhand knot in the rope to create a loop. This is then pulled back down by the person at the bottom. Keep the rope high and off the rock at this stage, to stop any chance of it snagging.
- A group member steps into the loop, and it is adjusted by the helper.
- Using a waist belay (or a direct belay in some circumstances), bring the climber up to you and across to the safe area. Ensure that he is not, at any time, unwrapping himself from the belay system, and that he will not end up leading on steep ground behind you.

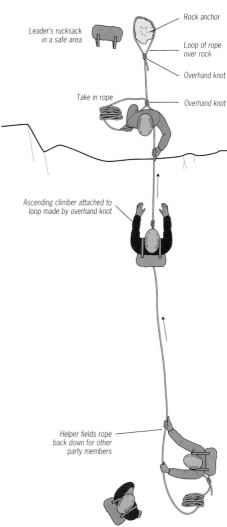

Rock anchor

Leader's rucksack in a safe area

Loop of rope over rock

Overhand knot

Take in rope

Overhand knot

Ascending climber attached to loop made by overhand knot

Helper fields rope back down for other party members

Start of loop system

Emergency Evacuation

WHAT IS EMERGENCY EVACUATION?

Emergency evacuation is exactly as it sounds – the removal of a casualty in order to position him in a safer place where first aid can be carried out, or a short-distance carry to move him to an area that is more suitable for awaiting the arrival of a rescue team.

It must be emphasised that any improvised carry in the mountains can only be over a short distance, often no more than a couple of hundred metres, and the method of carry will be dictated by:

- The equipment available.
- The nature of the casualty's injuries.
- The nature of the terrain to be crossed.

It is important to consider each of these points in turn in a realistic manner when practising, when training mountain leaders and when at a real incident.

OBSERVATIONS

It is worth mentioning the role of ski poles at this point. Many people carry them these days, and they have many benefits when travelling in the mountains. However, consideration should be made as to when they become a hazard, and at the following times they should be packed away or held with the wrist loops removed.

1 When acting as a leader on steeper terrain, they should be packed away. Neither you nor your group would benefit if you slipped, and you need to be ready to help a group member should they need assistance.

2 When crossing a boulder field, wrist loop should be removed to prevent injury.

3 When crossing a river, wrist loops should be off.

4 When traversing a narrow path, wrist loops should again be removed. It is possible to catch a ski pole between your legs and trip.

5 In winter, care should be taken that the stability offered by using poles does not get you on to ground where an ice axe should be deployed instead.

Equipment Available

With very few exceptions, you will not be taking to the hills with a purpose-designed mountain-rescue stretcher. You will also very rarely be out on the hills with a couple of 2.5m lengths of timber, much beloved of leader-training courses! Granted, you may be in a forested area that has the potential to provide poles suitable for improvised carry construction, but think back to when you were last in that situation.

However, you may well have some ski poles available, which are rather whippy when used on their own, but can be lashed together with tape from your first-aid kit to provide a much stronger and stiffer implement. You should also have with you a group shelter, a couple of heavy-duty plastic bivi bags within the group, a first-aid kit, maybe a rope and slings, and, possibly, a mobile phone. As well as this, you will have additional seasonal kit, such as spare clothing, ice axes, and so on.

The Casualty's Injuries

This is the most important factor determining if, how, and how far, a casualty is moved. Back and neck injuries are obviously a far more serious problem than a broken wrist.

The Nature of the Terrain

This must be considered, as it is counter-productive to organise a side-by-side carry and then to be faced with a steep narrow path where it is only possible to proceed in single file. Conversely, to arrange a weird and wonderful rope-stretcher system requiring many people to carry it, when the ground underfoot is flat hard snow, is somewhat more tiresome than simply putting the casualty on a bivi bag and dragging him over the ground, injuries permitting.

Never underestimate the effort it takes to move a person from one place to the next. This will only ever be over a short distance and consideration must be given to the fitness and well-being of both yourself and the rest of your party when organising a carry – you are no good to the casualty if you end up exhausting yourself. Similarly, watch out for your back when lifting; lift by pushing up with the legs and not by straightening your back when holding a weight.

GENERAL CONSIDERATIONS

From the many possible variations the following is a selection of the most practical evacuation techniques. The skill here, as in so many things, is having a good working knowledge of three or four possibilities, and being able to recognise where each should be deployed. It goes without saying that professional training in first-aid techniques is essential, and should be considered by any walker or mountaineer.

Thought should be given to the nature of the injuries before deciding on the final method of evacuation, and the process of getting the casualty onto the carry. For instance, someone with a lower-leg injury may well be perfectly capable of assisting by lifting his weight with his arms. The following assumes that simply picking up the casualty and progressing with him on a simple hand carry is not an option.

Scenario: the casualty has been injured in an area threatened by stone-fall. You must move him a short distance for his and the rest of the group's safety.

Method 1

Place the casualty on a bivi bag or some other smooth material. Drag them! This works well on snow, and is surprisingly effective on grass or heather, although you should watch out for hidden boulders. Care should be taken on snow that an easy drag does not become a terrifying toboggan ride as the slope steepens!

OBSERVATION

Method 2 is far more practical than the often-taught practice of placing stones at various points along the bivi bag and securing a rope or slings around these to provide a handle system. Organising a carry in this manner relies on too many variables, such as the availability of stones, rope and slings. Also, the finished article is very uncomfortable for the casualty, and the size of the bag, thus the carrying surface, is much reduced during the process.

Method 2

Place the casualty lengthways on a plastic bivi bag. The object is now to roll in the sides of the bag to hip-width to provide purchase for carrying. This can be done by rolling the edges in around ski poles, pieces of heather, or indeed anything that will give the plastic a little bulk and make either side's rolled section bulkier and thus the carrying easier.

We thoroughly recommend this method for a quick and comfortable carry.

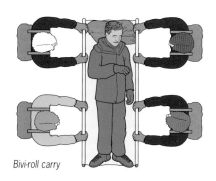

Bivi-roll carry

Method 3

Tape together two or more ski poles to strengthen them. Two group members of similar height stand side by side wearing rucksacks, and the poles are pushed through the shoulder-strap lower attachment point. The poles are padded to make a seat, and the casualty is helped on to this. He is supported by placing an arm around the back of each of the carriers, who in turn hold on to the casualty in a similar manner.

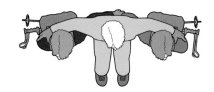

Pole sack carry

Method 4

If a rope is carried, it can be organised in tied-off coils, and half of the coils given to two group members of similar height. Standing side by side, they place the coils over their outside shoulders with the tied-off section at the lowest point between them. The casualty can sit on this, and be supported in a way similar to that described in Method 3 opposite. The rope coils should be padded at the relevant points for the casualty, and for the carriers if they are to travel any distance.

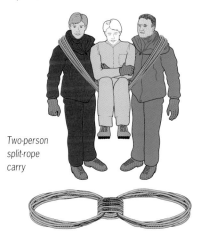

Two-person split-rope carry

EVACUATING CHILDREN

Even with a minor injury, a child is likely to be more distressed than an adult with a similar injury. However, if the nature of the injury allows a carry to take place, and having taken into account all first-aid considerations, evacuation is often easier due to the weight difference. It may be possible to evacuate a light person a considerable distance.

All of the other methods mentioned are valid, as long as you do not expect other children to be part of the carrying operation. The following may also be considered:

1 If a rope is carried, it can be arranged in coils tied off. Separate the coils so that you have half in each hand. The casualty steps into this and you can then lift him wearing the rope like a rucksack. The casualty is easier to pick up if he can be positioned on a suitable boulder at the right height, and the rope should be padded at the relevant points.
2 A small child can be carried by a method similar to the above, but by using a rucksack. With the sack off, he steps in with a leg through each of the shoulder straps. The rucksack is then put on as normal.

Method 5

This method requires three carriers and the use of ski poles or similar, but is the comfiest for both the casualty (injuries permitting) and the carriers. We recommend this method for slightly longer-distance carries on good terrain.

Tape ski poles together to make two strong carrying poles. Using a spare fleece or waterproof jacket, pull the arms through to the inside, do up the zip, and pass the poles through the arms so that they are running down the inside of the garment. All three carriers wear rucksacks. Insert two pole ends into the lower rucksack strap attachment points of one carrier from the back. This person will be at the front of the carry. One ski pole then goes into the inside shoulder strap of each of the two rear carriers. The casualty can then sit on the jacket, his back being supported by the lead carrier.

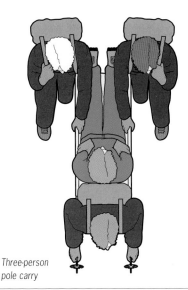

Three-person pole carry

Emergency Evacuation

The Rope Stretcher

It is quite possible, as long as there is a rope in the party, to construct a stretcher that is capable of comfortably supporting a casualty. A rope stretcher, though, has a number of drawbacks that may limit its use, not least that it is time consuming to make, and requires a lot of people to carry it even a short distance. However, it is useful to know how to construct one, and, of the various methods possible, we will concentrate on a version that uses clove hitches. A flat area of ground will help in its construction.

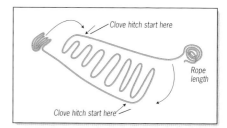

■ Ideally, a 50m rope will be used, although it is possible to use a shorter rope if that is all that is to hand. Starting with the centre of the rope, lay it out on the ground in a series of loops, six to ten either side of the centre, depending on the size of the casualty. These loops should be kept reasonably close together, and be around 2ft wide. It is important to keep the size and shape consistent throughout. Once the loops have been laid out, run the rope past either end to make a handle, then back down the opposite side. Now it is possible to start connecting the stretcher together. Tie a clove hitch on the side rope, and pass through the end of the corresponding loop. Repeat this for all of the loops on either side.

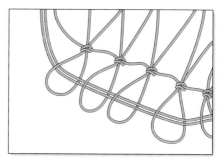

■ Now run the spare rope across the top and bottom ends of the stretcher, and thread it through the loops protruding from the clove hitches. Continue doing this until most of the rope has been used up, then securely tie the ends off. Push the clove hitches flush with the threaded rope and ensure that all attachments are tight. The basic stretcher is now finished. The base should be padded with mats, spare clothing or rucksacks, making sure that there is no chance of the casualty disappearing through any gaps in the rope-work.

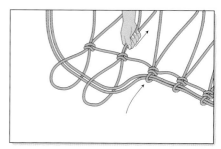

■ The stability of this basic design can be greatly increased by threading ski poles through the clove hitches as well as the rope. This makes the stretcher far easier to carry, as well as being a lot comfier for the casualty. When using a dynamic climbing rope, it will often be found that you need to make the stretcher slightly on the small size and stretch it to shape when complete.

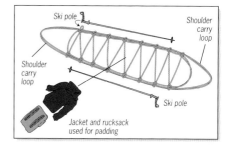

The rope stretcher

■ Knots pp42–6

Navigation

This chapter details a few ideas, both about teaching and about practising navigation. Compass skills are briefly mentioned, in order to help the novice find direction (!) and make a start, and some learning programmes are mentioned. It would serve the reader well to obtain a specialist navigation book from the library, in order to delve more deeply into the basic skills of finding his way.

■

coaching techniques in the teaching of navigation and offers some tips when navigating in summer and winter conditions.

Introducing Map Reading as a Skill
Map reading is the key to successful navigation, along with techniques such as map setting, map memory, linear feature navigation, and thumbing the map. It is these basic concepts that we need to be putting across in the first stages of teaching navigation.

The ability to interpret contours, measure distance, pace and time comes from a good understanding of the basics; without these, people may find it difficult to mountain-navigate efficiently.

Introducing Map Setting
Introducing map setting can be achieved in a number of ways.

1 Prepare an A4-size orienteering-scale map by cutting it into six or seven pieces of varying shapes and sizes, creating a jigsaw map. Present this jigsaw to a group of participants and ask them to piece the map back together within a set time, say half a minute. Then give them another jigsaw map with contours only illustrated on the map and give them half a minute to complete it. By doing this type of exercise, your students are beginning to recognise shapes and symbols along with having some competitive fun.

2 The next step is to map set. Place the letters N, S, E, W on each wall of the room. Have each

TEACHING NAVIGATION

Introduction
While navigation is a basic skill for walkers and mountaineers, the mountain leader and instructor will find themselves teaching navigation skills at all levels, from introducing the basic concepts to the advanced skills, enabling people to navigate confidently through the toughest of mountain-weather conditions and terrain.

There are many good publications on how to teach people the fundamental skills. Those who are orienteers will be familiar with the coaching aspects in the teaching of navigation.

The techniques illustrated below can be used for a wide range of age groups, although younger groups tend to have difficulty in grasping the concept of scale and representational distance, or map-to-ground relationships. However, with suitable coaching the skills of map reading can be attained within a short space of time by any participant of any age. This section will highlight and illustrate

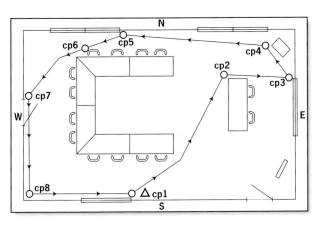

1 Wipe board
2 Table corner
3 Wipe board
4 Television
5 Window
6 Chair
7 Door
8 Corner of room

cp Control point
→ route
△ start point

member of the group draw a plan view of the room, including furniture, and ask them to mark N, S, E and W on their drawings. Then ask the participants to choose any furniture item and stand beside it. To map set, they simply match up the shape of their drawing to the shape of the room. The map is now set and orientated so that features on the classroom floor match features on the classroom drawing. The drawing has become a map of the surroundings.

3 Ask each individual to mark his seat position on his map by drawing a triangle, followed by marking with a circle the positions of all the other participants.

4 Ask the group to map read around the classroom by walking around the furniture and moving forwards, backwards, sideways, in effect driving their maps, turning them as they travel in order to keep them set to the letters N, S, E and W on the room walls.

5 Each participant should practise thumbing his map while map reading around the room furniture. By thumbing his map he can constantly follow his route as his thumb acts as a pointer. People should not just look across the room and head off to the next marker without using the map.

6 Each person should always have his map set; this means having the map positioned in front of his body at all times and always orientated in the direction of travel.

The next exercise is to have the group members draw a route on their maps, consisting of six control points, each indicated by a circle, starting at the triangle where they are sitting.

■ The route must start at the triangle, link up all the markers and return to the triangle.

■ Prepare six markers, using small squares of paper, and place them at various points around the room.

■ Make up a description of the feature where the marker is positioned, such as: the table is a knoll, the television is a boulder, where two windows join is a junction; this encourages map language.

■ Number each marker as you come to it. Place arrows along the line of the route to highlight the direction of travel on the map.

■ The route should not travel over any items of furniture you have drawn.

■ Be imaginative in the route drawing.

■ Participants can now follow the course set out and practise following a marked route, and they should swap maps with each other to practise different routes.

Map Reading

Using an orienteering map or a 1:25000 (a map with lots of detail and information), go for a short walk concentrating on map setting and thumbing of the map in order to check off features as you pass them. This is also called map-to-land relationship; it is simply matching features on the ground, such as a stream junction, to the correct stream junction marked on the map. This is also an important step to understanding micro-navigation.

Many different issues will arise such as, when walking with the map in your hand all the time, thumbing becomes difficult unless the map is folded small, and map-memory skills are required.

Contour Interpretation

For interpretation of the ground the most important information on a map is supplied by the contours. A contour is a line which joins points of equal height above sea level and collectively they display the shape, angle and height of the ground.

■ Each map will have a special colour indicating the contour for easy recognition. The vertical distance between them will be shown in the key, normally located at the side or bottom of the map.

■ The actual height of contours is also given on

OBSERVATION

There is strong evidence to suggest that introducing the compass at the same time as maps aids the speed of learning. Setting the map with the compass is frequently made excessively complicated, so ignore the magnetic variation which you really don't need for map setting by compass. Drop the compass onto the map, rotate the map until the magnetic needle points to the top of the map, remove the compass and you have set the map. It has only taken 5 seconds and is a very quick way of map setting.

most maps; this information will be in printed figures running through the map, often at 50m intervals. These figures will be facing the right way up when ascending and the opposite when descending. Where the ground becomes very steep, cliff symbols will be used. The tighter the contours the steeper the ground.

■ In poor visibility, contour-interpretation skills are the key to successful navigation.

Map Memory

Another simple way of developing map-memory and contour-interpretation skills is by using map-memory cards.

■ This process of learning can be fun. A plain postcard is an ideal size, with twelve cards in total. You will then require two identical orienteering maps. Cut the maps into 4cm squares and stick them on to the cards.

■ Now transfer the contour information from the small section of orienteering maps to the other six plain postcards; you can achieve this by tracing.

■ On the reverse side of the coloured maps number the cards 1 to 6 . On the reverse side of the contour postcards use letters from A to F.

■ With a small group, ask them to choose one of the numbered coloured maps and give them one minute to study the information on the map. Then ask them to make a note of the number chosen, then leave their workstation and quickly go to the other room where you will have laid out the contour maps.

■ The participants then try and match maps by using memory only; they take one of the contour maps back to their workstation and discover whether it matches.

OBSERVATIONS

1 It is very straightforward to design lots of different maps with varying shapes and routes. This will not only be good fun when learning: it also broadens your resource pack when teaching navigation.

2 It should be noted that further practical map-reading walks should follow map-memory exercises. This will help improve shape, angle and aspect identification.

When designing this sort of exercise you can vary the difficulty of detail from map to map, starting with easy features to technical features, depending upon the age and ability of the group.

MAP-SETTING EXERCISES

Designing your own maps can be fun and cost-effective.

■ For the above, all you will require is a postcard-size piece of coloured card. Highlight nine control points by using small circles, then draw a continuous line linking some control points, finishing on any point. A number of these cards can be prepared, all with different lines linking the points. There should be two of each map, so that the

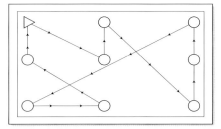

Including nine control points

students can pair up and watch each other progress.

■ This exercise will require nine control points; these can be small cones or cards. Place them on the ground, to the same shape on the above map. An ideal size is about tennis-court length. Encourage your group to practise map setting, first walking followed by running around the marked route. The idea is that they always maintain the map positions relevant to the ground as they follow the lines. This is map setting while moving.

■ Get the group to swap maps with each other a couple of times; this allows them to walk in a different set of directions.

■ Once you are satisfied that participants have the idea of continually orientating the maps to fit the ground, have them try the same exercise but *without* orientating the maps.

They should hold them close to their chests, and try to follow the lines. This should now prove to be a complicated task. By doing this, people can see the value of the exercise.

■ Once map setting has been introduced it is time to move on to map-reading skills. This can be best achieved by going for a short walk, in any environment where you have a relevant and detailed map, and map-to-land feature identification can be recognised and practised.

■ It is also a good idea to understand the scale of the map that you are using prior to any trip, as you will need to measure distance to plan your timing of your route.

■ Develop your understanding of the compass and learn how to use it correctly. There are many compasses to choose from and this can be confusing. In most circumstances people get lost because of poor management of the compass.

NAVIGATION TOOLS

Scale
The scale is the relationship of distance on the map to the distance on the ground, generally given as a representative fraction such as 1:50,000, 1:25,000 etc. This means that one unit on the map represents 50,000 of the same units on the ground. For example, 1cm on the map is 50,000cm, or 500m, on the ground. Using this formula you can now easily add and divide map scale to actual ground distance with a high degree of accuracy.

The Compass: What Type?
The best and most convenient compass for mountain use should be simple in design and layout. Its practicality in handling it while wearing gloves in foul weather should also be considered. If your present compass is unable to fulfil this role, then consider the following requirements:

Look out for good direction-of-travel arrow markings along with base-plate line markings for taking bearings. The compass should also be robust, accurate, light and versatile. In addition, its base plate needs to be transparent with a housing that doesn't move too easily, and it should have two-degree divisions around the rim. The length of your attachment string should be no less than 35cm and should be attached to a breast pocket located on the outside of your shell garment.

OBSERVATION
It is worth noting that a sighting compass has many limitations for mountain navigation, as well as short-base-plate compasses, and they are not recommended for serious use.

Feature	Benefit
A long base plate 12cm x 6cm	Comfortable to hold when wearing gloves
Three romers on base plate	Quick measuring, especially for grid references
Luminous material on base plate and compass housing	Easy to spot all the components for direction finding at night time
0 to 100mm ruler on base plate	Excellent for measuring longer distances
Magnifying glass	Allows you to study fine contour detail on map
Compass housing with coloured markings and degree markings from 0 to 360 degrees	Can easily identify bearings

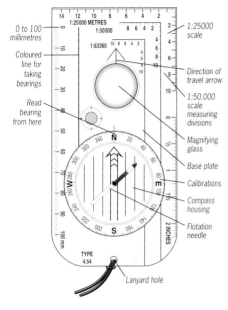

Compass and working parts

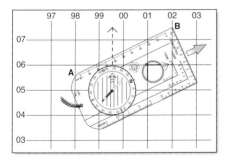

The compass and the map taking a bearing

Taking a Bearing

▨ Identify position A where you are, and position B where you wish to travel to.

▨ Using the edge of your compass or coloured line on the base plate, place the compass between A and B. Ensure that the compass direction-of-travel arrow is pointing to position B.

▨ Holding the compass firm and being careful not to move it off position, turn the compass housing so that the grid north arrow and lines in the compass housing point north on the map and run in parallel with the map grid lines.

▨ You have now taken a grid bearing.

▨ Add on any magnetic variation to align you with true north; this variation will be highlighted at the top of the map or located at the map key.

▨ Always ensure that the map being used is current.

Walking on a Bearing

▨ Place the compass flat in the palm of your hand in front of your body.

▨ Align the floating needle with the north arrow marked on the compass housing.

▨ Make sure at this point that the compass is in front of your body.

▨ Using the direction-of-travel arrow on the base plate, sight ahead a short way, maybe only a few metres, and observe a feature to walk to (boulder, clump of grass, etc), walk to it, then stop and repeat the process, always keeping the needle pointing to the north mark on the housing.

Good navigation comes with experience and practice, and the mark of a good navigator is having the ability to combine these techniques with a high degree of accuracy.

Walking on a Bearing without Stopping

This needs practice, but can become easy to do.

▨ Line up the compass as above, and sight on your first feature.

▨ Walk towards the feature but, as you approach it, let your compass needle settle.

▨ Line up your compass with your first feature, look through it and locate another feature on the same line.

■ Now ignore the first feature and walk towards the second. As you approach it, repeat the process of lining up, looking through it and keeping moving.

Accuracy is the most important factor and, although it is handy to be able to keep moving, if you feel that you need to stop then you must do so – do not be tempted to blindly walk on if you have any doubt that you may have sighted on the wrong feature.

OBSERVATION

A compass is an extremely useful piece of kit, but it can have its accuracy compromised. Be careful, when walking on a bearing, that no metallic objects are influencing the needle. Items that do so include ice axes, metallic rock elements, ski poles, cameras and, bizarrely, under-wired bras. It is also important to consider where to store your compass when at home. A common place to keep outdoor kit is under the stairs, but this tends to be the place where the power supply comes into the house, creating strong magnetic fields which can alter the balance of the needle.

Grid References

Knowing how to accurately take a grid reference is extremely important, if for no other reason than to be able to report the site of an accident accurately. The diagram shows how to go about it. Remember the phrase 'along the hall and up the stairs', as this should help you get the sequence of numbers right. Also, prefix the numbers with the map-sheet letter, which will make the reference unique.

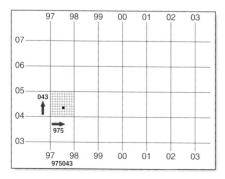

Working out a grid reference

TIP

Magnetic variation varies from country to country, and can be different in various areas of the same country. It is important to know what the variation is (this will be marked on the key of the map) and how to make the calculation. In the United Kingdom, for example, the variation has to be added to the grid bearing, to give a magnetic bearing. A useful way of remembering this is that the world is bigger than the map, so, when taking a bearing from the map, make the number bigger, ie add the variation. When going from the world to the map, the map being smaller, make the number smaller.

CALCULATING DISTANCE

Pacing and Timing

These are techniques used when navigating in poor weather conditions, when it is extremely important to know how far you have travelled and for how long you have been walking.

Pacing

Pacing is having a known amount of double paces for 100m. This is achieved by measuring 100m on the flat. Start walking and count every double pace, for instance every time your right foot hits the ground. The total that you reach, probably somewhere around 55 to 65 double paces, will only be for walking on the flat in ideal conditions. This number of paces will change as soon as you start going uphill, are wearing a heavy sack, have different boots on, are crossing differing terrain such as deep snow or boulder fields, or have the wind against you, etc. Time should be taken to find out these variables, and note the change in your stride.

Timing

One of the best formulae to use is known as 'Naismith's Rule'. When planning ahead, it is worth noting that you may find yourself tiring when a few hours into a journey, so it is wise to plan for a slower pace. Should you be travelling uphill, then you probably may not walk as fast.

In addition to the formula opposite add one minute for every 10m contour line of ascent. In the early stages of a trip, 30 seconds per contour may be sufficient, depending upon load carried, conditions underfoot etc. When descending, there is no need to add time for contours, unless the going gets steep. Other factors that will influence your time include:

- Tiredness
- Weather
- Steep ground
- Conditions underfoot
- Using a rope
- Using ski poles
- Not wearing crampons when appropriate
- Wearing crampons when inappropriate
- Poor navigation skills
- Poor route choice
- Physical fitness
- When there's nothing to sight on
- When unsure about the point you are leaving from
- When lost

Speed k.p.h. Distance m	2	3	4	5	6
50	1.5	1	45 secs.	36 secs.	0.5
100	3	2	1.5	1.2	1
200	6	4	3	2.4	2
500	15	10	7.5	6	5
1000	30	20	15	12	10

Naismith's formula

ESSENTIAL NAVIGATION TECHNIQUES

Attack Points

This technique is used when you intend to go to a small feature, say a small knoll by which you are camped. If you were navigating from some distance away, the chances are that you may find yourself way off target at the end of the leg. By splitting the one leg into two, and first travelling to a larger feature nearer to your objective, such as a big lake, you would have reduced the margin for error considerably. This

would leave a short distance to walk, resulting in greater accuracy, to the final objective, in this case the knoll.

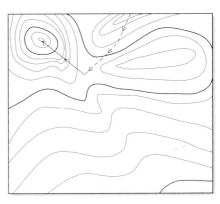

Attack point

Aiming Off

If aiming for a stream junction, for instance, in poor visibility, the chances are that you will end up one side or other of your intended destination. In poor weather, it would be difficult to decide in exactly which direction to travel to reach the junction. Aiming off is a most useful technique, with which you purposely aim a few degrees to the uphill side of the objective. When the stream, in this case, is reached, you would then know in which direction to turn to follow it to the junction.

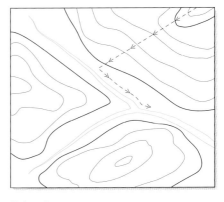

Aiming off

Boxing

Should you come across an obstacle in the way of your bearing such as a large gully cutting back some way into a cliff-top, it can be avoided by aligning your compass needle 90 degrees from your bearing then following this for a measured distance, say 50m, until the obstacle is cleared. Now walk on your original bearing for a measured distance past the obstacle, then stop and realign your compass needle 90 degrees and walk the same distance back. Continue on the original line.

Boxing

Dog Leg

This is when there is a huge dangerous feature that we wish to avoid. Take a bearing and follow it over a set distance past the danger then take a new bearing to rejoin the original direction.

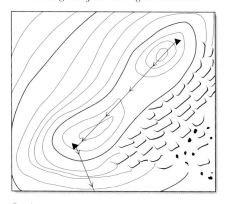

Dog leg

Slope Aspect

This is when you check the direction in which the slope faces, by using your compass. It can be a useful tool for re-location in poor visibility.

Take a bearing directly up or down the slope, then, having corrected for any magnetic variation, place the compass on the map in the area you have been walking, maintaining the north arrow in the compass housing parallel with grid north on the map. Move your compass across the map, maintaining north to north, in the area that you suspect you may be. Where the lines on the baseplate of the compass cross the slope at exactly 90 degrees will indicate your approximate position. However, you will still need to find out how far up the slope you are, and there may be other possible positions relevant to your current slope aspect that need to be eliminated.

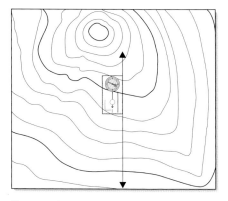

Slope aspect

Collecting Feature

This is a large, obvious feature a short distance behind your intended destination, that will immediately indicate that you have overshot your target. A collecting feature could be a change in slope, the edge of a cliff (care needed in winter or in poor visibility) or a river. A point will then be identified as an attack point, as mentioned above.

Hand-railing

This is a simple technique, which allows ground to be covered rapidly. It is the act of following an obvious feature, such as a river or an area of

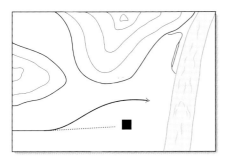

Collecting feature

major contour change, to help lead you to your destination. This may be gained by 'aiming off', the feature 'hand-railed', and then an 'attack point' used to reach your final objective. Navigation is often the linking of a series of line features (hand-rails) together to form a route.

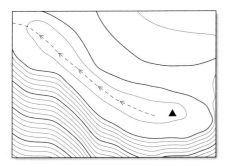

Hand-railing

Winter Considerations
Although navigational techniques are very similar from summer to winter, there are a few points that need to be borne in mind when travelling under winter conditions. For instance, features to sight on can be hard to find, and it may be necessary to have your partner travel ahead of you to give you something to sight on. White-out conditions occur when the sky, cloud and ground merge into one blank sheet, and it is very disorientating to be out in these conditions. Your eyes have nothing to focus on, and it is all too easy to travel too far or too close to an edge and simply walk over a drop. One

technique that is useful is to make a snowball and throw it in front of you. This serves two purposes: firstly it makes a mark in the snow, thus giving your eye something to focus on and a point you can use as a feature; secondly, it may help to determine if you are close to an edge by simply making a mark for a short distance and then disappearing.

Great care must be taken when hand-railing a steep edge, as there is a chance that it will be corniced. A technique that will make this safer is to use a rope. One person ties on the end, and follows the edge; at least two others tie in a minimum of 10m away from the edge, and walk on a parallel route. This means that if the one closest to the drop should fall, they will be counterbalanced by the others.

Another problem in winter is estimating distance travelled, even when using timing and

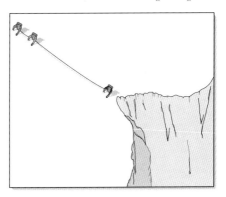

Roped up near to corrie rim

pacing. A climbing rope may well be to hand, and there is a very good chance that this will be 50m in length – simply use this, tied round you, as a distance guide. Very great accuracy can be gained, and this is useful when travelling on complicated terrain necessitating many bearings to be taken and legs to be followed.

PART ONE: SUMMER

Technical Skills for Summer and Winter Climbing

This section describes a variety of technical skills and techniques for use in summer and winter climbing and mountaineering.

Knots

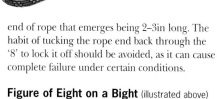

Figure of eight on a bight

Rarely does a subject bring forth as much fear or discussion as the subject of knots – what is the best for what application, which way is it best tied and so on. The number of essential knots needed for both summer and winter mountaineering and climbing is in fact relatively small. We have concentrated here on the knots that we regularly teach, a lot of which are transferable to various applications. The skill here is to be aware of the situations in which they can be usefully deployed.

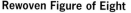

Rewoven Figure of Eight

The fig eight is one of the most useful knots, and it is the standard way of tying onto a harness. It is very simple to construct, and has a recognisable shape when complete. The loop created by tying the knot should end up the same size as the abseil loop of your harness – slightly less than fist size. The knot should be finished with an overhand or fisherman's stopper knot, pushed up snug to the fig eight when tightened, with the

end of rope that emerges being 2–3in long. The habit of tucking the rope end back through the '8' to lock it off should be avoided, as it can cause complete failure under certain conditions.

Figure of Eight on a Bight (illustrated above)

This is an excellent knot for belaying, relevant for all climbing and scrambling situations. It has the benefit of possessing dynamic properties, meaning that it will tighten slightly when loaded, thus taking a proportion of any shock loading away from the anchor points. It should always be considered first when constructing a system.

Start with a 2ft bight of rope through the harness tie-in loop. This means that when the knot has been tied, there will be approximately 1ft of tail left, which enhances its security. A little practice is needed in order to tie the knot in such a manner as to not introduce any slack into the rope between yourself and the anchor, but it will be time well spent.

Double Figure of Eight (see description at top of opposite page)

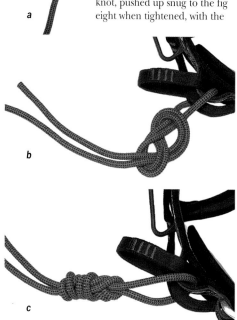

a

b

c

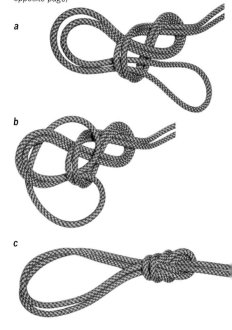

a

b

c

■ Tying In *pp54–7*

Double Figure of Eight (illustrated below left)

This knot is sometimes used as a rope method of bringing two anchor points down to one, but has now been somewhat superseded by the use of slings. Its main application, however, is in the rigging of rope systems, particularly bottom-rope rigs, and when used for these it is excellent. It allows a double loop to be used at the top-pulley karabiner section, thus markedly increasing its strength and security.

Bowline

The bowline (right) has been superseded in many cases by the figure of eight. It does, however, still have its place for a number of applications. One of its main plus points is that it is easy to untie once it has been loaded. It is sometimes used as a knot for tying onto the harness and, because of the ease with which it undoes, it is a useful knot for situations where a lot of falls are expected to be taken, such as when working a route on a crag or wall.

One of the main minus points is the position of the stopper knot on the inside section of the tie-in loop when it is used on a harness. This can get in the way of any subsequent knots and karabiners which need to be tied or clipped in. A stopper knot is essential with the bowline. Indeed, it could be said that the bowline is not complete until it has one as, under certain circumstances, a kink in the rope can cause the knot to undo and fail.

a

b

c

The Clove Hitch

This is one of the most frequently used knots (below), and is an essential tool for both summer and winter mountaineering. Its main use is as an anchor knot, where its ease of adjustment can be a big advantage over other systems. With a little practice, it can be easily tied with one hand.

It is best that an HMS karabiner is used with the clove hitch, as this will allow the knot to sit in the correct configuration. For this reason, it is important that only one knot is used per karabiner – the habit of clipping two or more clove hitches into one karabiner is potentially dangerous and should be avoided. It should also be noted that the correct way to clip the knot is with the load rope nearest to the back bar of the karabiner, along its strongest axis.

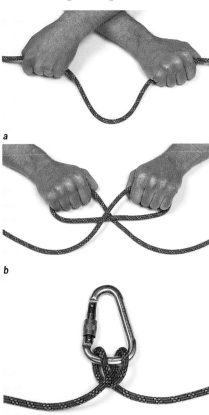

a

b

c

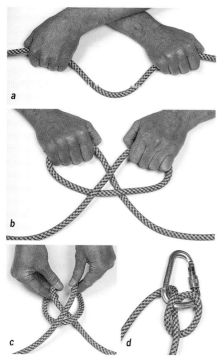

a

b

c

d

The Italian Hitch

This is an extremely useful knot, as it can be used for belaying, abseiling and rigging. For general climbing use, its main purpose is as a back-up should a belay plate be dropped from a stance, for example.

However, for group-activity use, the Italian hitch comes into its own as a belaying knot, allowing a huge flexibility in system design and operation. The knot is controlled from in front, as opposed to a belay plate which must be controlled from behind. Maximum braking is obtained by having the ropes parallel on the load side of the karabiner. This means that the breaking system on a top-rope set-up, for instance, can be rigged some distance back from the cliff edge, with the person controlling the system anchored well in front of it. The climber, upon reaching the top, is then still well protected as he walks away from edge.

Care must be taken when using the knot to ensure that the controlling rope at no time runs across the sleeve locking the gate of the karabiner. If it touches, there is a chance that it could unscrew and the gate open, resulting in complete loss of control. Particular care should be taken when abseiling.

Locking Off an Italian Hitch

There are a number of reasons why you would wish to lock off the Italian hitch. This could be when rigging a releasable abseil maybe, or when securing a second on a multi-pitch climb. An excellent and most useful feature is that the hitch can be locked off and released when the rope is under full load. The locking-off procedure consists of two types of knot, a slippery hitch and a half hitch, of which two are tied. Start the process with about 60cm of bight and you will be left with the correct tail length of 30cm when finished.

Locking Off the Belay Device

This is done in a similar manner to the Italian hitch lock off, except that the knots are tied around the back bar of the karabiner, avoiding

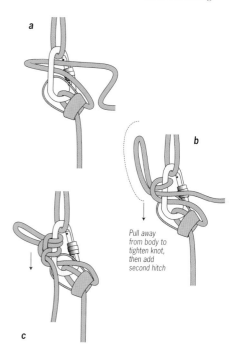

a

b

c

Pull away from body to tighten knot, then add second hitch

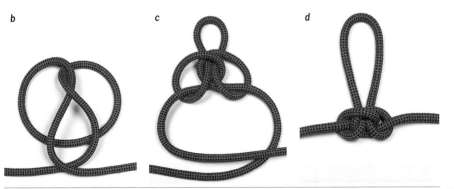

the gate. This must be practised before it is needed, unlocking as well as locking off. The finished product should have two half hitches; one is shown on the diagram for clarity.

The Overhand Knot
This simple knot is used for a variety of tasks, such as tying off the end of the rope after tying into the harness, for equalising slings, and it is an indispensable tool for the mountain leader.

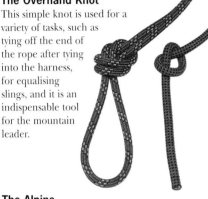

The Alpine Butterfly
This knot has been overlooked in recent years, as the overhand knot has gained favour. However, we feel that the butterfly is extremely relevant for a number of situations, such as in the rigging of group-abseil and bottom-rope systems, and for short-roping.

a

Double Fisherman's Knot
This knot is used more for construction of equipment than while on the move. However, it can be utilised on the hill to join together two ends of rope to make an improvised sling during retreat, for example, or for joining the ends of an Abalakov thread.

The Lark's-foot
The lark's-foot is included here, not as an essential knot but rather as one to avoid using. It will often be deployed in situations where a clove hitch should be utilised. The lark's-foot is a very weak knot, and it dramatically reduces the strength of a sling when tied around an anchor.

It is also often used ill-advisedly to join two slings together, a situation where a screwgate karabiner should be used.

The only time that a lark's-foot should be used is to attach a sling onto a harness to use as a safety line or 'cow's tail'. In this situation, the sling is threaded through the leg loop and waist-belt central points, taking the same line as the abseil loop, the lark's-foot tied and pulled in snug.

b   **c**   **d**

The Tape Knot

This knot (above) originated as a way of constructing slings, in the days before sewn slings were readily available. It is now rarely seen, and can be considered mainly as a knot for emergency procedures. It is often a good idea to carry a couple of 3m lengths of tape in the rucksack, for use in case a retreat has to be made from a winter route, for instance. The tape knot is then the best way of securing the sling around an anchor.

The Reef Knot

This knot (above) has two main uses – for carrying the rope, and for creating a way of stopping a double fisherman's from tightening up when abseiling. Although simple, it is very easy to tie incorrectly. The best way to remember how to tie it is 'right over left, left over right', which describes the route taken by the rope when starting with the right-hand end. Both ends should then be pulled to help tighten the knot.

Prussiking Knots

The following two knots have taken over from the original prussik knot. This has lost favour due to its propensity for jamming when under even a small load, especially on wet ropes, and its difficulty of operation. However, the generic name 'prussik' has been retained to describe the loop with which the knots are tied; and the act of using the loops to ascend the rope is, and will be for evermore, known as prussiking.

The loops, two should be carried, are best tied from 6mm kernmantle cord, and they

should measure 30cm long when tied with a double fisherman's knot.

French Prussik

This will be the most regularly used of the two knots described here (below left). Its major advantage over the Klemheist is its ability to be released while under load, an essential property when abseiling or performing emergency procedures. When forming the knot, take care not to include the double fisherman's in the coiled section, and ensure that the knot wrapping is neat when completed.

Klemheist

This knot (above right) is similar in appearance to the French prussik, the main difference being that only one loop of rope connects to the karabiner, unlike the French's two.

This knot also pulls tighter, and is very difficult to release under load, a property which is essential under some circumstances.

OBSERVATION

There is a number of small devices on the market that claim to be the 'ideal' piece of kit to carry for use in an emergency. However, none of these will perform as well as a prussik loop utilising either a French or Klemheist knot. The main drawback of the majority of these recent additions is that they are incapable of being released when under load, an absolutely essential quality of any attachment to the rope in a prussiking or emergency situation.

■ Tying In *pp54–7*

Abseiling

As a climber, you will rarely be more vulnerable than when you are abseiling, and there are a great many reasons for needing to do so. Getting to the bottom of a route on a sea cliff, bailing out from a multi-pitch route, descending to help someone, or simply retrieving stuck gear are all common reasons for abseiling. Many factors must be considered when an abseil has to take place: anchor selection, rope length, abseil length, rope retrieval, direction, destination, objective dangers and so on. Anything that we can do to reduce the risk is of value, and protecting ourselves with a back-up device is one of the most important.

Below we look at a couple of the ways of organising a personal abseil, as well as a method of looking after a number of novices.

APPROPRIATE EQUIPMENT FOR AN APPROPRIATE DESCENT

There is a huge number of devices on the market that are designed for belaying, and an equally large number designed for abseiling. The wise mountaineer will select an item of equipment that does both jobs, negating the need to carry around extra gear. It is common to see climbers sporting both a modern belay device and a figure-of-eight on their harnesses, where either one or the other would suffice. Modern belay devices are excellent for abseiling with, while figures of eight are not particularly efficient when used for belaying. Thus, for the purposes of this section, we will assume that the climber will be carrying a modern multi-purpose belay device.

The mechanics of setting up a group-activity abseil, and techniques using just the rope with no extra equipment, are covered elsewhere.

TIP

Abseiling is just one of the many reasons why it makes life easier to have the middle of your rope marked. Some ropes will come with the centre marked but, if not, it is worth doing it yourself. Tape of a contrasting colour to the rope sheath is ideal. The use of 'marker' pens should be avoided, as they often contain solvents that can damage the rope fibres.

PERSONAL ABSEIL

The method described here is the best way to organise a personal abseil for the vast majority of cases where descent is either planned or performed in an emergency.

There is no extra equipment needed, other than that normally carried on a route.

■ An extender is equipped with two screwgates, one of which clips into the abseil loop on your harness; the other, which should be an HMS karabiner, has the rope clipped into it via the belay plate in the normal manner.

■ Ensure that the dead rope, the side that you will be controlling, is coming out of the lower side of the plate. Put a French prussik knot onto this, and clip it into your abseil loop below the extender with another screwgate.

■ The prussik knot is held loosely open with the controlling hand while abseiling, and released when needing to stop. The controlling rope can pass between the legs, allowing smooth control with either hand.

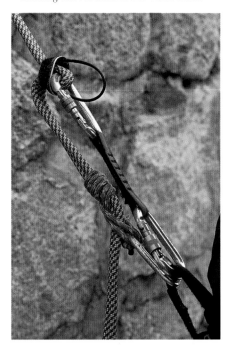

Abseil rig

For a number of years, it has been recommended that the prussik loop be clipped into a leg loop for ease of control, often with the belay plate being clipped directly to the abseil loop on the harness without being extended. This has a major drawback in that if the climber is knocked unconscious, he will have his back-up leg loop drawn upwards by the prussik attachment on the rope, which results in:

■ his body twisting in the harness so that he ends up supported simply by the waist section;

■ the back-up prussik having a real chance of touching the top of the plate and releasing.

THE ITALIAN-HITCH ABSEIL

This is a useful method if, for example, a belay plate has been dropped, or in winter if ropes are starting to freeze to the extent that they do not fit through a belay device. It is important that an HMS karabiner is used, to give a smooth descent with little chance of jamming.

■ If doubled ropes are to be used, one large Italian hitch is tied in both ropes together, and clipped into the krab. If two separate knots were tied, they would jam almost immediately. Ensure that there is no chance

Italian hitch with free krab on top

of the controlling rope ever touching the gate of the karabiner and undoing the sleeve. If you are right handed, clip the HMS onto your abseil loop with the gate opening to the left. This should ensure that the controlling rope runs across the back bar of the krab, staying well away from the gate.

■ The maximum breaking effect with an Italian hitch is achieved with both ropes parallel, the dead rope held in front of the krab. When abseiling, especially at the start of the descent, it is very difficult to hold the rope in this manner because of its weight, and just holding tight to control descent will suffice.

OBSERVATION

The Italian hitch tends to twist the rope as it passes through the knot, so care should be taken to remove kinks before any subsequent abseilers descend.

TIP

When retrieving the rope following an Italian-hitch-controlled descent, care must be taken that any twisting in the ropes is removed before pulling them down through the anchor. Before you leave the stance at the start of the abseil, clip a karabiner onto one of the ropes and let it slide down and sit on top of the Italian. As you descend, the ropes will twist slightly, stopping this free-running krab from staying with you. When you reach safe ground, unclip the Italian and start to untwist the ropes by hand. When the free-running krab drops down to you, you know that there are no more twists in the rope, and can start to pull it down.

THE STACKED ABSEIL

This is a method of attaching one or more less-experienced people to the rope, and controlling their descent from below. The main advantage of this method is that, on a multi-pitch route, you, as leader, can abseil first and set up an intermediate stance. For the purposes of this description, we will assume that there are two novices with you, and, for the sake of clarity, will not go into detail about personal and group security at the stances.

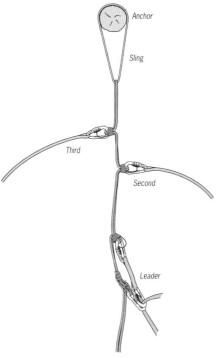

Anchor

Sling

Third

Second

Leader

It is worth describing here the process of changing from an ascent to descent, on either a single- or multi-pitch route. Retreat may be considered for a number of reasons: the onset of darkness, foul weather, being off-route, the climb getting too hard for you, illness, etc. The procedure is given in bulleted list form, in the simplest format for a logical progression. The climbers are using a single rope.

- The second arrives at the stance, belayed from a sling around a spike with an Italian hitch.
- The second is secured by tying off the belay knot, while plans for the descent are made.
- An abandonable anchor is rigged, such as a tape around the spike.
- Both climbers secure themselves to the new anchor with slings lark's-footed through their harnesses.
- The original belay system is dismantled.
- One climber unties from the rope and threads it through the new anchor until the middle mark on the rope appears.
- The climber who has untied holds the rope secure at the anchor as the other unties from his harness.
- The ends of the rope are knotted, it is flaked up and delivered down the crag.
- The first to descend connects up his abseil device plus back-up, collects all spare kit, unclips his safety sling from the anchor and stows it at the back of his harness, and descends.
- When he arrives at the next stance, he stays connected to the abseil rope while he rigs the next anchor.
- When completed, he clips himself onto the new anchor with the sling on his harness, and removes the abseil device and back-up. He can hold the ends of the rope loosely to help field the second.
- The second person can now descend in the same manner, clipping himself into the anchor when he arrives and removing his abseil device and back-up.
- The knots are removed from the ends of the rope.

- All three abseil devices are attached to the rope, the two for the novices being those closest to the anchor. Connect yourself to your device and back-up as usual. Attach a 4ft sling to each of the other devices, and clip these to their respective owners. These slings avoid your second and third being pulled around as you go down, and give them a little space to move. As you will be looking out for their safety, they will not need independent back-up prussiks. Get them to position themselves near to the rope, possibly sitting on the ground, and ensure that they are fully briefed as to what they must do once you are down. You can then start to abseil.
- As soon as your body weight is on the rope, the two other devices will be locked and unable to move. Once you reach the ground or the next stance and have made safe, the first of the two can start to descend. Hold loosely onto the end of the rope. They should be permitted sufficient rope to control their speed, but you must be attentive at all times, and ready to pull on the rope in order to stop them descending should the need arise. Once they are down, the second can join you in the same manner.

- One end of the rope is threaded through the anchor. This is then pulled down as far as the middle mark.
- When the middle mark appears at the anchor, it is held secure by one climber, while the other pulls on the second half of the rope.
- When the rope is down, the ends are knotted, it is thrown down the next pitch and the process repeated.

PROTECTION CONSIDERATIONS

There are two positions where the back-up prussik knot can be placed, below or above the device. Thought should be given to the mechanics of the system – if the knot is placed below the abseil device, the device itself holds the majority of the climber's weight, and the knot simply keeps the rope held back secure at the 180° angle required for maximum breaking. However, if the prussik is placed above the abseil device, all of the climber's weight is suspended by the knot, and the device is not loaded. The problem here is that the climber is now suspended by 6mm cord, and, if knocked, the French knot has a chance of releasing. If a Klemheist is used in this situation to prevent the knot from sliding, and it is loaded, it will be almost impossible to release again.

The only situation where the back-up knot could be positioned above is when using an Italian hitch. If the knot is used below the Italian, it can be argued that the hitch is being held in the open position, with the ropes at 180° to each other, the position of least friction.

At the Anchor

It is worthwhile carrying something with you from which to fashion an anchor, which can then be used in case a descent has to be made. This can be a couple of old slings, some untied tape from a reel, or, in a real emergency, a knife can be used to cut a short section from the end of the climbing rope. Once secured, this does not need to have a karabiner in it, as this is the only occasion on which we can sanction having the climbing rope running directly through, and in contact with, another piece of soft-wear. As you abseil, the rope will be static. When you

pull it down, it will rub against the sling and generate a lot of heat at the anchor end, but not on the rope itself.

It is for this reason that you should never use slings or bits of tat found in the hills – they may well have been used for retreat with the resulting heat build-up and loss of strength.

Knotting the Rope at the Ends

The ends of the rope should be tied in some form of knot, so as to avoid the possibility of abseiling off . The best method is to tie an overhand knot on each piece of rope. This means that any kinks chased down the rope as you abseil can come out of the end, and you will not finish up with a large twist-knot as you might if the ends were tied together.

Knotting the Rope in the Middle

When abseiling with two ropes, or if one has been damaged by rock-fall, you will need to join the ends together. One way is by tying them with a double fisherman's knot. This does tend to tighten when loaded, so an option is to tie a reef knot in the ropes first, then tie the fisherman's. The reef knot stops the whole knot sliding together and over-tightening. Either of these knots, though, are a little bulky, and have a chance of catching on the rock on the way down.

The recommended method, however, is simpler if a little more scary! Hold the ends of the rope together and simply tie an overhand knot in them, approximately 45cm from the end, and pull it tight. This means that when the rope is pulled down the crag, the overhand knot will automatically roll over to present the flat side of the knot to any obstruction, with less chance of it catching. It goes without saying that the knot should be on the same side of the anchor as the rope that is to be pulled.

Throwing the Rope

Better described as 'delivering' the rope, this may seem to be a minor point, but it becomes important at times when a wind may be blowing, or when the area through which the rope must go is narrow, such as in a gully. Start from the anchor end of the rope, and allow two or three metres of slack. Instead of coiling the rope,

Lowering

flake it over your hand, doubled, laying it across one way then back the other. Grasp the centre of these flakes, then throw the rope with some force at the target area. Flaking the rope is better than coiling, as it helps to stop it knotting as it unwraps in flight.

Rope Orientation at Anchor

This is a small detail, but extremely important. When pulling the rope through, the correct rope to pull down on is the one exiting on the inside of the anchor sling. If the rope on the inside of the anchor is pulled down, it prevents the sling and karabiner from being pulled into the rock and creating a lot of friction, and the possibility of you being unable to retrieve the rope.

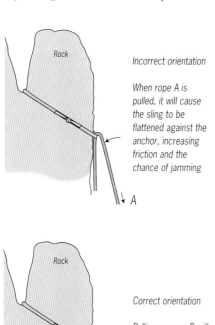

Rock

Incorrect orientation

When rope A is pulled, it will cause the sling to be flattened against the anchor, increasing friction and the chance of jamming

A

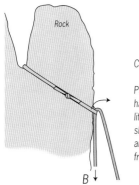

Rock

Correct orientation

Pulling on rope B will have the effect of lifting the sling slightly away from the anchor, thus reducing friction

B

What is lowering?

Lowering is a method used to protect the descent of a group member or members. There are a number of techniques; this section will illustrate two of the commonest methods using a direct belay.

Where is it used?

It is often used when traversing complicated ridges or descending routes where short, steep walls may be encountered. Instructors and guides around the world will use these techniques regularly, as it is faster to lower the climbing party than to have everyone abseil independently.

Prior to lowering a climber, you must first ensure that your rope will reach the bottom of the cliff and that a safe area is available for your party once they take the rope off. In the event that no safe area can be located at the bottom of the cliff, two options are open to you:

1 Manage the descent using multi-pitch techniques.

2 Find an alternative route.

Method 1: Using a Belay Device

Find a suitable direct anchor away from the immediate cliff edge. This will provide more space for controlling the dead rope, and will ease organising the group's descent. It is important that the leader be positioned below the anchor and that they are tied on.

■ Once you have located an anchor/s, bring it/them to one point using a sling.

■ Tie an overhand knot in the sling a few inches from its end, creating a small loop. Beware of sling angles; less than 90° is fine. Clip one HMS screwgate karabiner into the small loop, and one into the main part of the sling. Ensure that the screwgate is positioned correctly, with the gate facing upwards and the wide end pointing down hill.

■ Fix the belay device to the HMS on the small loop.

■ Flake the rope out and secure one end to the anchor so that it does not accidentally fall down the cliff.

■ Tie a figure of eight on the bight on the other end, and clip an HMS screwgate karabiner into it.

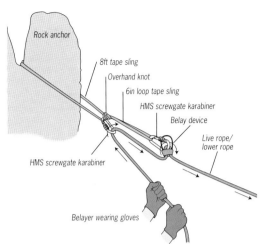

Single anchor set-up

- Clip the rope into the belay device. Now, clip the dead rope up and back into the HMS in the main part of the sling.
- Clip the figure-of-eight loop onto the harness abseil loop of the descending climber.
- Position the descending climber below the belay plate, hold the dead rope using both hands and lower the climber down.

By using this method you have created a 180° angle that is easily lockable and releasable while under tension. This additional friction allows comfort and smooth control when lowering.

OBSERVATION

It should be noted that the person controlling the rope must not be positioned above the belay device but should remain in front of it to maintain control.

The belayer should always tie himself on at the cliff top so he can comfortably observe the descending climbers; this can be easily organised using a tape sling from anchor to harness.

The belayer should wear gloves when lowering, and always lower slowly as the lower rope will experience abrasion when moving under tension over rocks.

It may be necessary to place a protective cover between the rock edge and the rope, such as a small strip of duct tape or a stuff sack.

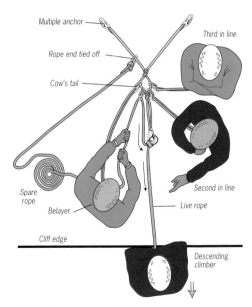

Cliff-top stance management with small group

OBSERVATION

It is obviously critical with either type of lower that the belayer controlling the descent does not let the rope release at any time. Problems that can lead to this occurring include: lowering too fast and losing control; the belayer not wearing gloves; the belayer being incorrectly positioned; and the rope diameter not being appropriate to the lowering device, in other words too thin.

■ Belay Methods *pp58–63* • Tying In *pp54–7*

Method 2: The Italian-hitch Lower

The Italian-hitch lower is an ideal technique when lowering climbers over a short section of rock, snow or ice. Unlike the belay-plate lower, only one HMS screwgate karabiner is required.

- Establish a solid anchor system, brought to one point with a sling.
- Clip an HMS onto the sling in the direction of load, and ensure that the gate is facing upwards with the wide end pointing downhill.
- The leader should position himself down-slope of the anchor and be tied on if appropriate.
- Flake out the rope, tying one end onto the anchor, and prepare the other end for clipping onto the abseil loop of the climber about to descend.
- Clip an Italian hitch into the HMS.
- Clip the rope end to the climber.
- The leader should hold the dead rope with both hands for lowering, and be wearing gloves. Again, it is important that the belayer is on the down-slope side of the anchor, in order to create the correct amount of friction.

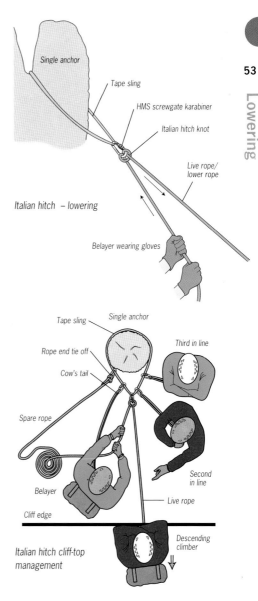

Italian hitch – lowering

Italian hitch cliff-top management

OBSERVATION

The integrity of your anchor is critical. It is important that you follow our guidelines for setting up a single- or multiple-anchor system. It is worthwhile organising your group in order of descent and ensure that members are either sitting or standing in a safe position back from the edge while the system is being prepared.

Once the descending climber has been lowered you should ensure that the figure-of-eight knot clipped to his harness is completely untied so that the rope does not snag when being pulled back up the cliff. Each member of your group should carry his own HMS screwgate karabiners. This prevents the need for gear to be hauled up the cliff, which has the potential to cause snagging problems.

It is also important to encourage the descending climbers to maintain their weight on the rope using an abseil position, feet wide apart and leaning back. Their hands will probably be used for balancing themselves away from the rock, although this will depend upon the rock shape and the situation of the descent. Once the group has descended it is likely that the leader will need to abseil.

TIPS

1 When using an Italian hitch to lower it is advisable to use a full-weight 11mm rope as it is easier to handle and will achieve greater friction.

2 Kinking of the rope can sometimes occur when feeding the dead rope through your hands to the Italian hitch on the HMS. To help avoid this, flake the rope out onto the ground and ensure that the rope feeds from the top of the pile and not from the underside.

Tying In

WHAT IS TYING IN?

Tying in is the term used for attaching the rope to your harness. When tying into a harness, you should always follow the manufacturer's recommended guidelines. We recommend a harness type that has a fixed abseil loop linking your leg loops to the waist belt. Alpine-style harnesses with a loop located on the top of the waist belt, or those with more than one attachment point, are not recommended.

The Knot
When tying into the harness, we recommend that you use a rewoven figure of eight with a stopper knot. When completed, the tie-in loop should be the same size as the abseil loop on your harness. If using a bowline with a stopper knot, you need to ensure that the stopper is properly butted against the bowline, or there is a slight chance that the bowline will loosen and release. The stopper knot on a bowline has the undesirable effect of cluttering the belay loop.

Belay Loop
By tying in you have created a belay loop that will accommodate your belay device. When belaying you should *always* use your tie-in loop as the attachment point. Avoid attaching your belay device directly to the abseil loop.

TYING ON TO ANCHORS

Single Anchor
Before tying on to a single anchor, you should ensure that the anchor is completely sound. This means testing by inspecting, tapping, pushing, pulling and kicking it. There should be no question as to its integrity, be it a sling through a thread or the rope wrapped around a 30ft oak tree.

Within Reach
This means you are within arm's reach of an HMS screwgate karabiner located at the anchor. Clip a clove hitch into the HMS screwgate karabiner.

By tying off in this fashion, you can easily adjust your position on the stance by simply adjusting the clove hitch, maintaining tension between the anchor and your harness.

Out of Reach
Establish where you need to belay from. Clip the rope to a screwgate karabiner clipped into the anchor. Take up your position and tie off into your belay loop using a figure of eight on the bight. When tying the figure of eight, start with a bight of rope 60cm long; this will ensure that the correct tail length is left once the knot has been completed.

TIPS
1 Always ensure that your hips are lower than the anchor; this maintains a downward pull in line with the ascending climber and will maintain position of the protection placed at the anchor.
2 Never compromise the integrity of your anchor by 'making do', either with placements or your belay position.

Tying into harness

Tie off to a single anchor point within reach

■ Knots pp42–6

Tie off to a single anchor point out of reach

Tie off with clove hitch at belay loop

stance. It is used whenever security cannot be guaranteed by just one anchor, or when one substantial anchor is out of line to the possible direction of loading. The important point to remember about any multiple-anchor system is that there must be *no* chance of one anchor point being shock-loaded if the other fails for some reason. To ensure this, equalised-tension methods have evolved of tying into multiple anchors by using both the rope and slings.

OBSERVATION

When tying off with a figure-of-eight knot you should ensure that when you take a bight of rope from the live, you must include the dead rope leading to the ground when making your turns. In other words, tie the knot around the two lengths of rope that form the loop. Once the knot has been tied, gently pull it tight. An indication that it is firm enough is when no daylight can be seen through the knot.

A figure of eight will absorb energy better than many other knots, as the knot will reduce in size when loaded, helping to lessen forces transmitted to the anchor.

To tension the rope while standing or sitting in position, simply lean a few inches towards the anchor and tie the knot with the ropes from the anchor pulled snug. When you lean back into position, the rope will be correctly tensioned.

It is also possible to use a clove hitch clipped into an HMS screwgate karabiner positioned at your belay loop. This has an advantage of being easy to adjust. However, the figure of eight has dynamic properties, which means that it will tighten somewhat when loaded, thus reducing the amount of shock-loading transmitted to the anchor in the event of a fall. It also does not require the use of any extra equipment. The figure of eight should always be considered as first choice.

Multiple Anchors

A multiple anchor is the use of two or more points of attachment to the rock or ice at a

Within Reach Using Rope (1: overleaf)

Clip one HMS screwgate karabiner to each anchor point. Take off the rope coming from your harness tie and clip on to the first point using a clove hitch. Leave a little slack, and clip a clove hitch into the second point. Tie off the rope back to your harness using a figure of eight on the bight. Adjust the clove hitches to equalise the tension on both sections of rope leading to your harness. The anchor is now said to be equalised.

Out Of Reach Using Rope (2)

This is a repeat of tying into one anchor using a figure of eight on a bight. Clip the rope into one anchor, bring it back to your harness and tie a figure of eight. Then simply repeat the process for the second anchor. Practice will ensure that both rope lengths are tied with the same tension.

The habit of bringing two clove hitches back to a karabiner on the belay loop is to be discouraged, as it loads the karabiner incorrectly and is extremely difficult to adjust.

Variable Anchor Positions (3)

Once the method of tying in using either a clove hitch or figure of eight has been practised and understood, the only limiting factor for attaching yourself to anchors will be the amount of rope available. An anchor system that has one out of reach and one in reach can be easily solved using first a figure of eight, then a clove hitch, and more than two anchors points can be tied into using a variety of these knots.

1   2   3

OBSERVATION

It is vital that you leave a slack but short length of rope between the two anchor points when using the in-reach clove-hitch method. This allows a two-way dimensional pull downwards, avoiding a cross-load or three-way dimensional load which would be highly dangerous, leading to a possibility of the anchor arrangement failing when extreme forces are applied. This section of slack rope also allows for a little further adjustment to the anchor-rope lengths if needed.

Using Slings at Multiple-anchor Points

There are a number of reasons why you may choose to attach yourself to a multiple anchor brought to one point with a sling: you may be short of rope, intent on leading the next pitch, be leading clients and need a central attachment point, or wish to use a direct belay method, sharing the load between the anchors. Here is a variety of methods we recommend. They are all very simple, and are to be recommended when leading multi-pitch routes in any season.

Method 1 (below left)

Attach a sling by clipping it into two screwgates at the anchors. Pull both lengths of sling downwards to a point of tension, in the direction of possible loading. Tie an overhand knot in the sling, creating a small loop. Clip an HMS screwgate karabiner into this. This will now be your attachment point. Should one anchor fail then the other will not be shock-loaded.

You can now tie into this central point using either the in-reach or out-of-reach rope method. If you are right next to the anchor, the karabiner in the sling can be simply clipped into your belay loop.

Method 2 (left)

Tie a loose overhand knot in the middle of the sling, which has the effect of creating two independent loops. Clip one loop into each anchor. Decide on the possible direction of loading, and equalise the anchors by adjusting the overhand knot.

Clip an HMS screwgate karabiner through both loops above the overhand knot, and attach yourself to this.

■ Knots pp42–6

Method 3

Attach a sling to the first anchor using a clove hitch. Create a short length of slack between both anchors and attach a second clove hitch to the second anchor. Tie an overhand knot in the sling. This creates a central point for attachment.

Method 4

You will require two slings for this. Clip one sling into each anchor. Pull the slings towards the possible direction of loading and, holding them together, tie an overhand knot near their ends. Clip an HMS screwgate karabiner into both

shortened sling sections above the overhand knot. Should the loops below the knot be even and equalised, this will be OK to clip into.

TIP

With all of the above methods, take a moment to think about the position of the sewn section of the sling. Ensure that it is not part of any knot, and that it is not the part of the sling in contact with a karabiner.

Slings with a circumference of 8ft are very common, but those of 16ft are more versatile. It is a good idea to have one 16ft sling per person when on multi-pitch mountain or winter routes.

Thinner slings are easier to tie knots into, but the knots will tend to be difficult to undo if subjected to a loading. You may decide to use a figure of eight or a figure of nine (tied the same as a figure of eight but with half a turn extra) instead of an overhand knot if a loading is certain, such as on a lowering rig.

If tying on to three anchor points, a 16ft sling is very handy. Clip the sling into all anchor points, gather all sections of the sling together (you will end up with three loops in your hand) and adjust them to the same length. Tie an overhand knot in the loops, and clip a karabiner through this as the attachment point.

Three anchor points with a sling

OBSERVATIONS

1 There is a method of arranging a sling with a twist in it so that it is self-equalising, the karabiner moving with the belayer, and it is often suggested as the best method for use with ice screws to permit constant tension. However, should one anchor point fail, there is no captive knot and the second anchor will be shock-loaded with the chance of it failing. This method should be avoided, any of the above being far more relevant, up to date and safer.

2 It should be noted that the integrity of your anchor set-up is based upon the sound placement of your protection, and the direction of pull when loaded.

Always avoid using snapgate karabiners singly at anchor points. If snap karabiners are required because no screwgates are available, double them up and position them back to back, as this will vastly reduce the chance of a gate being opened unintentionally.

3 Double- and twin-rope systems are quite common when climbing multi-pitch routes. When tying directly into two anchor points, it is worth using just one rope for the two anchors. This has the advantage that the second rope is out of the system, and can be used as a spare rope in an emergency.

Belay Methods

There are many different types of belay devices in the market place, and almost as many techniques. When using the right belay method everything should run smoothly, with the leader and second experiencing no difficulties.

When using an incorrect method for a particular situation problems arise. It is worth asking yourself each time, 'Should the climber slip will I, as the belayer, be able to hold a fall without causing injury to myself and to him?'

This section describes the correct use and appropriateness of the three 'normal' methods. Never forget that no matter how good a belayer you feel you may be, should your stance position be poor or incorrect then the integrity of your belay system is in doubt and your ability to hold a fall could be impaired.

SEMI-DIRECT BELAY

What is a semi-direct belay?

The construction of the true semi-direct belay contains four key parts:

1 Tie the rope end into your harness thereby creating the belay loop.

2 Create a single or multiple equalised anchor, whichever is appropriate.

3 Attach yourself to the anchor.

4 Attach a belay device to your belay loop. The belay device in the belay loop is ready to be used as a *semi-direct* belay.

This method absorbs any load through the belay device, the belay loop and the rope to the anchor. It should be noted that the belayer must be tight to the anchor and in line with any possible direction of loading.

Any force applied is taken away from the belayer's body, allowing him to comfortably lock off and pay out the rope when under tension.

DIRECT BELAY

There are a number of ways to arrange a direct belay, depending upon the situation. A direct belay is constructed to take the load of a fall directly to the anchor. It must be able to take a large load without any concern about it failing. The belayer can be attached or unattached to an anchor when controlling the rope, again depending on the situation. There are two common methods.

Method 1

You can belay directly by taking the rope round a rock flake, spike, boulder or tree, generating friction along the surface of the anchor. Whichever type you decide to use, it is imperative that the anchor is solid and unmovable. It is then a matter of holding the rope with both hands and taking in or paying out hand over hand as required.

TIPS

1 It is very wise to wear gloves when using this method of belay as it is solely dependent on friction; skin is sensitive and burns easily.

2 You should always have the rope-end secured, either to your harness, with chest coils or with a knot tied in it. This will prevent the accidental loss of the rope and the second, particularly when lowering!

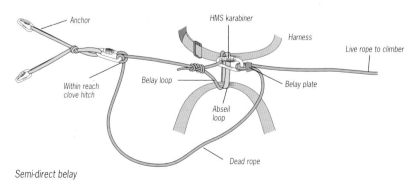

Semi-direct belay

Labels: Anchor · HMS karabiner · Harness · Live rope to climber · Within reach clove hitch · Belay loop · Belay plate · Abseil loop · Dead rope

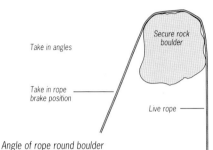

Take in angles

Secure rock boulder

Take in rope brake position

Live rope

Angle of rope round boulder

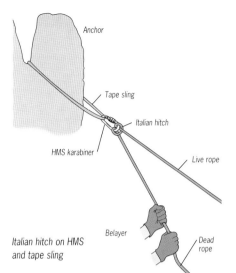

Anchor

Tape sling

Italian hitch

HMS karabiner

Live rope

Belayer

Dead rope

Italian hitch on HMS and tape sling

Method 2: Italian hitch

When using a single- or multi-point anchor system, the direct-belay method can still be used. Once you have ensured your own security, clip an HMS screwgate karabiner into the anchor. Orientate it so that the gate faces up and the wider end is away from the anchor, and clip in an Italian hitch. Stand in a comfortable and braced position, remembering that you must always be in front of an Italian hitch for it to work properly. You can now operate the belay, with any loading being transmitted directly through the system to the anchor. A major advantage of this method is that it is easily possible to lock off the Italian hitch, and remain out of the system all of the time.

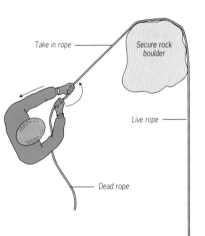

Take in rope

Secure rock boulder

Live rope

Dead rope

Belay technique hand over hand and stance

OBSERVATIONS

1 The most important factor is the strength of the anchor. You should progressively test the anchor before committing to it by first gently tapping it, then shaking it and finally kicking it. However, don't kick it off down the mountain as it may cause injury to your partner, client or others.
2 Before belaying you should ensure that your stance is solid and comfortable, that you are in a braced position, and that there is no chance of the rope lifting off from the anchor as your second reaches you.
3 The direct belay is only advisable when belaying an ascending second/climber, or when lowering off short awkward steps.

OBSERVATION

This type of friction knot is very simple to use and has a big advantage in that it is very fast to belay with, and so can be used where speed and security are prime concerns. It is common practice to use this method when moving together such as when short roping or when traversing serious ridges where it is often critical to move fast.

TIPS

1 Ensure that you flake or place your spare rope in a suitable position so it doesn't knot, snag or drop down the route.
2 The Italian hitch can easily be transferred to a clove hitch, should the second need to be locked off at the stance, or the Italian locked off using the slippery hitch and two half hitches.

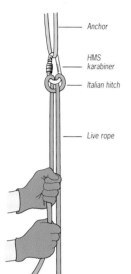

Anchor

HMS karabiner

Italian hitch

Live rope

The brake position

In harder snow conditions, it is possible to take a direct belay from a snow anchor. Careful judgement is required, as direct belay anchors must be impeccably solid. The following could be considered as being practical and safe anchors for a direct belay under good conditions:

- A buried or reinforced axe anchor. The sling must be correctly clove-hitched and great care must be taken to ensure that the load is directed along the surface of the snow. A shallow pit a couple of inches deep can be cut at the karabiner position, to ensure that the Italian does not jam if loaded.
- From a dead-man. The above considerations apply.
- From a snow bollard. The rope can be used as follows: tie a large loop in the end of the rope by using a fig 8 on the bight. This loop should be large enough to fit around the bollard. Tie a second but much smaller fig 8 on the bight just below the knot, into which an HMS screwgate and the Italian hitch is clipped. The rest of the rope is then used to effect the lower, and it should be stored on a ledge prepared for the purpose.

INDIRECT BELAY

This is often known as the body belay. The rope is taken round the belayer's back and positioned at the top of the hips. A turn of the dead rope is taken round the arm to act as a friction brake should force be applied. It is important that the belayer is tied on to an anchor in such a manner as to prevent him from being pulled off the stance and accidentally releasing the rope. In exceptional circumstances when winter climbing you may only have a bucket seat for security when belaying with this method.

This type of belaying is often the most appropriate in winter where snow and ice anchors may be limited, scarce or of dubious quality, and absorbing the load through the body becomes important to reduce any loading on the anchor.

Method

- Once you have tied on to your anchor and correctly adjusted the tension between it and your harness, sit down and brace yourself with your feet shoulder width apart. Take in the slack rope between yourself and the climber, then arrange the rope round your back above your hips to the front, ensuring that it runs over the top of the rope from the anchor.
- When using a front attachment harness, it is *essential* that the rope to the climber is on the same side of your body as the rope from the anchor.

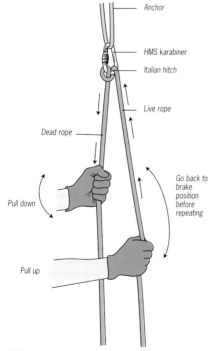

Anchor

HMS karabiner

Italian hitch

Live rope

Dead rope

Go back to brake position before repeating

Pull down

Pull up

Taking in

OBSERVATIONS

It is worth noting that whenever you decide to use a body belay there is a number of basic principles you should adhere to.

1 Sit down whenever possible, as you can brace your feet to help prevent being pulled off the stance.

2 Never stand and body belay when not tied-on to an anchor.

3 Always make sure that the rope runs in a straight line from the climber, past you to the anchor. If the rope to the climber and anchor run on opposite sides to your body and a fall is held, severe injury to your spine could occur.

4 Never take a twist round the live-rope arm. This could result in injury.

5 Ensure that the rope around your body is running low down behind your back, and that it has not got caught up on your rucksack if worn.

6 Wear gloves when belaying, even in summer.

7 The rope around your body must go over your head, and not be stepped into. It should be resting on top of the rope coming in from the anchor.

■ The process of controlling the rope during a leader fall is also important, as you should never stop the leader suddenly. Let the rope slip a little, bringing your braking arm across the front of your body to increase the friction. This will dilute any shock-loading to the system and prevent the belayer from being pulled off his stance.

This technique is applicable to all seasons. However, semi-direct or direct belays may well be more relevant for the majority of situations.

SELECTING A BELAY DEVICE

There is a vast range of belay devices to choose from, with each one designed differently in its shape and use. When choosing one, you should consider purchasing a modern multi-purpose device. Not every belay device will be appropriate for your rope diameter, as some are designed for 8.5 and 9mm ropes only, while others are designed for 9.5mm to 11mm ropes. Using the correct gauge of rope with your belay plate is essential.

You should ensure that you receive a manufacturer's instructional leaflet when purchasing a device and follow the directions given. Time spent practising with the device before using it on the hill will be well spent. When using a modern belay device, you are no longer required to have spent a year in the gym working out. Your arm strength plays little part in the use of a belay device when used correctly.

Method

■ To rig a belay device, a bight of rope is simply pushed through it then clipped to your belay loop using an HMS screwgate karabiner. Most devices will have a leash attached that requires to be clipped into the HMS alongside the bight of rope, which prevents the device from sliding out of reach when belaying.

■ We recommend that the leash be a fixed steel or wire loop, as this type does not get damaged or tangle as easily as a cord loop. The belay device and its method of use creates a braking force that's designed to slow down and stop a falling climber. The braking force and mechanics of a device will vary; the manufacturer's guidelines should highlight these braking forces in kilograms.

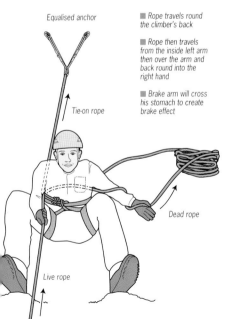

Equalised anchor

■ Rope travels round the climber's back

■ Rope then travels from the inside left arm then over the arm and back round into the right hand

■ Brake arm will cross his stomach to create brake effect

Tie-on rope

Dead rope

Live rope

Indirect belay

BELAY-DEVICE ORIENTATION

When attaching your belay device, *always* clip it to the loop created by tying on to the rope.

Paying out Rope to Lead Climber
It is important to clip on to the *top* of your belay loop above the figure-of-eight knot, ensuring that there are no twists and that the rope runs smoothly through the device (below left).

Taking in Rope
Clip your belay device to your loop *below* the figure of eight, again ensuring that there are no twists and that it all runs smoothly (below right).

Controlling the Dead Rope
It is important to pay attention before belaying, and to check that the belay-device orientation is correct before giving the climber the command to climb.

To safeguard the climber, it is critical that

TIP
If, on a multi-pitch route, the belay device needs to be ro orientated when the second arrives at the stance and the anchor points are within reach, they can simply clip themselves to the anchor system before the device is moved. However, if the anchor points are out of reach, this can be attained by the following method. Once the second arrives at the stance, tie an overhand knot on a bight in the dead rope, and clip this loop to your harness tie-in point with a screwgate. The belay device may now be removed, re-orientated, replaced, the overhand knot untied, and the second can now lead through.

you never let the dead rope release from your hand. You must take a firm hold at all times and never compromise this when sliding your hands forwards and backwards on the dead rope. If your rope from the anchor runs to your right side, your right hand should hold the dead rope and vice versa.

Common Belaying Mistakes	Remedy
Always relying on a single anchor.	Single anchors are good as long as they are absolutely solid. Always test them before using. If in any doubt, use a multiple anchor.
Standing to belay with anchors arranged below waist height.	If no good high anchors can be found, then sit down low to belay.
Anchors not equalised.	Adjust the system and check that should one anchor fail the other will not be shock loaded.
Not in line with an anticipated direction of pull.	Redirect the ropes running back to the anchor or adjust your belay stance.
Belay device clipped to abseil loop on harness.	Always clip on to your tie-on belay loop.
Incorrect orientation of belay device.	Ensure that it is in the correct position for taking in and paying out.
Not having free movement of control hand on the belay device.	Extend yourself from the anchors away from the obstruction, or go under the anchor attachment rope and belay on the other side with the correct hand.
Ropes jamming in belay device.	Belay device may be twisted and incorrectly orientated or belay device is too small for the rope diameter. Rope fed to belay device may be kinked or knotted, indicating poor attention to stance management.
Rope not feeding out slack when required.	Using an inappropriate mechanical direct-belay device.

OBSERVATIONS

1 It is important that you learn to belay using either hand for taking in the dead rope, as you will not always have a stance position that would allow you to use your stronger hand. It is very possible, if using the incorrect hand, that a shock-load would rotate your body and make it very difficult to lock off the belay device.

2 Remember to watch the lead climber as he will require slack rope when clipping into placed protection. Should you not provide enough slack rope you may accidentally pull the leader off-route. When taking up your belay position for protecting a leader, ensure that the rope to him is running up the line of the route.

3 *Always* belay from your tie-in loop, rather than from the abseil loop on your harness.

Summer/Winter Multi-pitch Changeovers

What is a route change-over?

This is the process of rope management, allowing climbers to alternate between leads or for one climber to lead the entire multi-pitch route.

This section will illustrate different methods of route change-overs in both summer and winter conditions. In addition, we will highlight some of the common problems climbers experience, particularly those who are making the transition from summer multi-pitch climbing to winter multi-pitch climbing. When selecting a route, you should consider alternative options in the event that your choice is not suitable for any reason.

Planning Your Trip

- The weather: the effects on you and your partners.
- Avalanche forecast: potential hazards at the chosen venue.
- Route choice: consider the length and how long it will take.
- Maintain flexibility: is the route in condition?
- Equipment: personal and team needs.
- Climbing ropes: single- or double-rope techniques.
- Adopt a rope system: how many people are climbing; rope management.
- Climbing partners: their experience; are you instructing or guiding?

Once you have carefully planned your trip the next stage is to consider whether you have the appropriate skills, techniques and equipment to do a route.

STANCE MANAGEMENT

One of the key areas that may often slow down climbing teams is poor stance management. Climbers often become benighted on routes because they have simply moved too slowly.

What is a stance?

A stance is a position on a cliff face where you have chosen to stand or sit by attaching and tying yourself to an anchor.

What is stance management?

Stance management is one of the most important aspects of climbing. When climbing multi-pitch routes, it is crucial to get your ropes organised and seconds positioned correctly. This allows the seconds to belay safely and the leader to climb smoothly. This is achieved by adopting a rope method appropriate to your situation.

Managing your stance includes:

- Location of stance.
- Equipment required.
- Rigging appropriate anchor/s.
- Tying yourself on.
- Positioning yourself for belaying.
- Preparing a position for seconds/thirds.
- Belay-plate orientation.
- Position for spare rope taken in.
- Climbing calls.
- On arrival at stance, positioning and locking off your second/third.
- Preparing the dead rope and belay-plate orientation for leader climbing on.

EQUIPMENT

Careful consideration must be given when choosing your belay device. When leading on 8.5 or 9.5mm ropes it needs to be an appropriate fit for the ropes in order to lock off without experiencing slippage.

OBSERVATIONS

1 Often, instructors will have two people climbing together while belaying them independently. To achieve this, careful selection of the belay device is important as is the position of the spare rope taken in. If two people can climb one above the other safely, then this will save much time.

2 On some routes, climbers may have enough space to climb side by side, which will help prevent debris from falling onto others. Alternatively, seconds may need to move one at a time on each pitch to reduce the hazard from falling debris. In winter climbing, a stance should be located in a reasonably safe position, protected from falling debris dislodged by the lead climber or another climbing party above.

3 To achieve a smooth transition on multi-pitch changeovers, you should consider trying relevant techniques in a controlled situation. A steep route is no place to be when practising for the first time.

Mountain Weather pp10–14 • Avalanche Awareness pp107–15 • Gear Lists p159 • Tying-In pp54–7 • Knots pp42–6

MULTI-PITCH STANCE MANAGEMENT

Method 1 One to One

Scenario: the route will be climbed swapping leads. The route continues up the wall behind the stance.

■ The leader constructs and connects himself to an anchor system.

■ The leader ensures that the belay-device orientation is correct. This means that any loading should not allow the live and dead ropes to cross at the device, which could potentially cause a lack of friction, affecting the device's ability to lock off the rope. Ensure that the dead rope is being placed in an accessible position, very close to the belayer.

■ When the second arrives at the stance, he secures himself by either clipping into the anchor, or by the belayer tying a big overhand knot on the bight on the dead rope close to the belay device. If the device needs re-orientating, the second should clip into the anchor while the belayer unclips and re-clips the device.

■ The belayer passes the equipment to the new leader.

■ The belayer now ensures that his stance is appropriate to the direction that the new leader will be taking.

OBSERVATION

In winter the leader should secure his ice tools, either to the anchor or in a safe position near the stance.

It is important to have a ledge well prepared, not only for the leader and second to stand on, but sufficient in size to allow the rope to be flaked onto it. In some situations, it may be that a separate ledge is dug in the snow to accommodate the rope.

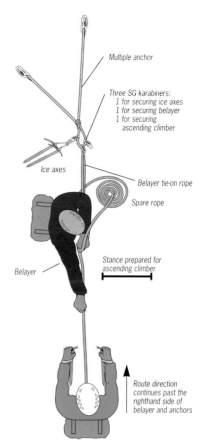

Multiple anchor

Three SG karabiners:
1 for securing ice axes
1 for securing belayer
1 for securing ascending climber

Ice axes

Belayer tie-on rope

Spare rope

Stance prepared for ascending climber

Belayer

Route direction continues past the righthand side of belayer and anchors

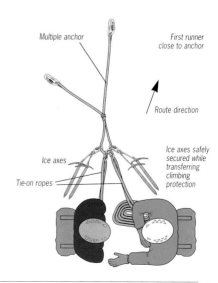

Multiple anchor

First runner close to anchor

Route direction

Ice axes

Ice axes safely secured while transferring climbing protection

Tie-on ropes

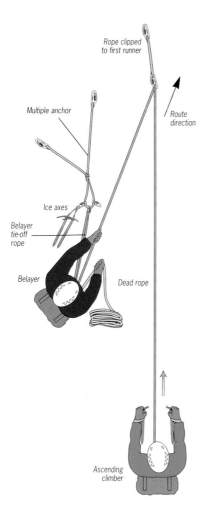

Rope clipped
to first runner

Multiple anchor

Route
direction

Ice axes

Belayer
tie-off
rope

Belayer

Dead rope

Ascending
climber

One to Two

Scenario: you are climbing a winter gully with two clients. You will be leading all of the pitches. You have decided to use a plaquette direct-belay method for both of your seconds. Two ropes will be used.

■ The leader arrives at the stance and creates an anchor, clipping into it and using it as a runner as he prepares the stance for the seconds.
■ Two HMS karabiners are placed in the central point of the anchor system. These will be used by the seconds as anchors.
■ The leader ties on to the anchor and prepares for belaying.

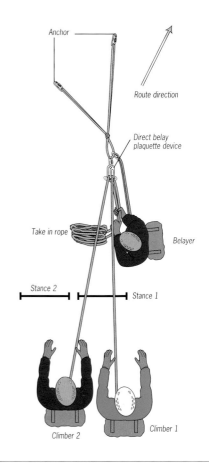

Anchor

Route direction

Direct belay
plaquette device

Take in rope

Belayer

Stance 2

Stance 1

Climber 2

Climber 1

Method 2 One to One

■ With this method, the leader, upon reaching the stance, prepares an anchor as normal. However, he also pre-places the first piece of protection on the next pitch, clipping the rope to the second through this.
■ The leader will then take up a belay position facing into the rock, with the rope running from his plate, up through the runner, and down to the second. When the second arrives at the stance, he has simply to take the gear off from the belayer, and continue climbing. No re-orientation of any part of the system is needed.
■ This method, though not always possible, is to be recommended. Anchors capable of taking an upward pull should be considered, in case the system needs to be escaped for any reason.

OBSERVATIONS
Method 2 One to One

It should be noted that it is extremely important to place runner above the stance as soon as possible when in a multi-pitch situation. This helps to reduce the shock loading to the system and avoids a factor-two fall occurring. The placing of an early runner should be of prime concern.

One to Two

1 The leader should remember to instruct the seconds on how to extract climbing protection from both the anchor and while on the route. Organising equipment extracted from the route is important so that expensive and much-needed gear does not get lost.

2 Should you have two seconds climbing together on two ropes, either have them climbing one above the other at not too great a distance between them, or have them both climb side by side. You should think about objective dangers, such as falling debris, in winter conditions.

In most cases you may choose to belay your seconds one at a time, or, when the first arrives at the stance he could belay the last second. Whichever person is free while the other belays the final person, they should prepare the rope for the next pitch.

Although an extremely useful device, a plaquette has a major drawback in that it is not easy to pay out rope when it is loaded. For this reason, we would only recommend them for use where there is no chance of your second/s falling into a free-hanging situation.

■ When the seconds arrive they should be stacked in order of climbing, close together and one above each other, or side by side.
■ The leader should be positioned in such a way as to be on the outside of the seconds when they arrive at the anchor.
■ When the seconds arrive at the stance, both dead ropes should be run through so that the lead rope runs from the top of the pile.
■ The seconds then belay the leader. Both seconds may belay the leader, or just one using a rope through the belay plate while the other rope trails and is hand fed by the other second.

One to Three

Scenario: you are leading a group up a buttress route of a moderate grade. Two ropes are being used.

Method of Attaching Three Seconds to Two Ropes

- The leader ties on to one end of each of the ropes.
- Two of the climbers tie on to the other ends using a rewoven figure-of-eight knot.
- The third climber ties on approximately two metres from one of the other climbers. First tying an isolation loop, he must then use either a rewoven overhand knot with the tail loop clipped back into the belay loop using a screwgate karabiner, or a rewoven figure of eight on the bight (using a screwgate karabiner to clip in should be discouraged when climbing).
- The leader will tie on to both ends of the rope to create an Alpine 'V' shape, then start to ascend the route. It is important to advise the person tied on part-way up the rope that he must not climb past the isolation-loop knot; also, that the two seconds climbing together be briefed to maintain the 2m distance between them.

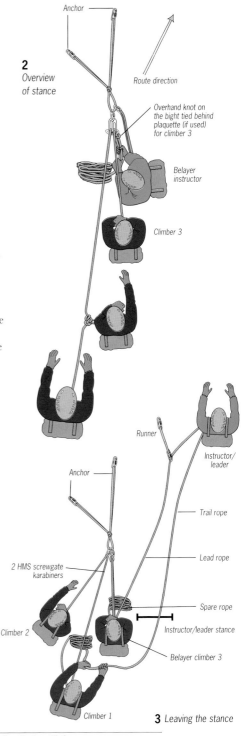

2 Overview of stance

Anchor

Route direction

Overhand knot on the bight tied behind plaquette (if used) for climber 3

Belayer instructor

Climber 3

Runner

Instructor/ leader

Anchor

Trail rope

Lead rope

2 HMS screwgate karabiners

Spare rope

Climber 2

Instructor/leader stance

Belayer climber 3

Climber 1

3 Leaving the stance

1 *Attaching three seconds*

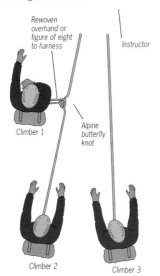

Rewoven overhand or figure of eight to harness

Instructor

Climber 1

Alpine butterfly knot

Climber 2

Climber 3

■ Tying-In pp54–7 • Belay Methods pp58–63 • Anchors pp21–3 • Knots pp42–6

On Arrival at the Stance

■ The leader creates an anchor, secures himself, and clips two HMS screwgate karabiners into the central point in readiness for the arrival of seconds.

■ He then prepares the belay device and calls the seconds to climb in the pre-arranged climbing order. The rope with one climber attached is taken in first, as he will often be climbing faster than the two.

■ The first second is clipped into one of the HMSs, in a position next to the belayer.

■ When the final two climbers arrive at the stance, clip them into the second HMS using the short section of rope between them, so that they are counterbalancing each other. A clove hitch could also be tied here if thought necessary.

■ Flake the ropes and run them back through.

OBSERVATION

When two climbers are moving together in winter, especially when sharing the same rope, there is a danger of injury through contact with each other's axe or crampons. It is essential to train in the art of ice-axe and crampon use before attempting a route, and to employ a full briefing about maintaining the distance between each other.

Stance Management: Common Problems

Whether climbing for fun, or professionally instructing, you should always ensure that your partner or client understands your stance management system and procedures. Should any seconds be unsure as to what is required of them, or lack training with interpretation of procedures, then problems and serious delays will arise.

Think about problems that you have experienced while organising your stance: do the same problems recur again and again?

Problem	Cause	Remedy
Ropes twisted at the stance.	Leader positioning seconds incorrectly, inhibiting direction of travel of leader.	Leader positions seconds to the inside of route and stacks in order of climbing.
Rope running between seconds at stance.	Inefficient check of belayer and poor belaying. Dead rope stowed in wrong position.	Consideration should be given to the position of the person belaying the leader, and the location of the dead rope.
Seconds and leader can't hear climbing calls.	Poor location of stance, inefficient briefing on climbing-call interpretation.	Stay in sight of seconds, shorten the pitch length in bad weather, check and understand climbing call terms.
Debris falling down on seconds.	Poor location of stance, poor route choice, poor technique, seconds dislodging debris onto each other.	Good location of stance protecting seconds from the line of debris, improved route selection, improved technique. Ensure that seconds moving together maintain a short maximum distance.
Seconds drop the dead rope down route which then jams.	Inefficient stowing of dead rope and inattentive belaying.	Good stance-management skills. In winter, dig a ledge for the rope.
Seconds incorrectly positioned at the stance.	Leader has not prepared climbing order, creating rope twisting and confusion. The seconds depart from the stance in the wrong sequence.	Good stance management; on arrival the leader positions himself on the outside edge of the stance and route direction, then prepares for seconds' arrival.
Poor orientation of belay device, thus the lead rope sticks and twists creating rope drag. Belay device cannot then be locked off properly.	Lack of knowledge or practice in the correct method of use.	Ensure that you have an appropriate device for your rope types; learn how to orientate for taking in a second and belaying a leader.

Tying-In pp54–7 • Belay Methods pp58–63 • Anchors pp21–3 • Knots pp42–6 ■

Stance Management: Common Problems continued:

Problem	Cause	Remedy
Seconds get very cold.	Leader moving too slowly and seconds not adequately clothed for mountain temperatures.	Preparation; ensure that you take clothing into consideration when planning, especially extremities. You may also have chosen the wrong route if the climbing is too difficult for the leader.
Seconds unclipping from anchor in wrong stacking order with ropes getting twisted and knotted.	Inefficient instruction. Confusion as to which second de-rigs the anchor.	Before committing to a route it is worthwhile practising the order of climbing and communication calls. This can easily be achieved on a small outcrop of rock or ice.
Losing your ice tools from the stance.	Ice tools not attached to anchor or secured into the ice. Often it is the belay rope or lead rope snaking between axes that catches them and pulls them out.	Clip ice-axe straps to the anchor at the central point of attachment or stow the axes into the ice away from rope movement.

Aim	Need	Action
Remain in sight of seconds.	Choose an appropriate and safe location for the stance.	Consider the level of seconds' experience. Ensure that you can see the seconds, and that they can hear your calls.
Rig an equalised anchor.	Create a multiple anchor that allows the leader to carry on through with minimum disruption to the system.	When instructing and leading you may decide to avoid rigging the anchor with spare rope and simply use a tape sling to create a central clip point.
Safety of yourself.	Tie yourself on at the anchor before you call 'safe' to the belayer.	Ensure that your position at the stance is appropriate and is suitable for the climbing order of the seconds.
Stance and anchor prepared to accommodate the seconds.	In winter you should dig or cut slots in the snow/ ice for the seconds to stand or sit in, and then position them in climbing order.	Prepare screwgate karabiners in correct orientation at the anchor central point of clipping, prior to seconds arriving at stance.
Prepare a position for the dead rope.	Ensure that the rope taken in will be stowed at the appropriate position for the belayer.	Arrange the rope neatly on the ledge, round your leg or over your anchor attachment point. In winter, cut a slot or dig out a hollow in the snow to place it in.
Ensure that you have an appropriate belay device, and that it is orientated correctly.	Be familiar with your belay device. Check that it is orientated for taking in and paying out the rope.	Learn how to lock off the belay plate to safeguard seconds on arrival at the stance prior to clipping on to anchor.
Preparing take-in rope for leading on.	Re-flake the rope.	The leader's rope should now be running from the top of the pile. The second attaches the rope to his belay plate. Leader climbs on.

Tying-In pp54–7 • Belay Methods pp58–63 • Anchors pp21–3 • Knots pp42–6

Rock Climbing

This chapter looks at a few of the more important considerations when rock climbing, with the emphasis on learning to lead, and the way an instructor may be able to assist by being close by. There is a variety of instructional books that devote many pages to the placement of runners and anchors, and you are directed towards one of these if you are requiring basic information.

◼

LEARNING TO LEAD

This section is aimed at preparing the novice to lead by learning through best practice, but the comments within are equally relevant for consideration by anyone undertaking to instruct rock climbing.

Following the experience of climbing on indoor walls, and bottom roping and top roping on a crag, the next stage in the leading process is to practise clipping pre-placed protection on a route. This should take place on a single-pitch crag. To practise this safely for the first time, the novice leader can work on a bottom rope. This method allows him to practise placing and clipping runners without the worry of clipping incorrectly and falling any great distance. There are three methods to choose from:

1 Place all the protection on the ascent while being protected by a bottom rope.
2 Abseil down the route and pre-place all the protection.
3 Use an instructor to set it up.

Method

Two ropes will be needed, one for the bottom rope set up, the other for a 'lead' rope used to clip the runners. If learning from an instructor, he will often climb beside you on a fixed rope anchored to the side of your route. This allows him to offer coaching as you climb and to give any assistance should you feel uncomfortable.

◼ Once you have arrived at the top of the route, the belayer will gently lower you back down.
◼ The trail rope will simply run through the pre-clipped protection as you descend. Now you can untie the trail rope and pull it back through all the pre-placed protection, then prepare to climb back up practising the extraction of the protection.

OBSERVATION

It should be noted that the trail rope used by the lead climber to practise clipping protection should be properly uncoiled and flaked on the ground for it to run smoothly, with the leader's end running from the top of the pile, and it should be close to, and on the correct side of, the belayer.

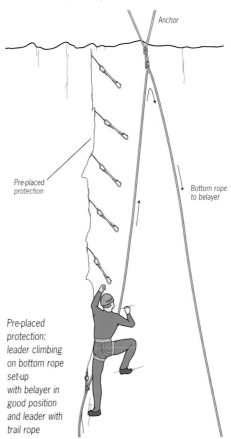

Anchor

Pre-placed protection

Bottom rope to belayer

Pre-placed protection: leader climbing on bottom rope set-up with belayer in good position and leader with trail rope

COACHING NOTE

This is the first progression towards leading, and as such should be made as realistic as possible, erring on the side of safety. For instance, the bottom rope can be left reasonably slack, in order to simulate the feeling of leading. The climber can be allowed to place his own gear, and it can be discussed on the descent with the instructor alongside. If you are instructing, do not forget the role of the second, as he is performing an important task and may feel a little isolated if all of your attention is with the leader.

Knots pp42–6 • Anchors pp21–3 • Abseiling pp47–50 ◼

Learning to Lead without a Bottom Rope

The next stage is when preparing to lead without the security of a bottom rope. It is advisable to pre-place your protection, either by abseil or by using a bottom rope. Check that the belayer is correctly positioned and has correctly orientated his belay plate.

- A good belayer is part of the key to success. The belayer should be anchored at the bottom of the route, using one of the methods for setting up an anchor already mentioned in previous chapters.
- It is also critical that the belayer is belaying close to the base of the route. This is necessary as the further the belayer is from the crag the more chance that the first, and possibly subsequent, protection will pull out, as a tensioned sideways pull will be created. The lead rope requires to run smoothly through the extenders.
- The leader will, after checking with the belayer, climb.

The leader should be careful as to the position of the lead rope while ascending and clipping. It is very easy for the rope to slip round to the back of your leg, and should you take a fall with the rope in this position then you may be inverted with the possibility of injury. Once the leader gets to the top he should set up an anchor and prepare to belay the second. After the correct call sequence, the second can now climb and extract all of the gear.

Leader climbing with pre-placed protection in place

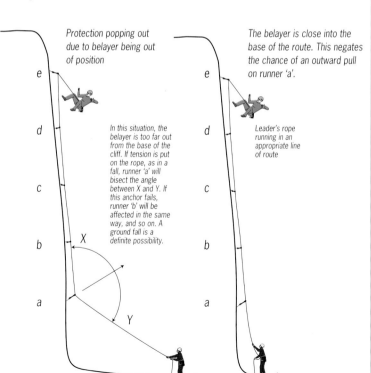

Protection popping out due to belayer being out of position

The belayer is close into the base of the route. This negates the chance of an outward pull on runner 'a'.

In this situation, the belayer is too far out from the base of the cliff. If tension is put on the rope, as in a fall, runner 'a' will bisect the angle between X and Y. If this anchor fails, runner 'b' will be affected in the same way, and so on. A ground fall is a definite possibility.

Leader's rope running in an appropriate line of route

With rope wrapped dangerously round leader's leg

■ Tying In *pp54–7* • Belay Methods *pp58–63*

When leading your first route, you will obviously not have any pre-placed protection. If you are concerned about this, it would be wise to abseil the route and place two or three key runners that will act as 'islands of safety' should you need them. Having an instructor beside you on a fixed rope is a definite advantage. It is important to choose a route that is well within your climbing capabilities.

Method

■ Once you leave the belayer, stay calm and focused; your aim is to place protection as soon as possible after leaving the ground and at 3–5ft intervals. Consider that, if your first piece of protection is at 8ft above the ground, your second piece cannot be 4ft above that, as that means there will be sufficient slack rope for you to hit the ground.

■ If the climbing is getting too difficult and you haven't placed any protection and are thinking you may fall, remain cool and down climb before you get into real exposure and trouble.

■ It is also important to ensure that placed protection is adequately extended, which will avoid unnecessary rope drag.

■ Belaying from the ground is difficult to perform slickly and safely. The rope should be sufficiently slack as to not inhibit the leader as he moves up, but not so slack as to allow him to travel some distance in the event of a fall. The belayer needs to pay particular attention when the lead climber asks for slack rope, possibly for clipping a runner. At this point, the lead climber is vulnerable, from pulling through some slack, failing to clip and falling off. Ensure that slack is given straight away, and the unused slack retrieved when the piece of gear is clipped. The belayer should remain constantly alert, continuously adjusting the rope through the belay device.

■ When you have led the route and reached the top, you may wish to have a rest for a minute or two, in order to clear your mind before bringing up your second. Remember your own safety, and communicate properly with him before proceeding.

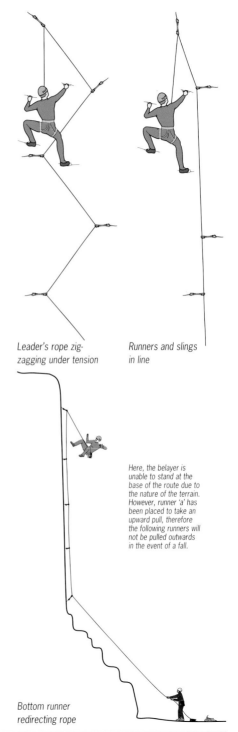

Leader's rope zig-zagging under tension

Runners and slings in line

Here, the belayer is unable to stand at the base of the route due to the nature of the terrain. However, runner 'a' has been placed to take an upward pull, therefore the following runners will not be pulled outwards in the event of a fall.

Bottom runner redirecting rope

Rock Climbing

Comments on Gear Placement

This book concentrates on the more technical aspects of mountaineering in all its forms. Therefore, we are not including a chapter on the basic placing of equipment, since this can be read about in great detail in other publications. There are, however, several observations about equipment placements that need to be discussed. The object of this short section is to bring a few of those to light as a series of notes.

- There is a bewildering variety of different items of equipment on the market, both hardware and software, all designed for a particular job, and usually tested to stringent safety standards. All of these items of kit can be dramatically weakened by misuse and abuse, high impact, a load or a fall, corrosion, abrasion, cuts in textile components, prolonged ultra-violet light, incorrect loading over sharp edges, age, poor storage conditions, temperature, sea water, and chemical contamination. You should make a habit of *always* inspecting your kit before and after use.

- It is a matter of personal choice where you carry your kit while on a route. The gear loops on a harness are good, as long as the gear is easily accessible. A bandolier is another option; this is easier to pass over when swapping leads on a multi-pitch route, but it can cause the kit to bunch together making gear selection awkward. A compromise might be extenders on a bandolier, the rest of the kit on your harness. Whichever method you prefer, ensure that the kit is easy to get at and racked in a logical order.

- It is advisable to have a wide range of wire sizes: a set of 1 to 9 is good with an additional set advisable. For carrying the wires, it is best to split them into two sets of 1 to 5, and 6 to 9, clipped to two snap-gate karabiners.

- When placing a piece of equipment, summer or winter, as a running belay or as an anchor, ensure that the direction of load is compatible with the position of the device being used.

- When a wire has been placed, it is good

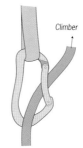

Climber

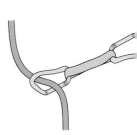

Incorrectly clipped. The rope could unclip from the karabiner in the event of a fall

Extender incorrectly clipped. Movement through the rope will cause the extender to rotate, with the possibility of dislodging the wire placement

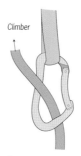
Climber

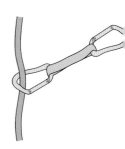

Correctly clipped. The rope will run across the back bar of the karabiner in the event of a fall

Extender correctly clipped

practice to pull down sharply on the karabiner to which it is connected, to help ensure a good placement and minimise the chance of it swinging out with the movement of the rope. When seating the wire, only one firm pull is required: constant tugging is to be discouraged. Ensure that the hand that is not pulling has a firm grip on the rock, as a wire that flicks out of a placement when tugged may well send you off balance.

- A camming device with a rigid stem will not be able to be deployed in quite as many situations as one with a flexible stem. Care should be taken to avoid using a rigid-stemmed device in a horizontal crack, where the effect of a fall could be to snap it.

- Camming devices should not be used on

■ Gear Lists p159

main belay anchors, as they are prone to 'walking' into a crack, which will compromise the make-up of the belay system.

■ Care should be taken not to force a camming device too far into a crack, as, once the trigger is released, there is a high chance of it becoming irretrievable.

■ If there is a danger of a camming device 'walking' into a crack when being placed on the lead, it can be extended by clipping an extender on to the sewn tape loop.

■ It is important, before you begin to lead, that you position your karabiners correctly on your extenders. Ensure that the gates are opening the correct way; it is normal to have the karabiners facing opposite directions on each end.

■ It is important that the rope runs correctly up through the karabiner, allowing the extender to hang naturally and not twist the gear placement.

■ Bent gate karabiners are often seen on extenders. These are designed to make clipping the rope easy; unfortunately, in some circumstances, they allow the un-clipping of the rope to occur in the event of a fall. It is essential that the rope runs in a manner that lets it run across the back bar of the karabiner so that, in the event of a fall, the rope will stay well away from the gate.

■ When a piece of gear has been clipped, ensure that neither of the karabiners will have their gates pushed against the rock and opened in the event of a fall. A karabiner's strength is compromised many times when the gate is not in its correct position.

■ Great care should be taken when using bent gate karabiners on long routes in summer or winter, as it cannot be guaranteed that they will sit in the safest configuration, with the rope running across the back bar.

■ Bent gate karabiners should only be used on the rope end of the extender, and never be clipped directly into the projection.

■ Care should be exercised when using extenders on bolted routes. The karabiner that attaches to the bolt is easily marked on the inside surface when falls occur, and these abrasions could consequently damage a climbing rope. It is wise to keep a set of

karabiners simply for the purpose of using on bolted routes.

■ Slings are the traditional piece of gear for threading around anchors, but do not forget that wires can be threaded, too. They can be placed in such a manner that the head of the nut sits loosely on top of a constriction, having been placed by first passing the wire loop down through the hole and then clipping it with an extender.

■ Often, the first piece of gear on a pitch is placed to avoid ankle injury on the initial moves, thus it may not need to be extended. It might be an advantage to simply clip it with a spare karabiner, increasing the distance for which it will be of an advantage to the leader.

INSTRUCTING LEADING

Below are given a number of pros and cons of soloing alongside a novice when teaching leading. It should be fairly obvious that using a

Soloing CONS	Roped Ascent CONS
Need to be competent climbing several grades harder.	Time consuming to set up.
No use to panicking leader.	Need access to top of route.
Chance of being grabbed by panicking leader.	Rope may be in way of leader.
Chance of being accidentally knocked off by leader.	
Chance of serious injury if fall occurs.	
PROS No setting up required.	**PROS** Complete safety for instructor.
Ease of movement around route.	Ability to clip leader to system if required.

rope for your own security will be the safest, both for yourself and for your student. The importance of having the ability to clip your student to your system should he begin to feel uncomfortable should not be underestimated.

Using Rope Ascenders

The safest way to teach leading is by the use of rope ascenders. Many different types are available, but the way of connecting them to yourself stays basically the same. Considering that an average beginner's pitch will be less than 25m in height, the instructor's rope in this case has been doubled, secured to an anchor at the top, and the ends lowered down. The system that we recommend is as follows:

■ Two handle ascenders are being used on one half of the rope. One is connected to your abseil loop with a 4ft sling, and will be the upper of the two when clipped to the rope. The second one is connected to your foot with an 8ft sling, possibly with a couple of twists in it to shorten it to a suitable length. This ascender is also connected to your abseil

loop with a 4ft sling – this provides extra security.

■ An Italian hitch may be clipped, taken from the second rope, into an HMS connected to your harness abseil loop, if felt necessary, or if there is any chance of your rope being damaged on the rock above. The slack can be fed through this at intervals. This second rope can also be used to secure a nervous leader, as loops may be tied into it at required points, and the leader's rope clipped into these. This allows: a) an impromptu 'runner', adequate until a proper suitable runner is located, or b) the means to enable the belayer to lower the leader to the ground.

■ If using devices other than standard handled ascenders, be careful that they are being used for the purpose for which they were designed. It may be sensible to make a series of overhand knots in the rope below you to avoid any chance of sliding down.

■ Sometimes, instructors might be seen using a cow's-tail from their top ascender into which a failing leader can be clipped. This should be avoided, as the loading on the ascender when being placed under even a small shock-loading is sufficient to strip the rope sheath, or to cause complete failure of the system.

CLIMBING CALLS

Climbing calls have evolved to give clarity to communication between leader and second. It is important that they are called out loudly and clearly, and are not confused by adding non-standard calls within any sequence. If climbing on a busy crag or near other climbers, remember to use your climbing partner's name to avoid potentially disastrous confusion between teams. There may be slight variations when on a multi-pitch route, and it is important to clarify these with your partner before starting out. Indeed, a series of rope pulls may be employed when communication is difficult. The essential calls are listed opposite.

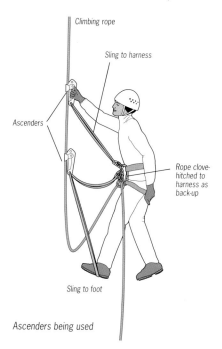

Climbing rope

Sling to harness

Ascenders

Rope clove-hitched to harness as back-up

Sling to foot

Ascenders being used

■ Gear Lists *p159*

TAKING IN	Call from the leader that he is pulling up, hand over hand, all of the slack rope between himself and his second.
THAT'S ME	Call from second to indicate that all of the slack rope between himself and the leader has been pulled up.
CLIMB WHEN YOU ARE READY	Call from leader, which only comes after he has put on his belay device, checked all knots, gates shut and done up, tight on belay, in line with belay and able to brake correctly.
CLIMBING	Call from second, but he does not start climbing until he has had the OK from the leader.
O.K.	Call from leader to show that he has heard that the second is about to climb.
TAKE IN	If the rope has not been taken in for some time, or slack rope has been introduced due to unclipping a runner, etc.
SLACK	Indicates slack rope is needed, maybe to reverse a move or unclip a runner. **Note**: never shout 'take in slack', as these are two countermanding orders. If just the word 'slack' were heard due to the wind, etc, spare rope would be paid out when you were needing it to be taken in.
TIGHT	Often called by the second, either when making an awkward move, or when expecting to fall off.
SAFE	From the leader, to indicate that there is no possibility of him coming to harm. The second will normally say 'safe' at the top of a route to the belayer out of courtesy.
YOU'RE OFF or OFF BELAY	From the second, following the 'safe' call from the leader. (In some countries, 'off belay' is used in place of 'safe'.)
RUNNER ON	From the leader, to indicate that the first runner has been placed and the second must now be ready to hold a fall from a different direction.
BELOW	From anyone who has accidentally dislodged a stone, etc, from a crag or route. This call must be shouted at full volume! If you hear the call, do not look up as you may receive a facial injury.
ROPE BELOW	A courtesy call used when lowering or throwing out a rope for abseiling, top roping, etc.

Gear Lists *p159* ■

Short Roping

What is short roping ?

Short roping is a group of techniques where instructors will plan to safeguard their clients, moving roped together over steep and exposed mountain terrain. Short-roping techniques are among the most misunderstood of mountaineering skills.

Why does short roping differ from confidence roping ?

As opposed to confidence roping, short roping is a planned event whereby the instructor will be controlling up to two clients at one time on a rope.

Where is short roping used ?

In summer conditions it is used on steep narrow ridges and scrambling ground in both ascent and descent. In winter it can be used for the approach and exit slopes of winter climbs, and for descending moderate-angled snowy headwalls.

What is moving together ?

Moving together is a technique used to secure one or two persons on the end of a rope, while constantly moving over steep and exposed terrain, speedily without having the safety of the group members compromised.

The ability always to maintain control derives from the experience, skill and judgement of the instructor.

Tying-on techniques used by the instructor and clients can be varied. However, it is essential that the tie-on is tidy, practical and efficient. Remember, you can be moving on steep exposed ground, so an error in rope-work techniques means you will lose control.

It will not always be possible to find a suitable area to stop and rope-up; this is why you must be constantly planning ahead and always be interpreting the terrain. When moving together, you may also find it necessary to stop and pitch short sections. Remain flexible.

Method

Distance apart should be as short as possible but this will depend upon the terrain. For example in summer you may have your two clients spaced 1.5m apart, then you may change that distance

when you need to pitch, say a new distance of 2–3m to create safe and comfortable climbing for an ascent. In winter you will use the same techniques to adjust length.

■ Tie on the end client using a rewoven figure of eight.

■ Tie on the second client using an 'isolation loop', an Alpine butterfly or overhand knot with a loop approximately 30cm long, with an overhand knot on the bight tied on the end. Clip a screwgate karabiner into the client's abseil loop. This system of tying on the second with a screwgate is only appropriate on short sections of scrambling or winter terrain.

■ Should you be short roping on graded ground, anywhere of a serious nature or on longer sections of ground, then the second should be tied in through the harness with either a re-threaded overhand knot with the tail clipped back into the abseil loop, or a rewoven figure-of-eight knot.

■ The instructor will tie on and will then take chest coils. The distance that he ties himself off from the second person will vary

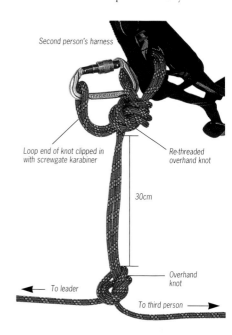

Second person's harness

Loop end of knot clipped in with screwgate karabiner

Re-threaded overhand knot

30cm

To leader

Overhand knot

To third person

■ Knots pp42–6

depending upon the terrain, but will usually be in the region of 5–8m. The spare rope between instructor and client will be carried in hand coils with a final locking twist.

Tying off Chest Coils: Method 1

- Prior to taking chest coils, tie into your harness. You should be wearing your rucksack at this point.
- Place your left hand facing out, palm down, at a point near the front of your harness belt. This will act as a guide for the coil size.
- With your right hand, take the rope from your harness up round your neck from left to right, and round your left hand, maintaining tension. Ensure that the coils are neat (1). Take in coils until the required length of rope is left.
- When enough coils have been taken, move your left hand and put your left arm through them. Adjust them so that they sit tidily on your shoulder (2).
- Standing upright, the coils should feel nice and snug, but must not restrict breathing.
- To lock off the coils, take a bight of rope and pass it through your central tie-in loop, up behind all of the coils, through and back down to an HMS karabiner that has been clipped between your harness leg loops and waist belt (NOTE: this should be the only time that a karabiner is ever connected to your harness in this manner). Clip in this loop of rope, do up the gate, and pull on the main rope to tighten the knot. The coils will now be firmly locked off through the friction created by the way it has been threaded (3).
- To take hand coils, hold the rope and stretch

your left arm forward.
- Using your right hand, hold the main rope length and take coils over your left hand. Alternatively, flake the rope backwards and forwards over it. To lock off either hand coils or flakes, take the main length of rope round the back of the coils via your knuckles and through your index and middle finger, closing your hand to create a tensioned grip.

OBSERVATIONS

1 It is vital that the hand coils are locked off, as this will prevent hand coils sliding through your hand and resulting in a complete loss of control.

2 We recommend that gloves be worn when short roping.

3 It is important to have an arm's length of rope between the chest coils and the hand coils, allowing you to shock-absorb a fall.

4 With Method 1, you can take off the coils if required by simply unclipping the loop in the HMS and pulling the main rope – there are no knots to undo – and coils can very quickly and easily be removed.

5 It is important to practise on a variety of terrain types. Being able to tie off the coils does not mean that you can operate effectively on steep mountaineering terrain; any user of this technique needs to be competent, highly trained and practised.

6 When undoing the chest coils it is important to reverse the way you coiled them, one by one. If you take off all of the coils at once and drop them on the ground, you will most likely end up with a huge knot.

Knots pp42–6 ■

4

5

Tying off chest coils: Method 2

- Take coils around your body as above, but this time ensure that the live rope is exiting forwards from underneath your left arm (4).
- To lock off the coils, take a bight of rope from the main rope of approximately 35cm in length. Pass this bight from left to right underneath and back round the rope leading from your harness tie-in to the first chest coil (5).
- Holding the bight with your right hand, pinch both the bight and the chest coils with your left hand.
- Now pass the bight in your right towards the left, then up behind (on your chest side) the coils. Bring it through to the front, then back down through a small half hitch that has

been created by the bight.
- You should now have a small loop of about 10cm; clip this loop into the main tie-in loop using a screwgate karabiner.
- Pull the main rope, and your coils are locked off (6).

Maintaining Control in Ascent and Descent

The further apart the instructor is from his second/s, the more difficult it is to hold a slip/fall. It is important at all times to maintain control in ascending and descending. The main problem arises when you need to traverse and only one line can be taken, then you must keep the rope distance between seconds short to maximise control. The other option is to protect a traverse using runners, moving together while placing protection, or to drop the coils and pitch the section if appropriate and realistic.

- When moving together the rope must always be snug; this provides reassurance and confidence to the clients and gives the instructor the ability to react quickly to hold a slip or fall.
- It is important that the second client, tied on the isolation loop, is independent, which helps to prevent a knock-on effect should the third person slip.
- The second person should be briefed to not overtake the knot that forms his isolation loop, as this will permit him to slip a longer distance and will mean that it is harder to control from the front.
- When traversing with either one or two others on the rope, it is important that they always

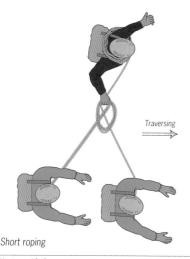

Traversing →

Short roping

remain on the downhill side of the instructor.

▪ On a traverse section, an appropriate technique is to protect the two seconds by 'en fleche' or 'arrowhead'. To perform this, hold the centre of the rope between the two people, and twist it 180 degrees to form a handle. The instructor now stays up-slope of them, and is able to provide a good deal of support.

Holding Coils on the Move

▪ The instructor should always have the coils held and locked off in the downhill arm; this arm should be at a right angle with the elbow 15–20cm from the side of his waist. This powerful position allows the arm to draw in and out to maintain constant tension in the rope between himself and his second/s.

▪ The uphill arm must be free to climb with, and in winter this arm will be holding the ice axe. It is also crucial that his stance be as solid as possible to be able to resist a downhill pull.

▪ The seconds should be briefed as to the position of the rope between them and the instructor, particularly when traversing. The rope leading to the second client and on to the guide should be positioned on the uphill side of their legs. It is also important that the isolation loop is not too long as the second could easily trip over it.

▪ Clients should always receive a briefing on working together when short roping. This will allow the system to run smoothly and ease any potential frustration when moving together.

Changing Direction in Winter

To change direction in the winter, the following procedure should be adopted. This is assuming the ascent of an uncomplicated snow slope.

▪ The instructor stops, still with his arm bent in a powerful position.

▪ He tells the second/s to kick themselves a ledge, stand in it facing up-slope, and push their ice axes into the snow, holding on to the axe heads. The person on the isolation loop can push his axe shaft down through

the rope loop for extra security.

▪ The instructor, having been moving with his right-hand side up-slope, turns to face down-slope.

▪ He places the ice axe under his left arm, unlocks the coils, swaps the rope to the right hand, the left hand then retrieves the axe.

▪ He continues to turn until he is facing the right direction.

▪ The instructor then tells his second/s to turn to face the right direction one at a time, the person on the isolation loop carefully stepping over it.

▪ The group continues.

The instructor may decide to simply place the axe in the snow and turn round but, as this is possibly on more technical terrain than with confidence roping, it is recommended that a grip be kept on the axe at all times.

OBSERVATIONS

1 It is vital that the instructor be alert at all times and be continuously looking ahead, anticipating any potential problems and looking out for running belays, stances, alternative routes etc.

2 The instructor must remain aware at all times of the comfort of his seconds, and, if there is any indication that either is struggling with the gradient, that section should be pitched.

3 Should the instructor be uncomfortable or uncertain at any time, then he should stop moving together with the clients and pitch.

4 When moving together it is important to think about your clients' strengths and weaknesses. It is generally best to position your clients according to weakness, placing the weakest to the front and shortening the distance of rope between instructor and that person.

5 When the seconds are of a different size, the heaviest needs to be closest to the instructor.

6 It is important to move at a continuous and regular pace suited to the clients' ability and fitness; while doing this the instructor will be constantly adjusting the length of rope to maintain tension.

Improvised Rescue Techniques

Much is made of improvised rescue, often too much when in a practical situation. It is frequently referred to in instructional books, which give a bewildering variety of ways of constructing systems. Here, we are dealing with the major issues that can occur, and give a reasonable response to each one. Practise these, and you will find that answers to more complicated scenarios will become apparent with ease. Remember that it will often be the simplest procedure that will get the best result. The following techniques are a selection of tools that are designed to be used individually or collectively to solve a variety of problems, often in a multi-pitch situation.

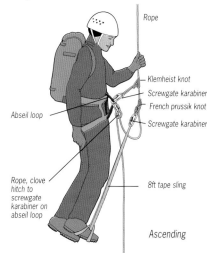

Ascending

If you get into the habit of bringing all of your anchors down to one point, this simplifies the execution of the hoisting and rescue systems greatly.

Be practical and think ahead. Do you have to spend hours constructing an elaborate anchor system when on a ledge only 30ft up, or would lowering your second solve the problem simply and effectively?

Finally, when practising scenarios, or being asked by others to demonstrate them, consider this: when in real life did you last have to perform a counterbalance abseil from out-of-reach anchors to a traversing second who was choking on his tongue after being hit by a falling asteroid?

Ascending the Rope

Scenario: you need to ascend the rope to render assistance to a stuck, unconscious leader.

- Clip a Klemheist directly to abseil loop with screwgate.
- French prussik for foot, placed below Klemheist, connected to an 8ft sling to act as a foot loop. A couple of turns can be taken around the foot to shorten the sling to the required length.
- Clip an HMS karabiner on to the abseil loop. Connect a clove hitch to this, tied with the spare lower length/s of rope. This will act as your safety back-up.
- Move up the rope, alternately moving the Klemheist and French prussiks.
- Every few feet, adjust the rope through the clove hitch to limit the distance it is possible to slide.

Changing from Abseil Descent to Ascent of Rope

Scenario: having made an abseil descent of the rope in poor visibility, you find that you are hanging free and have passed the last safe ledge. Ascending the rope is the only option.

- Clip a clove hitch, taken from the dead rope below your back-up prussik, into your abseil loop via an HMS screwgate.

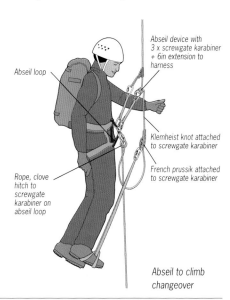

Abseil to climb changeover

■ Knots *pp42–6* • Tying-In *pp54–7* • Belay Methods *pp58–63* • Gear Lists *p159*

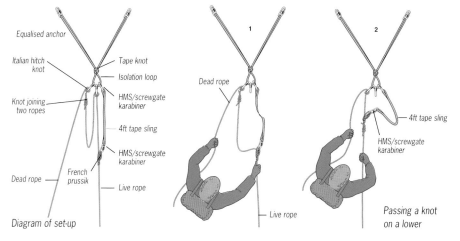

Equalised anchor

Italian hitch knot

Tape knot

Isolation loop

Knot joining two ropes

HMS/screwgate karabiner

Dead rope

4ft tape sling

HMS/screwgate karabiner

French prussik

Dead rope

Live rope

Diagram of set-up

1

2

Dead rope

4ft tape sling

HMS/screwgate karabiner

Live rope

Passing a knot on a lower

■ Tie a Klemheist immediately above the abseil device, connect a screwgate to it but leave it hanging.

■ Clip an 8ft sling into the abseil back-up French prussik with a separate screwgate, immediately next to the existing karabiner.

■ Placing your foot in the sling (a couple of turns around your foot may be required to attain the correct length), grip the main climbing rope above the Klemheist with both hands, stand up, and clip the Klemheist's screwgate into your abseil loop. Gently lower your weight on to it.

■ Slide the French prussik down the rope a few inches, and remove the abseil device.

■ Remove the screwgate connecting the French prussik to your abseil loop, leaving the prussik on the rope, still with your foot in the sling.

■ Ascend rope, taking in on a safety clove hitch at regular intervals.

Passing a Knot on a Lower

Scenario: you are lowering an injured partner with two ropes tied together, allowing a greater distance to be covered and less stances to be taken.

As for passing a knot on a free abseil, this technique is hopefully rather rare! Things are greatly eased if the person being lowered can get his footing on the rock or snow and take his weight off the rope, which will normally be the case. Remember, though, to be careful of a French prussik placed on a rope that will be unloaded. There is a chance that the French will release and not sit back in its correct position once the rope is re-weighted.

■ Set up an anchor system brought down to a single attachment point.

■ Clip in two HMS screwgates, and one extra screwgate attached to a prussik loop via a 4ft sling. One of the HMSs has an Italian hitch tied into it, with a French prussik being placed on its live-rope side.

■ Holding the French released, lower the casualty until the rope knot is about 2ft away from the HMS. Allow the French to take the weight.

■ Without letting go of the dead rope, tie an Italian hitch on the dead-rope side of the rope knot and clip it into the second HMS, with the knot hard up against the karabiner.

■ Unclip the first Italian hitch.

■ Holding firm on to the dead rope, pull up on the French prussik to release it and allow the weight of the casualty to come on to the new HMS.

■ Undo the French prussik and replace it above

OBSERVATION

In many emergency procedures, when a French prussik is being used as part of the load-bearing system, there is a slight chance of either the climbing rope creeping through the prussik, or the prussik jamming, especially when wet and under full load. An extra back-up may be placed in the system by connecting the prussik to the anchor using a narrow-diameter sling. This should be attached to the anchor by using an Italian hitch tied off; thus, if the French prussik now slips or jams, the system can be released by simply undoing the Italian. This consideration is relevant for the majority of the procedures detailed here.

Knots *pp42–6* • Tying-In *pp54–7* • Belay Methods *pp58–63* • Gear Lists *p159* ■

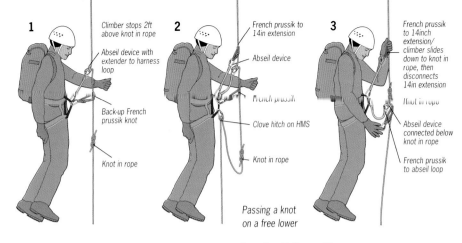

1 Climber stops 2ft above knot in rope

Abseil device with extender to harness loop

Back-up French prussik knot

Knot in rope

2 French prussik to 14in extension

Abseil device

French prussik

Clove hitch on HMS

Knot in rope

3 French prussik to 14inch extension/ climber slides down to knot in rope, then disconnects 14in extension

Knot in rope

Abseil device connected below knot in rope

French prussik to abseil loop

Passing a knot on a free lower

the rope knot, just below the new HMS. It is *extremely* important during this process that you do not release your hold on the dead rope.

■ Continue lowering, holding the French prussik just released.

Passing a Knot on a Free Abseil

Scenario: two ropes have been tied together to allow a single abseil on to safe ground to be made. This abseil will be free for part of its length.

It should be mentioned that there are not many times that this is likely to have to be used! It is usually the case that you can get some foot purchase on the rock or snow, which makes the whole process far easier.

■ Abseil to approximately 2ft above the knot and stop.
■ Put a French prussik on to the rope above you, extended for 14–18ins (the length of an 8ft sling folded into thirds) clipped into your harness.
■ Abseil a little further, stopping 1ft above the rope knot, with your weight being taken by the extended French prussik.
■ Clip a clove hitch to your harness via an HMS karabiner as a back-up.
■ Remove your abseil device and abseil-protection French prussik, and replace them below the rope knot, ensuring that they are replaced as close to the underside of the knot as possible.
■ Remove safety clove hitch.
■ Release extended French prussik by pulling down towards you, and take it off the rope.
■ Continue abseiling.

Leader Falls on Traverse

Scenario: the leader has climbed a short way above you, then traversed to the right. He has fallen off, and is hanging in an area of unclimbable rock.

■ Lower the leader so that he is on a line just above the height of yourself and the stance.
■ Lock off the belay device.
■ Pass a loop of rope from the anchor end of the system to the leader. It will often be possible to throw this to him, otherwise it will mean escaping the system, prussiking up the rope, throwing or lowering the loop to him, then regaining the stance.
■ The leader connects the loop to himself using a screwgate karabiner.
■ Clip an HMS karabiner on to your anchor system and tie an Italian hitch on to it, on the side of the rope loop coming back from the leader.

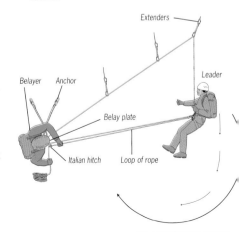

Extenders

Leader

Belayer   Anchor

Belay plate

Italian hitch   Loop of rope

■ Knots *pp42–6* • Tying-In *pp54–7* • Belay Methods *pp58–63* • Gear Lists *p159*

- Pull the rope in as tight as possible through the Italian and lock it off.
- Release the belay device and lower the leader a couple of feet.
- Lock off the belay device, release the Italian, and pull the leader across as much as possible.
- Lock off the Italian, undo the belay device, lower the leader a couple of feet.
- Repeat the above processes until the leader has reached climbable ground, or has been hoisted in an arc towards you and is now at the stance. The climb can now be continued, or the ropes pulled through and a retreat made.

Second Climbs past Runner

Scenario: your second is so involved in the climbing that he climbs above a runner that has been extended with a sling, and ends up on desperate ground tight on the rope which is now coming up from below him. It is not possible for him to down-climb.

- Lock off the belay plate.
- Using the dead rope at the point it connects to the anchor, clip a screwgate to a loop of rope and lower it down to the climber. He clips this to his rope tie-in loop or his abseil loop on the harness.
- Clip an HMS karabiner on to your rope tie-in loop and clip an Italian hitch on to this, on the side of the loop coming back up from your second.
- Holding on to the dead rope from the Italian hitch, undo and release the belay plate. You can now belay your second down to retrieve the runner.

Assisted Hoist (see p86)

Scenario: the last few feet of a climb are too hard for your second, and lowering is not an easy option.

- Lock off belay device around the back bar of the karabiner.
- Attach French prussik on to live section of climbing rope in front of the belay device, ensuring that there are plenty of turns. Clip it directly to the belay-device karabiner with a screwgate, and push it snugly down the rope.
- Clip a screwgate on to a loop of rope coming from the dead side of the belay device, and

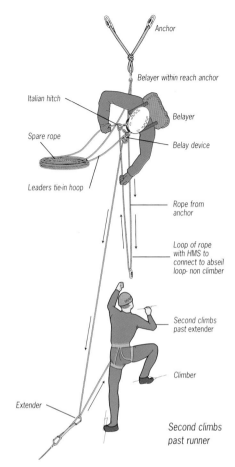

Anchor

Belayer within reach anchor

Italian hitch

Belayer

Spare rope

Belay device

Leaders tie-in hoop

Rope from anchor

Loop of rope with HMS to connect to abseil loop- non climber

Second climbs past extender

Climber

Extender

Second climbs past runner

lower it down to your second.
- Instruct him to clip it on to the abseil loop of his harness.
- Holding on to the dead rope with a couple of wraps around your wrist, untie the belay device and pull in the slack rope as you go. Be careful not to shock-load the prussik knot in the process.
- Instruct your second to pull on the rope coming to him from what was the dead-rope side of the belay device; you pull on the rope feeding up from his recently attached karabiner. Co-ordinating the pulling helps greatly with the amount of effort needed.
- As you both pull, your second moves up towards you on a 3:1-ratio pulley system. The French prussik will slide up to the belay device and release.
- When you need to stop for a rest, or to remove a runner, first slide the French

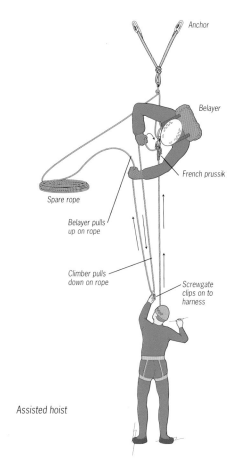

Assisted hoist

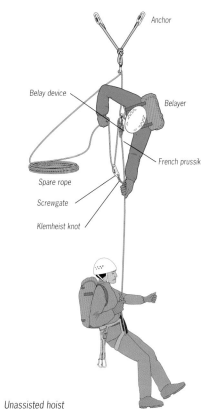

Unassisted hoist

prussik down the rope as far as it will go. You can then both gently reduce the pull on the rope, and let the prussik take the weight. DO NOT let go of the rope, as it is still possible for the knot to slide.

Unassisted Hoist

Scenario: your second has slipped off a bulge, and is hanging some distance from you in mid-air. Lowering is not an option either owing to him being injured or insufficient rope being available.

This process is *much* easier if you have escaped from the system first, although the time factor will go a long way to determining if this is possible. The following is the basic process if still part of the system.
■ Lock off belay device.
■ Attach a French prussik on to the live section of climbing rope in front of belay device,

ensuring that there are plenty of turns. Clip it directly to the belay-device karabiner with a screwgate, and push it snugly down the rope.
■ Reaching as far down the rope towards the victim as is possible, attach a Klemheist to the rope, and clip in a bight of climbing rope from the dead side of the belay device with a screwgate.
■ Holding on to the dead rope with a couple of wraps around your wrist, untie the belay device and pull in the slack rope as you go. Be careful not to shock-load the French prussik in the process.
■ Pulling on the dead rope now has the effect of a 3:1 pulley system as before. Pull in the rope until the Klemheist is a short distance from the belay device.
■ Holding the dead rope secure, push the French prussik down the rope as far as it will go.
■ Gently release the weight of the victim on to the French prussik.
■ The Klemheist can now be moved back down the rope, and the process repeated.

■ Knots pp42–6 • Tying-In pp54–7 • Belay Methods pp58–63 • Gear Lists p159

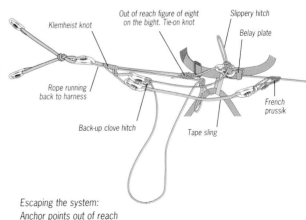

Within reach tie-on
clove hitch

Slippery hitch
lock off knot

Clove hitch
back-up from
lock-off knot

French
prussik

Belay plate

8ft tape sling

Escaping the System:
Anchor Ponits within reach

Escaping the System: Anchor Points within Reach

■ Lock off the belay plate.

■ Attach sling to anchor point, adjusted so that the end of the sling is just in front of the belay device.

■ Attach French prussik on to live section of climbing rope in front of belay device, ensuring that there are plenty of turns. Clip it into the sling from the anchor with a screwgate.

■ Clip an HMS into the anchor point and put a clove-hitch on to this, taken from the dead rope coming out of the plate lock-off knot. This will eventually act as a safety back-up in case the French slips.

■ Ensuring that the system is as snug as possible from the anchor through the sling to the French prussik, slowly release the locked-off belay device, making sure that you do not shock-load the French.

■ Take in the slack rope introduced into the system by taking it in through the clove hitch.

■ The belay device may now be removed from the rope. This means that the rope between the back-up clove and the French now has a little slack in it, this is by design and should be left.

■ You are now free to untie from the rope, first ensuring your own safety by the use of a cow's-tail or similar.

taken from the dead rope coming out of the plate lock-off knot. This will eventually act as a safety back-up in case the French slips.

■ Ensuring that the system is as snug as possible from the anchor through the sling to the French prussik, slowly release the locked-off belay device, making sure that you do not shock-load the French.

■ Take in the slack rope introduced into the system by taking it in through the clove hitch.

■ The belay device may now be removed from the rope. This means that the rope between the back-up clove and the French now has a little slack in it; this is by design and should be left.

■ You are now free to untie from the rope, first ensuring your own safety by the use of a cow's-tail or similar.

■ When untied, tie a knot in any ends of rope left to prevent any chance of the sling sliding off.

Escaping the System: Anchor Points out of reach

■ Lock off the belay plate.

■ Use a sling and tie a Klemheist around the anchor rope/s (escaping the system is far easier if all anchors have been brought to one point). Organise it so that the end of the sling is just next to the belay device.

■ Attach a French prussik on to live section of climbing rope in front of belay device, ensuring that there are plenty of turns. Clip it into the sling from the anchor with a screwgate.

■ Clip a second screwgate into the sling. Put a clove hitch on to this,

Out of reach figure of eight
on the bight. Tie-on knot

Slippery hitch

Klemheist knot

Belay plate

Rope running
back to harness

French
prussik

Back-up clove hitch

Tape sling

Escaping the system:
Anchor points out of reach

Accompanied Abseil from Stance: System Escaped

Scenario: your partner is feeling unwell enough to cause you concern about his ability to organise and safeguard his own descent.

■ Select the most appropriate position for the casualty – either side by side or suspended just above and in front of you, at 90 degrees across the rock face.
■ Organise abseil device with 8ft sling tied off to suit the situation – equal lengths for side-by-side descent, or have the casualty suspended from one-third of sling length for assisted descent. If casualty requires evacuation via the assisted-descent method, ensure that he is correctly supported and cannot slip back in his harness. It may be necessary to construct a temporary chest harness for him.
■ Ensure that your personal-abseil back-up French is correctly positioned.
■ Release any temporary cow's-tail system, and descend.
■ With the assisted method, it will be necessary for you to carefully select your footing on the way down, and to field the casualty away from the rock and any obstructions.

Converting to Counterbalance Abseil: Anchor in Reach

Scenario: your second has been injured by a rockfall, and needs your assistance to descend. It is not possible to safely lower him to a ledge.

■ Escape from the system, remembering personal safety.
■ Clip a screwgate into the anchor, and run the climbing rope through this, with the end of the rope thrown down the crag (now referred to as the 'dead' rope).
■ Put abseil device on to dead rope, extended with sling as required, as well as personal back-up French. Move up close to anchor.

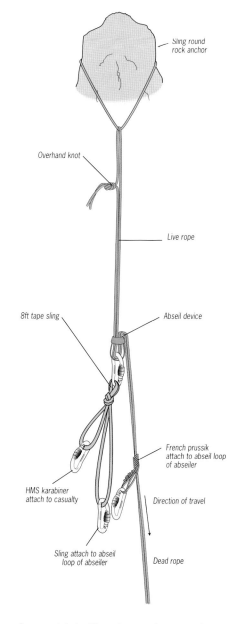

Sling round rock anchor

Overhand knot

Live rope

8ft tape sling

Abseil device

French prussik attach to abseil loop of abseiler

HMS karabiner attach to casualty

Direction of travel

Sling attach to abseil loop of abseiler

Dead rope

Accompanied abseil from stance: system escaped

■ Knots *pp42–6* • Tying-In *pp54–7* • Belay Methods *pp58–63*

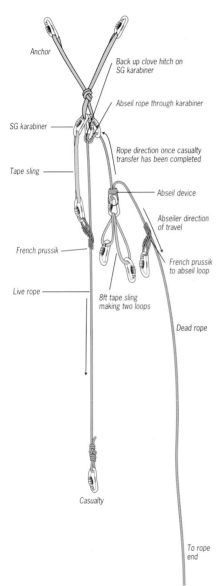

Anchor

Back up clove hitch on
SG karabiner

Abseil rope through karabiner

SG karabiner

Rope direction once casualty
transfer has been completed

Tape sling

Abseil device

Abseiler direction
of travel

French prussik

French prussik
to abseil loop

Live rope

8ft tape sling
making two loops

Dead rope

Casualty

To rope
end

Converting to counterbalance abseil: anchor in reach

■ Undo back-up clove and remove karabiner.
■ Take in slack through belay device and
French, moving close to the anchor again.
■ Lean out from anchor with plenty of weight
on the rope, and release the French prussik
placed when escaping the system. Strip
prussik, sling and any spare karabiners from
the anchor.
■ Remove personal-safety sling/rope.
■ Abseil to casualty. Remember that, from this
moment on, you are counterbalancing the
weight of the casualty, so ensure that you do
not un-weight the rope at any point.
■ Strip any runners from above the casualty if
relevant.
■ On reaching casualty, connect him to you by
using a short sling or extender, and arrange
him either next to you or across in the
assisted mode. It is important that even a
seemingly completely able second is
connected to you, as there could be a
difference in your respective body weights,
which will be amplified by the friction
existing in the system.
■ Abseil to next ledge/safety.

Converting to Counterbalance Abseil: Anchor out of Reach

■ Escape from the system, remembering
personal safety.
■ Clip a screwgate into the original anchor, and
run the climbing rope through this (now
referred to as the 'dead' rope).
■ Put your abseil device on to the dead rope,
extended with a sling as required, as well as
personal back-up French.
■ Lean out from anchor with plenty of weight
on the rope, and release the Klemheist sling
and French prussik placed when escaping the
system. Strip prussik, sling and any spare
karabiners from the anchor.
■ Remove personal safety sling/rope.
■ Continue as above.

Single-pitch Climbing Sessions

The idea of the following chapter is to help clarify the role of a rock-sports' instructor, involved in providing climbing and abseiling sessions for novices. These may be held for one or more people and could involve either friends or paying clients. The intent here is to look at both the hard and soft skills involved in providing a safe and enjoyable time on the rock.

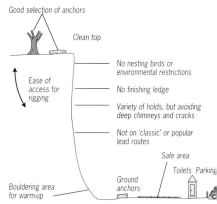

An ideal single-pitch venue!

VENUE SELECTION

What makes a crag qualify as 'single pitch'?

There is a very convenient decription of a cliff or crag which can be designated as suitable for use with novice groups. As safety is paramount, these guidelines should be well considered when choosing an activity venue. A true single-pitch crag will be no more than a rope length in height, and will be described as single pitch in a guide book. It must be climbable without intermediate stances, and must allow a second to be lowered to the ground at all times. It must be non-tidal, and have no navigational nightmares involved in reaching it. There should be little objective danger, and should allow easy access to top and bottom.

What else would make a crag good for single-pitch activities?

Apart from conforming to the above necessary criteria, an ideal single-pitch crag will have a variety of features that make group management and route choice simpler. A few of the more important features are listed below, together with some elementary considerations.

- **Car parking.** It would be very useful if this were off the main road. Having a group, especially younger participants, around your transport on a busy or narrow road could lead to an accident.
- **Short walk in.** Not only because there may well be a lot of equipment to carry, but also in case a return has to be made to the transport for any emergency.
- **Safe area at crag.** This needs to be a defined safe area, perhaps a flat area of grass surrounded by rocks or bushes, which is unmistakable to the group members. It should be easily in view from the activity area,

without being in a dangerous position too close to the edge or too near to the bottom of the crag.

- **Toilet area.** This could either be properly designed public toilets, or a designated area near the crag. If the local area has to be used for the toilet, EXTREME consideration must be given to environmental impact, line of water courses, etc, and thought given to the carrying out of solid waste.
- **Crag accessible by public or by consent.** Consideration should be given to any access agreement and landowner's requirements, as well as to any nesting bird or environmental restrictions.
- **Warm-up area.** It would be useful to have an area in which your group could warm up, or be introduced to the different ways of using holds. An area with large holds and a safe landing underfoot would be ideal.
- **Variety.** A variety of routes and abseils would be useful. These should allow the novice to achieve early on; to put a beginner on a desperate overhanging prow as a first route would guarantee his failure and subsequent lack of interest in the rest of the day's proceedings.
- **Other users.** Consideration must be given to other crag users. Avoid blocking routes that are popular leads, 'classics' or abseiling down those with delicate holds. Avoid covering steep hard slab routes with mud from boots. Talk to other crag users to ensure that you

TIP

It can prove very useful to have a large plastic bag or bin liner to hand. This can be placed in the centre of the safe area and not only be used as a receptacle for rubbish, but also act as a physical reminder to your group about the location of your designated safe area.

are not getting in their way – remember that a couple leading will always take precedence over a group. Remember group control: noise is also a very anti-social thing to many people.

■ **Route choice.** Your choice of route can either cause or save you so many problems, it is really worth taking time to select carefully. The steepness of the route should be considered, taking into account the proficiency of your group. A route with no defined finishing ledge is ideal, especially for novices, as it can help to negate the problem of the crag-fast climber. A variety of holds is ideal, but avoid deep chimneys and cracks.

■ **Anchors.** A good selection of anchors at the top of the climb will obviously be necessary, for either top-rope or bottom-rope sessions, and ground anchors will be extremely useful for direct belays when bottom roping.

■ **Access to top.** Ease of access to the top is important when rigging, especially if group members are helping to carry equipment for you. Remember that one of the criteria for group use of a single-pitch crag is that access must be simple. That means that if any group member has to use his hands to get up the path, its suitability as a venue should be questioned.

TOP- AND BOTTOM-ROPE SYSTEMS

It is necessary to be aware of what is meant by 'top roping' and 'bottom roping'. Top roping simply means that the belayer controlling the rope is at the top of the climb, bottom roping means that the person controlling the rope is at the foot of the climb, with the rope running up and back down to the climber through a pulley-type system.

Both systems have their pros and cons, and there will be many factors to consider when deciding which option to use. Below are listed a number of the main for-and-against points of each method. It will be noticed that the bottom-roping system appears to have more going for it than its counterpart, but it should be

OBSERVATION

To make your activity session more enjoyable for your group, it will be necessary to consider the weather and its effect on the day. For instance, if the crag is north-facing and the weather is forecast to bring cold winds with blustery showers, would a different venue be more appropriate? Conversely, if the crag is south-facing and you are in the middle of a heatwave, is it still a sensible choice?

remembered that it is only by true top roping that a climber will get to complete a route from bottom to top, surely the reason for climbing in the first place.

TOP-ROPE SYSTEMS

Careful thought must go into setting up a top-rope system when dealing with novice climbers. If climbing with peers, the simplest and most popular method would be to belay with a device attached to your tie-in loop. However, in a group there may be more of a chance of having to escape the system and leave the stance, and a direct-belay system will be more appropriate. The diagram below shows a very simple and safe way of organising the system, and allows a lot of flexibility for the position of the belayer.

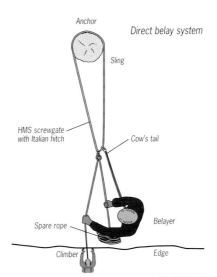

Anchor

Direct belay system

Sling

HMS screwgate with Italian hitch

Cow's tail

Spare rope

Belayer

Climber

Edge

OBSERVATION

Although there is a method of using a belay device in a manner similar to this, the system shown above is to be recommended due to its ease of set-up and operation.

Knots pp42–6 • Tying-In pp54–7 • Belay Methods pp58–63 ■

The Top-rope System

PROS

- Quick to rig.
- Allows for traditional topping out and feeling of achievement.
- Good approach to climbing for those progressing to leading, multi-pitch routes etc.
- Nervous novice is approaching a friendly face, can be encouraged upwards and has something to focus on.

CONS

- Difficult for belayer to see all the moves on the climb.
- Creates maximum distance between belayer and climber at start.
- Communication can be difficult and confusing to the novice.
- Novices feels that they have 'failed' if they do not reach the top of the cliff.
- Assisting and/or rescuing a stuck climber can be difficult.
- Group management at top of cliff requires close attention.
- Some group members remain at bottom of crag during part or all of the activity – difficult for management.
- Difficulty of checking attachment of climber to rope.
- Very difficult for group members to belay other climbers.
- Top roping causes general wear and tear to cliff top.
- Group needs managing on descent paths, with resultant wear and tear.

The Bottom-rope System

PROS

- Allows an instructor to move around freely and supervise more than one rope at the same time.
- Students are able to belay under supervision, and several can be occupied at the same time.
- It can be easier for a novice to learn how to use a variety of belay techniques correctly.
- The instructor is with his group, making group management easier.
- The instructor is 'right there', and can offer close encouragement and assistance to anxious novices making their first moves on a climb.
- Cliff-top and descent-path safety concerns are removed.
- Students do not feel that they have failed if they do not reach the top.
- It can reduce cliff-top erosion and unsightly descent paths.
- 'Stuck' novices can be easily rescued.
- Correct attachment of the climber to the rope can be guaranteed.

CONS

- Each system takes time to rig correctly and the anchors are out of sight.
- Anchors need to be bomb-proof as loading can be at least two times the force exerted by a climber.
- It prevents students from 'topping out' and thus gaining a feeling of real achievement.
- May encourage the assumption that bottom roping is the 'normal' way to climb.
- Care must be taken not to be monopolising a route.
- A nervous novice ends up a long way from a 'friendly face' and may have trouble committing himself to a lower.

■ Knots *pp42–6* • Tying-In *pp54–7* • Belay Methods *pp58–63*

Attachment to the Rope

This must be carefully considered for both top- and bottom-rope sessions. Our recommendation for either is that the climber is *always* tied in through the harness, rather than be attached by a screwgate karabiner. Although a krab may be convenient, there is a danger of a sideways loading occurring across the gate, seriously weakening the system. There is also the chance of the gate rubbing on the rock and unscrewing. When using a top-rope system, it would be very convenient if there were a helper at the bottom to assist and check that each of the climbers was tied on before they started.

OBSERVATION

Ensure that all group members are fully briefed as to what is expected of them *before* you go to the top of the crag – shouted instructions rarely make sense. Once they have climbed up to you, have a safe area designated behind you well away from the cliff edge, to which they can go before taking off the rope.

Also make sure that they will not end up taking the lead as they go past you. This could occur if you have organised the stance a little way down an eroded exit; great care must be taken to prevent this from happening. It is not acceptable for a novice to be leading, as the consequences of a slip on the final moves are dire.

TIP

If you have opted to use an indirect belay, with the belay device clipped to your tie-in loop, and you need to escape the system, it can be rather difficult. However, instead of starting a technical escape using prussik loops and knots, there is an even simpler solution. Once you have tied off the belay plate, take off your harness!

BELAY METHODS

There are various ways of securing a climber, and below are listed some of the most common. The main emphasis of this is on protecting a climber during a group bottom-roping session. Often, the choice will be determined by the

Method	Pros	Cons
Belay plate onto harness.	Easy to operate, good control.	Awkward to escape the system.
Italian hitch onto harness.	Simple, good control.	Twists the rope, takes in less rope than with plate, awkward to escape the system.
Belay plate onto direct anchor.	Smooth take-in, belayer out of system.	Awkward to control, 'floppy' action, belayer must be behind plate, relies on availability of ground anchors.
Italian hitch onto direct anchor.	Smooth take in and pay out, easy to control, belayer can be in front of anchor, belayer out of system, easy to lock off.	Twists rope, relies on availability of ground anchors.
Belay plate or Italian hitch controlled by student on his harness.	As above, plus belayer out of system, group members occupied.	As above, plus care needed when teaching novices.
Two or three novices clipped together and walking back as climber ascends.	No technical kit needed, keeps group members occupied.	Dependent upon having lots of space and flat ground, anti-social to other crag users, danger of belayers 'larking about'.

OBSERVATION

Make sure that you are clear about the difference between direct and indirect belays. The best way to remember it is that the direct belay goes directly to the anchor, without being clipped to the belayer in any way, while an indirect belay is controlled by the belayer from his tie-in loop or similar.

experience of the people you are climbing with, the equipment available and the availability of ground anchors.

It can therefore be seen that belaying with an Italian hitch onto a direct anchor is often the best method. It goes without saying that any anchor selected must be completely sound. If there is no suitable anchor available, then belaying with a plate from the harness comes a close second. If students are belaying in this manner, ensure that they are in no danger of being dragged into the rock in the event of a fall, and provide them with a solid anchor, either from the ground or by linking them to a second person with a sling.

BOTTOM-ROPE SYSTEMS

There is a number of ways of rigging a bottom-rope system, but whichever is chosen it should have the same result – total security and ease of operation. Given below is arguably the best of the many possible systems. Here, we will assume that two anchor points are being used.

EQUIPMENT

Low-stretch rigging rope, slings, screwgates, climbing rope, rope protectors.

Method

Assuming that the anchors are roughly equal distance from the edge of the crag, tie a double figure of eight in the centre of the rigging rope.

- Decide how far down you want the loop to be, place it over the edge, then tie an overhand knot on the rigging ropes 1–2ft back from the top of the cliff. This overhand knot helps to direct the forces efficiently, and reduces rope movement and rubbing on the edge of the cliff top.
- Run one length of the rigging rope back to an anchor point and clip it in with a clove

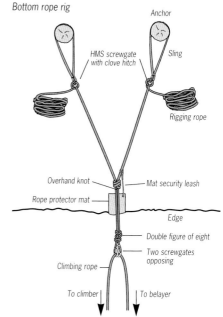

Bottom rope rig

Anchor

HMS screwgate with clove hitch

Sling

Rigging rope

Overhand knot — — Mat security leash

Rope protector mat

Edge

— Double figure of eight

— Two screwgates opposing

Climbing rope

To climber | To belayer

hitch. Clip a screwgate karabiner into the rigging rope loop, together with the centre of the climbing rope, the rest of which can be dropped down the crag. Ensure that the sleeve of the screwgate does up downwards, to prevent vibration from unscrewing it.

- Now clip in a second karabiner with the gate facing the opposite way to the first, but still with the sleeve doing up downwards.
- Run the second length of the rigging rope back to the other anchor and clip it in, again with a clove hitch. Now that the rigging rope has the weight of the climbing rope hanging from it, it will be easy to adjust the two sides until the loop is in the desired position. (This is judged by ensuring that the rope, when controlled from the bottom of the crag, will run smoothly and in a straight line up and through the top karabiners, nowhere rubbing on the rock.)
- Place a rope protector under any wear points, have a final check of all screwgates, and that is the rig finished.

If climbing with younger people, it may be an idea to use a pulley in place of one of the karabiners, with an extended karabiner backing it up. There will be a large reduction in the amount of friction which can make lowering easier, but it will make controlling the descent of a heavier person more difficult, so care must be taken.

■ Knots pp42–6

OBSERVATIONS

1 Be very careful to look after your own safety when rigging a system; it is easy to clip yourself in as you work and it makes a lot of sense to do so.

2 Check your kit after use for wear and tear, particularly karabiners. These have a hard life being used for group sessions, and can become worn and pitted quite quickly. Steel karabiners wear more slowly than alloy, so they could be used as the two top krabs in the rig where the rope runs.

TIP

Rope protectors are very useful, not just to stop your rope from possible damage on edges, but also to save areas of soft rock from eroding. They are available commercially, or can be made very simply. Use a square of carpet, about 1ft x 1ft, such as are commonly used as samples by carpet showrooms. Make a hole about 2in in from the centre of one side, lark's-foot through an old sling, and attach a prussik loop to this. The prussik loop or the sling can be used to secure the protector in the right place.

OBSERVATION

It is usual to use low-stretch rigging ropes for the anchor part of the set-up. Using standard dynamic climbing ropes is OK, but as they tend to stretch they can make the rig feel somewhat springy. However, the main reason to avoid using them is that, if they run over an edge, the weight of the abseiler will cause them to stretch and contract many times causing damage to the rock and, rather more seriously, damage to the rope.

GROUP-ABSEIL RIGGING

The following is the standard method of organising a group-abseil rig. It is assumed that there are three excellent anchors available.

Method

■ Ensure that all anchors are sound and equipped with screwgate karabiners. Tie a figure of eight on the bight on one end of the rigging rope. Clip this into the first anchor point and run a loop of rope from here loosely on the ground towards the edge of the crag.

■ Bring the rope up to the second anchor point, clip it in and repeat the loop on the ground,

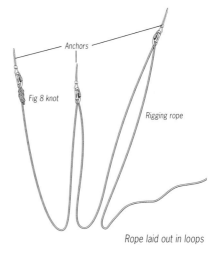

Anchors

Fig 8 knot

Rigging rope

Rope laid out in loops

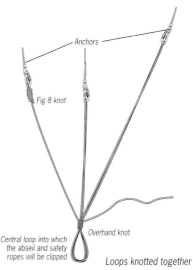

Anchors

Fig 8 knot

Central loop into which the abseil and safety ropes will be clipped

Overhand knot

Loops knotted together

then take it to the third anchor point, clip it in and carry the remainder of the rope back to the end of the loops. The position of the knot on the rig is critical, as everything will be operated from here. It must be near enough to the edge of the crag so that you can reach it at all times, but not so close that someone using the system ends up hanging over the edge before all of the slack is taken up.

Knots pp42–6 • Belay Methods pp58–63 ■

OBSERVATION

There are commercially manufactured 'rigging plates' available on the market, designed to replace the central rigging loop. These are flat plates in each of which there is a series of holes. Each anchor's rigging line, and each utility such as the abseil rope, safety rope, etc, is clipped into separate holes. The problem with this is that you substantially increase the number of karabiners required and, more worryingly, have a situation of metal on metal, with the plate dictating the angle at which the karabiners are held. The chance of a sideways loading on the karabiner is a real possibility. These plates are best rejected, as the simple rope-loop system described above does a far better job.

In practice, this means that the knot will be tied around 6ft back.

■ Take the rope loop from between the first and second anchors, adjust it so that it is the right length and tension (make it slightly longer than required as you will need to tie a knot in it, thus reducing its length), take the rope from between the second and third anchors and repeat the process. Then lay the rope coming from the final anchor on top and create a loop in that as well.

■ Ensure that all of the loops are the same length and tension and, holding them together, tie an overhand knot. All of the subsequent pieces of kit will clip into this central loop.

RELEASABLE ABSEIL

What is a releasable abseil?

A releasable abseil is one that allows the abseil rope to be slackened off while still under tension.

When would it be used?

This method of securing the rope should be encouraged as the standard system for all group-abseiling activities, allied with a safety rope.

What is its advantage over other systems?

If the descendeur should jam for any reason, this method allows the weight of the abseiler to be taken on the safety rope and for the abseil rope to be loosened. This will let the abseiler

release any obstruction jamming the descendeur, and he can then either be lowered to the ground, or the abseil rope tied off so that he can continue the descent himself.

If a non-releasable system is used, for example a figure of eight on the bight clipped into the anchor krab, and the system is loaded, it will prove extremely difficult, and often impossible, to haul up the abseiler to a degree at which the abseil device can be un-jammed.

Method

The setting up of the releasable system is extremely simple. An HMS karabiner is clipped into the rigging loop, turned gate up with the wide end facing down hill. An Italian hitch is tied in the abseil rope. This can be tied either singly or double, depending on a number of factors but usually decided by the amount of friction required. The Italian hitch is then clipped into the krab, and the gate done up.

■ The knot should be rotated on to the down-hill side of the krab, and it should then be locked off using the standard method of a slippery hitch followed by two half hitches, leaving a bight of rope of at least a foot in length. This bight should be laid neatly at the side of the set-up, and should not be knotted or clipped back with a krab in any way.

■ The amount of abseil rope used is very important. It should just touch the ground at the bottom of the abseil, and not be allowed to lie on the floor in a heap. To have an excessive amount of rope at the bottom of the crag will almost certainly contribute to problems, and it should be ensured that there will always be

Italian locked off

■ Knots pp42–6 • Learning to Lead pp71–2

plenty of spare rope at the top to allow for lowering procedures to take place, without having to let go of the end. The spare abseil rope at the top of the crag must be carefully coiled into a pile, making sure that there are no knots or twists, with the rope leading neatly from the top of the pile to the Italian hitch.

■ Should the need occur for the abseil rope to be released, such as someone's hair becoming entangled in the abseil device, firstly the safety rope is pulled up tight. Then, the locked-off Italian hitch on the abseil rope is released which allows slack to be paid out and the obstruction cleared.

TIPS

1 Stop a problem before it occurs. Make sure that the knot that you have tied into the end of the safety rope at the abseiler's end has got an extremely short tail on the stopper knot, otherwise there is a chance of it catching in the abseil device.

2 Once down, a common problem, especially for younger folk, is caused by them having trouble taking the karabiner off the harness once they have unscrewed it. This is because they get the notch on the nose of the karabiner hooked on their abseil loop. There are screwgates on the market that have been designed with the notch on the inside of the gate, and the nose presents a smooth surface to anything being clipped in and out. A karabiner of this type is excellent for using with safety ropes and abseil devices.

OBSERVATION

The HMS of the safety rope can often jam up against the HMS of the abseil rope, which is clipped into the same part of the rigging loop. To prevent this happening, clip a short extender onto the rigging loop, and put the safety-rope's HMS onto this. There is now little chance that they will jam together.

GROUP-ABSEIL SAFETY ROPE

It is not acceptable, in group activities, to allow participants to abseil without the security of a safety rope. Quite apart from the obvious problem of them hitting the bottom at speed, the safety rope is your insurance that if anything should go wrong, you have the means with which to go about doing something to rectify it.

OBSERVATIONS

1 One of the main causes of nervousness amongst novice (and indeed experienced!) abseilers is a low take-off point. If the rigging rope is high, then the angle at which the abseiler steps over the edge is greater, and he will feel better supported.

2 Take great care with your group management at the top of the abseil. Ensure that they are sitting in a safe area, and know what to do when called forward. It is very tempting for folk to creep forward to see how their mates are getting on.

3 It is important to ensure that your group members have been told to tuck away any 'flappy' bits of clothing or loose hair, and check that helmet straps have been secured and tucked in. Carry out a quick individual check as each person comes forward to abseil.

Method

A dynamic climbing rope should be used. One end should have a figure of eight on the bight tied in, with a screwgate clipped through it; the other end can be clipped out of the way on one of the anchors.

■ An HMS screwgate is clipped into the rigging loop, with the gate facing up and the wide end towards the edge of the cliff. An Italian hitch is clipped into this, and the end of the safety rope is clipped into the group-member's abseil loop before he starts.

■ Once he is connected to the abseil device and has started going down, the Italian hitch can be controlled as normal, but ensure that you are not holding him too tight – pay out slack with your free hand as he descends. In the case of an emergency, if necessary the safety rope can be pulled in tight and locked off at the Italian hitch.

PERSONAL SAFETY

Your own safety is extremely important – you are of no use to the group if you are lying at the bottom of the crag in a strange shape. When rigging, running an activity and de-rigging, always look after yourself and don't take risks.

Method

■ The simplest safety system is an 8ft sling lark's-footed between your leg loops and waist belt,

TIPS

1 It is possible, when exiting over a sharp edge, for the rope to catch and lark's-foot over the abseil device, in particular when using the figure-of-eight descender. The remedy for this is simple – instead of threading the rope up the big hole and round the little hole, which puts the rope on the lower side of the device, thread the rope *down* the big hole and up over the little hole. There is now no rope on the underside that will catch.

2 To help reduce the chance of a group member catching his hair or a pull cord from his clothing in the abseil device, extend it with a sling. This can be either a 4ft or an 8ft sling doubled and, if using a figure-of-eight descender, it can be simply threaded through the small hole, removing the need for an extra karabiner. Another advantage is that the abseiler now has somewhere to put the hand that is not controlling the rope; before, there was a danger of him getting his fingers too close to the device.

3 It is worth carrying a few hair ties or elastic bands on a small krab on the back of your harness. These can be given out to the group members who will inevitably have 'forgotten' to bring their own, and will help to keep their hair out of the way of the abseil device.

in the same line as the abseil loop. Have a screwgate karabiner on it, and it will be instantly ready to use by clipping into an existing anchor or rigging loop. This method is extremely useful if you are moving between a variety of sites. When not being used, the sling can wrap around your waist and the krab can be clipped into stop it flapping about.

■ If you are running the abseil session, a better method may well be to use the length of rigging rope you had coming in from the third anchor then out from the central knot, the end of which is not attached to anything. You can connect yourself to this by using either a clove hitch or a figure of eight on the bight, adjusted to give you good eye contact with the abseiler all the way down the crag.

LEADING NOVICES

There will come a time when you find yourself in the position of leading novices; often this will be when introducing a friend or friends to the art of climbing. It may be that you have been coaching them on a climbing wall for two or three sessions, and now the time has come for them to sample outdoor rock for the first time. Running through the basics with a couple of visits to a wall is very worthwhile, not only because they can pick up the mechanics of moving on rock, but because they can become familiar with belaying a leader in an atmosphere with few distractions. After practice, this will then allow them to belay you on outdoor routes. The decision as to whether you can trust someone enough to belay you is yours. It must be remembered that being belayed by someone who is not proficient is the same as soloing, with the added worry of injury to your second if something goes wrong.

Climbing with Two Novices

Attaching a second to your climbing rope is a simple process, and this allows him to learn quickly through individual contact. If you are in a situation of having two novices to follow you, then a bit of thought must go into their attachment point and method on the rope. There are five practical methods, any of which may be used.

■ The first is the least efficient, in which one rope is used. When the second reaches the top of the climb, he unties and the end is thrown down to the third, who ties on and climbs.

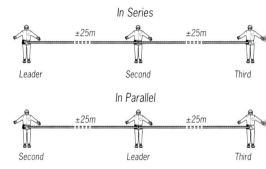

Attaching three climbers to one rope

This method can only be recommended for shorter routes with more experienced novices because of the following points:

1 You are unable to check whether the third person has connected himself to the rope correctly.

2 There is a chance of the rope snagging when it is thrown down. The habit of throwing down the rope with a knot and a karabiner in the end, and getting the second to clip into his abseil loop, is to be discouraged.

■ Two more methods, using just one rope, rely on the certainty that half a rope length will be more than ample to reach the top and belay, for instance on a shorter route with good anchors near the edge at the stance. The leader ties on to one end, with the second in the middle and the third at the other end; this is known as 'climbing in series'. Alternatively, the leader could place himself in the middle, with this system being known as 'climbing in parallel'. Whoever ends up as the middleman must be attached by tying into the harness, as opposed to clipping in with a karabiner. The knot can be a standard figure of eight rewoven on a bight with a stopper, although this does end up as being rather bulky and some may find it feeling a little restrictive. The other method is to tie a rewoven overhand knot on the bight, and clip the loop end back into the harness with a karabiner to prevent the knot from unravelling.

■ The fourth and fifth methods use two ropes, and are recommended as the best way of organising things. Rope handling and stance-management dynamics are greatly eased if these rope are of different colours. The leader ties on at one end of a rope, with the second attached at the other end. The second is then connected to the other rope, with the third climber tied on at the far end (in series). Alternatively, the leader could tie both ropes into his harness, and have one climber on each (in parallel).

■ One of the biggest pros of the first method is that, when the second reaches the top, his rope can be connected to the belay system and he can then belay up the third person. The rope between the leader and second is then free to be used for another purpose, such as rigging an abseil, to be coiled up ready for the descent, or it can be deployed in case of an emergency.

Clipping into Runners

If climbing with one other person who is going to follow you, clipping into runners while leading should present no problems. When climbing with a second and a third, though, some thought must go into the process. When leading in series, the simplest solution is to have one person belaying you and clip the runners as normal, with the other person just observing. If climbing in parallel, it is possible to have either one or both people belaying. If both are involved, this will allow you to clip each rope into a variety of runners, and lets both the second and third remove gear thus learning about placements. It also avoids having one person sitting at the bottom doing nothing while the other belays.

An extremely important consideration, whichever method is used, is the run of the rope if the route necessitates a traverse of any kind. If you have placed gear to protect yourself and the second while traversing, and the gear is removed, the third person may not be protected. It is important to bear this in mind, and to ensure that any briefings contain concise information on what the second is required to do when unclipping a runner – clipping it back on behind him to the rope trailing to the third is often the answer.

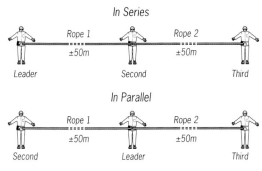

Attaching three climbers to two ropes

Improvised Rescue Techniques *pp82–7* • Knots *pp42–6* ■

COMMON GROUP-ACTIVITY PROBLEMS: PREVENTION AND SOLUTIONS

It should be realised that the chances of a problem arising during a single-pitch climbing or abseiling session are greatly reduced if there has been proper planning, preparation and briefings. For instance, the common problem of a helmet strap caught in a descendeur is prevented, not by running into a full-blown releasable-abseil scenario, but by checking that the strap was properly tucked away in the first place. Below are given a few of the commonest problems that may occur during a session, the cause and the remedy. This list is non-exhaustive, and is designed to demonstrate that the simplest solutions are normally the best. It will be noted that *the cause should become the remedy for the following sessions*, with the lesson having been learnt.

It cannot be emphasised enough that briefings and preparation are the key to a successful and trouble-free session. All of the scenarios in the table could have been easily avoided by a little thought beforehand, and by paying attention to the activity involved. If

practical action is needed, then the simplest remedy and course of action will normally be the best. Massively complicated rope systems, hoists and pulleys are fine in their place, but there will always be a simpler alternative. Safety, efficiency and speed are what is required, in that order.

EXAMPLE

You are running an abseiling session for a group of twelve- to fourteen-year-olds. Even after your best attentions, one of the girls gets halfway down the slab and a tuft of her hair blows forward and gets trapped in the abseil device. She is crying out in pain, gripping the abseil rope for all she's worth. Do you:

1 call out to her not to worry; bend down and tie off the safety rope with a slippery hitch and two half-hitches while keeping her informed of what you are doing; untie the locked-off Italian on the abseil rope, at the same time as letting her know you are untying it; slowly release her weight on to the safety rope, then call down to see if she is able to free her hair from the device? Or:

Problem	Cause	Remedy
Helmet strap caught in abseil device.	Inefficient checks.	Pulling on safety rope; release of abseil rope.
Refusing to commit weight to rope on bottom-rope lower.	Did not brief and practise lowers before allowing climb to start.	Verbal encouragement; assistance from above; assistance from below; rope tricks.
Freezes on ledge.	Poor route choice, reading of client's ability.	Verbal encouragement; assistance from above; assistance from below; rope tricks.
Climbing up rope hand-over-hand.	Inefficient briefing, inattentive belaying.	Verbal instruction.
Climbing off route.	Inefficient briefing, poor route choice.	Verbal instruction; tight rope.
Climbing past runner when following led climb.	Inefficient briefing, inattentive belaying.	Verbal instruction, rope loop passed down with krab.
Climbing beyond top krab on bottom-roped climb.	Inefficient briefing, inattentive belaying.	Tight rope; careful verbal instructions.

■ Improvised Rescue Techniques pp82–7 • Knots pp42–6

1 As far as this abseiling incident is concerned, it is worth thinking about the instructions that you give. Keep any verbal instructions simple, loud and clear, and remember that if someone is in distress hanging from her hair on a scary piece of rock in a gale in the pouring rain, the last thing that she wants to hear is you calling down, 'Right, I'm now going to undo the abseil rope ...'!

2 With a jammed abseil device, there are two types of situation. One is where a body part, such as hair, a finger, etc, has stuck in the device – this will need a very quick remedy, with lifting the abseiler's weight on to the safety rope being the quickest and normally the most efficient. If you are unable to pull his weight up sufficiently, perhaps because you have rigged a free abseil, you may have no choice but to release the abseil rope.

2 pull hard on the safety rope as soon as it is apparent that something is wrong, lifting her weight off of the abseil rope, and call down for her to free her hair?

Even here there could be a shortcut, in that it may not be necessary to go through the procedure of locking off the safety rope – a couple of wraps around the hand and a tight grip could be all that is necessary. If, however, the problem has been caused by a piece of clothing jamming, you have the luxury of time and will be able to go through the full locking off/unlocking process if need be.

3 It may be noticed that some instructors working on single-pitch crags carry a pocket knife with them, hanging from the back of their harness. It can only be hoped that these implements are to be used in the event of personal attack, and are not for use during a group session. It cannot be emphasised enough that EXTREME caution should be shown when wielding a knife, as climbing rope under tension cuts very easily indeed.

The point here is that, although there may be a textbook way of doing things, a simpler remedy is often available given just a little thought.

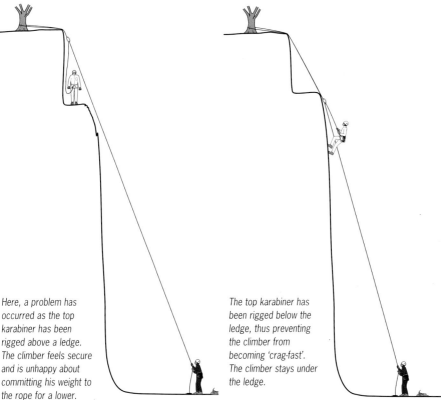

Here, a problem has occurred as the top karabiner has been rigged above a ledge. The climber feels secure and is unhappy about committing his weight to the rope for a lower.

The top karabiner has been rigged below the ledge, thus preventing the climber from becoming 'crag-fast'. The climber stays under the ledge.

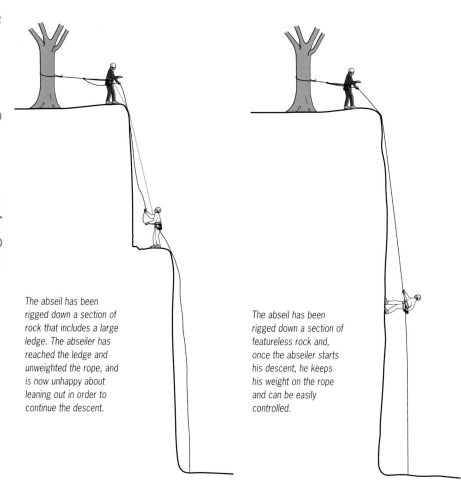

The abseil has been rigged down a section of rock that includes a large ledge. The abseiler has reached the ledge and unweighted the rope, and is now unhappy about leaning out in order to continue the descent.

The abseil has been rigged down a section of featureless rock and, once the abseiler starts his descent, he keeps his weight on the rope and can be easily controlled.

Thoughts on Route Choice

The four diagrams (above and previous page) show very simply how important route choice is, and how a problem can be avoided with ease. In the first example, the top karabiner of the bottom-rope system has been situated above a large ledge at the finish of the route. This allows a nervous climber to stand on the ledge and feel safer there rather than committing his weight to the rope for a lower, even though one will have been practised at the bottom. To avoid this problem ensure that, when rigging, the karabiner has been lowered down on the

rigging rope to just below the ledge, ensuring that the climber is unable to climb on to it in the first place.

In the second example, an abseil has been set up over a route that has a ledge part way down. This is asking for trouble, as a nervous abseiler will automatically stand up when he reaches the ledge, un-weight the system, and be very wary about leaning back out again. As it is not possible to lower the top of the abseil down the crag, a different route must be selected, one which allows for a straight descent with no obstacles to be negotiated.

■ Improvised Rescue Techniques pp82–7 • Knots pp42–6 • Abseiling pp47–50

TECHNICAL EMERGENCY PROCEDURES

As we have said, proper planning before and throughout the session should negate all of the problems. There should be no call for a large amount of 'rope tricks' to be used to solve a situation. For instance, knowing how to lock off a belay plate under load may not be relevant. If a plate is loaded with a person's body weight, then he can simply be lowered to the ground, from either a top- or bottom-rope set-up, and there should be no occasion on which a person is left locked off and suspended in mid-air while climbing. However, it may well be relevant to know how to secure a plate and pass it over to another group member when the plate is not fully loaded, for instance when the climber has become 'crag-fast' and refuses to move either up or down from a ledge.

Four of the following procedures should be practised until they become second nature, and they are in the technical rope-tricks category. The fifth procedure, the solution of the stuck screwgate, has been included to indicate the many ways there are to solve a simple problem.

Locking Off and Escaping from a Belay Plate on a Bottom-rope System

Scenario: the climber has become crag-fast, and refuses to move up or down. You have been unable to find a suitable ground anchor, and did not wish for your group members to belay, hence controlling the plate yourself.

▨ Call over one or two of the other group members. Clip an HMS karabiner onto the abseil loop of one of them. Tie a clove hitch in the dead rope close to the belay device and clip it into the krab, doing up the gate.
▨ If the group members are young or very inexperienced, or if there is a large weight difference between the new belayer and the stuck climber, clip a sling between the abseil loops of your two helpers.
▨ With little slack between the climber and new belayer, undo your belay device screwgate and

take it off your harness. The plate can either be left on the rope, or removed in case it is needed later. The new belayer/s should now sit on the ground.
▨ Brief them to stay put until told otherwise, and remember to keep talking to the stuck climber while all of this is going on. You are now free from the system.

Retrieving a Stuck Climber from the Top of a Route on a Bottom-rope System

Scenario: despite your best efforts and after having practised lowering at the start of the climb, a climber reaches the top karabiner and refuses to commit his weight to the rope. You are not part of the system, having either selected a ground anchor, allowed group members to belay each other, or have escaped the system as above.

▨ Remember that the climber may not have to be lowered to the ground – he may be able to climb up and over the top. This will avoid you having to rig a complicated abseil system.
▨ Get to the top of the route quickly (via the path!), and immediately gain eye contact with the stuck climber, and continue reassurance.
▨ Select an appropriate anchor, clip in an HMS krab and, using either a spare rope or the end of the rigging rope, tie a figure of eight on the bight and clip in a second karabiner. This is then passed down to the climber, who clips it into his abseil loop and screws up the gate.
▨ Be very attentive at this point, and ensure that the screwgate has been correctly done up by both visual inspection and by getting him to perform a squeeze test, where the climber squeezes the krab across the back bar and gate with one hand. An Italian hitch on the new climbing rope is now clipped into the HMS on the anchor.
▨ The belayers on the ground are at this stage able to undo the clove hitch and let the rope go, as you have the climber held safely from above. The climber can now climb over the top and be fielded well back from danger.

Abseiling to Retrieve a Marooned Climber

The following is a technique that is amongst the most advanced of the skills needed for running a single-pitch session, and should be seen as being more relevant to the skills required by the multi-pitch climber and instructor. However, there is an argument that it could be used during group-climbing sessions as a remedy for one or two very rare and awkward scenarios, hence its inclusion in this section.

Scenario: the climber has become stuck on a ledge part way up the route, and is unable to move for whatever reason. You are not part of the belay system, or have escaped from it as above.

■ From the top of the crag, drop down a spare rope and attach it to a solid anchor. Prepare to abseil to the climber. This is organised by using an 8ft sling doubled, with an overhand knot on the bight tied at the centre. The karabiner and abseil device will clip into this knot. You will be clipped on to your abseil loop with one half of the sling; the other half will be left hanging free so that you can clip the stuck climber to it.

■ Tie an overhand knot halfway up the spare sling side, so that you have some flexibility when deciding where to attach the climber.

■ Protect the abseil in the usual manner, with the French prussik being connected to the rope via your abseil loop. Descend to the stuck climber. Attach him to the spare sling loop with a screwgate karabiner: at the end of it if he is going to walk down next to you, above the middle knot if you need to assist him down, such as with an unconscious casualty.

■ This assistance is accomplished by you swinging him horizontally across in front of you so that he is suspended from the abseil device, you keeping your feet out in front of you and flat on the rock so that he does not swing into it.

Sling set-up for assisted abseil

■ For multi-pitch assisted abseils, there will be a need to improvise some form of chest support, but for use on a single-pitch crag, it is much better to get him straight down to the ground.

■ Once he is securely clipped to the sling, the original climbing rope can be released. This can be done either by untying the knot to his harness, or by getting your helper on the ground to release the belay plate. Proceed to the ground.

■ Improvised Rescue Techniques *pp82–7* • Knots *pp42–6*

Prussik in front of plate

Safeguarding Yourself on an Easy Slab Climb

Scenario: you need to ascend for some reason to assist a climber who is having difficulty on an easy slab route.

■ Assuming you are belaying through a standard device, place a French prussik on the live rope immediately above it, clipped into the belay plate's HMS with a separate screwgate. When the dead rope is pulled through, the prussik acts as a back-up, and you can make your way up the ground to the climber, pulling through the slack rope as you go. Every few feet, tie an overhand knot in the dead rope to act as a stopper in the event of a slide.

■ When you reach the climber, you can render any assistance that may be necessary, which may include attaching him to you with a short

sling, then abseiling to the ground, a method known as the 'counterbalance abseil'.

Although a handy technique to be familiar with, this method of ascent has a couple of severe limitations. First, if the ground is anything more than very easy, then it is extremely hard to make any headway at all. Second, remember that you are relying on the weight of the stuck climber as a counterbalance; therefore, if he is somewhat lighter than you, he will be in for a reasonably uncomfortable time!

Undoing a Stuck Screwgate

Scenario: a person has abseiled to the ground, but is unable to undo the screwgate connecting the safety rope to himself. This is either because it has some grit stuck in the sleeve, or because it has been overtightened.

There are a number of remedies; these are in a logical order:
■ Check he is unscrewing it the right way.
■ Get him to hold the screw sleeve with a piece of material to improve grip.
■ See if there is someone else close by who could help.
■ Get him to tap the gate with another karabiner – this often helps to dislodge debris.
■ Have him sit on the ground, then you pull hard on the safety rope. This can stretch the karabiner shape sufficiently to allow the sleeve to turn.
■ Tell him to undo the knot on the rope.
■ Get him to take off his harness.
■ Go down to him.

OBSERVATION
It should be remembered that if a prussik loop is being used for anything more than a back-up for a personal abseil, it is probably an inappropriate technique and outside the usual remit of skills associated with running a single-pitch group session. If rope tricks are to be employed, they should be simple, quick, effective and safe, and employed only after all other possibilities have been considered.

PART TWO: WINTER

Avalanche Awareness

This section presents a number of considerations for safe travel in the hills under winter conditions, as well as some practical methods of appraising snow stability.

The Snow-pack

Snow falls, it's a fact of life. What we are interested in as mountaineers is how anchored each layer is to its partners throughout the snow-pack. Weak cohesion between adjoining layers or between the snow-pack and the ground could very well lead to ideal avalanche conditions. There are three ways in which the snow-pack will consolidate.

Isothermal Metamorphism

Also known as settling, it is the natural conversion of the crystal structure within the pack to a single compact layer; the whole process is speeded up as the snow temperature rises towards melting point.

Melt/Freeze Metamorphism

This is, as the name suggests, a process during which the temperature within the snow-pack alternates between below and above freezing point. A continued MF Met cycle gives fine hard snow, when it is frozen, that is good to travel over and climb on. But care must be taken during the melt process that moisture has not invaded the pack to such a degree – this could be to its full depth after lots of rain – that it may avalanche.

Kinetic-growth Metamorphism

This is the effect of the temperature gradient between the base layers and surface layers of the pack. Where a large gradient exists, water vapour migrates through the pack and forms extremely fragile cup-crystals, also known as depth hoar.

FACTORS DETERMINING SNOW STABILITY/INSTABILITY

Surface Hoar

Crystals are formed on cold, clear nights when the surface temperature of the snow-pack becomes colder than that of the air surrounding it. The danger from surface hoar becomes real after subsequent snowfall covers the crystals and leaves a fragile layer within the pack which may exist for some time.

Snowfall

This has a large effect on pack stability with most avalanches occurring during or immediately after a heavy fall of snow. For the purposes of clarity, heavy snowfall is defined as being at a rate of 2cm per hour.

Angle of Slope

Obviously a factor, and it is not often realised that a slope with an angle of as little as 15 degrees can avalanche. The most prone to avalanche are those between 30 and 45 degrees, with slopes of more than 60 degrees rarely accumulating enough snow.

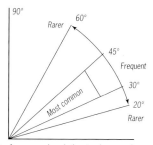

Avalanche frequency in relation to slope angle

Shape of Slope

This can affect stability: at the back of a concave slope the snow is compressed and so reasonably stable; however on a convex slope, such as at the top where it reaches a plateau, the snow is stretched within the pack and on the outer surface, and cohesion can fail.

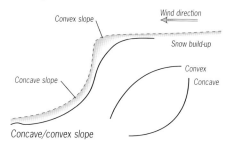

Concave/convex slope

Air Temperature and Wind

The snow-pack is profoundly affected by this. Cold temperatures allow the snow to remain in an almost-unchanged state for long periods, warmer temperatures allow crystal change and conversion of the crystals to a different state. The presence of wind, or lack of it, is a major factor.

TYPES OF AVALANCHE

Loose Dry-snow Avalanches
May be quite large and form from a single point, and occur when cohesion is lost due to isothermal met. The avalanche will flow at speeds of up to 40mph, and if it exceeds this speed it may become airborne.

Airborne Powder
Such avalanches are extremely destructive, and in the Alpine regions can be immense. They may start as a loose dry-snow avalanche or slab, but become airborne after around 40mph is reached. Other types of avalanche such as hard or soft slabs may be pulverised by their own motion and may turn into airborne powder. The destructive power can only be imagined as the speed of the avalanche can be around 175mph.

Slab Avalanches
There will be a marked lack of cohesion under the layer, sometimes with the slab being completely unsupported over a large area. Soft slabs are associated with accumulation of snow on lee slopes owing to wind action, with winds of up to 30mph. Most soft-slab avalanches are released by their victims, so all slopes, not just those in the lee of the wind, should be treated with suspicion until the snow settles, remembering that this may take some time in cold conditions. Straight-edged blocks breaking away under your boot are a sure sign of soft-slab danger. Bear in mind that it need not have been snowing for the snow to have accumulated; wind transportation will do the job on its own.

Hard slabs are one of the greatest hazards in the mountains. Wind speeds of over 30mph help hard-slab formation on lee slopes, and the slab will feel underfoot as hard as concrete. Release is usually accompanied by a loud cracking noise, and the slab breaks up into huge angular blocks which remain intact during its descent. Hard slab has a dull chalky appearance and does not easily reflect light, often squeaking, sometimes booming, underfoot. This 'booming' sound will come from the inherent weakness underneath.

Wet Avalanches
Common in spring, and at any time following a thaw. They are caused by water weakening the bonds between layers or between the bottom layer and the ground. The danger is greatest when there is a heavy snow storm which starts cold and finishes warm. Wet avalanches can be loose or in slab form, and move either fast of slow. They will set like concrete immediately upon stopping, so the survival time for a buried victim is extremely short. They can be expected at the start of heavy rain, and for 24 hours thereafter.

Ice Avalanches
In their purest form these are uncommon in Scotland; however the danger is from a thaw when an icefall attached to a crag peels off and crashes down the hillside.

Cornice Collapse
Often associated with thaw conditions, although cornices may well collapse under their own weight given extra snowfall. As with slab formation, there need not be any snowfall to form a cornice; wind action alone will do the job.

To Sum Up
■ Lee slopes are very prone to slab build-up.
■ Low temperatures prolong avalanche risk.
■ A sudden increase in temperature increases danger.
■ High-danger slopes are between 25 degrees and 45 degrees.
■ The convex section of the slope will often be the fracture point.
■ A reliable indicator of unstable conditions is evidence of recent avalanche activity.
■ Snowballs rolling down-slope indicate rising temperature.
■ Angular blocks breaking away underfoot indicate slab conditions, as does a chalky appearance.
■ Danger period is up to 48hrs after snowfall, longer in cold conditions.
■ Accumulation rate of more than 2cm per hour can lead to a heightened avalanche risk.

AVALANCHE AWARENESS

It is a fact that mountaineers and skiers sometimes get caught in avalanches. Statistics show that many either had no knowledge of avalanches or safe-route- travel skills, or they

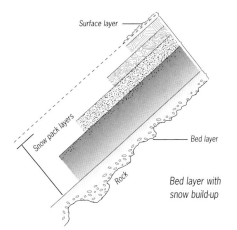

Surface layer

Snow pack layers

Bed layer

Rock

Bed layer with
snow build-up

simply ignored all the signs of instability and
convinced themselves that everything would be
all right and it wouldn't happen to them.

If you were caught in an avalanche what
would be the consequences? Statistically, the
more time you spend walking and climbing in
winter, the greater the chance you have of being
caught-out in an avalanche, or of observing
others trying to survive one. Victims of
avalanches often trigger the slide themselves,
with the same mistakes frequently repeated time
and time again.

Avalanches often occur during heavy snowfall,
during windy periods that re-deposit snow, and
up to 48 hours thereafter. To minimise risk when
travelling in the mountains where a moderate- to
high-risk condition may prevail, two courses of
action are open to you:
1 Improve your overall understanding of
avalanches and practise safe travel. **OR:**
2 Don't go.
It is very important to be objective according to
weather conditions and not to let personal goals
and ambitions cloud your judgement.

Warning Signs: Snowpack
■ Avalanche activity.
■ Fresh avalanche debris.
■ Snow cracking or easily breaking away in
    blocks underfoot.
■ 'Whumphing' noises underfoot.
■ Signs of snow-pack instability at test sites.
■ Rollerballs/sunwheels.

Warning Signs: Terrain
■ Slopes, in particular those between 30 degrees
    and 45 degrees.

■ Lee slopes and wind-sheltered gullies.
■ Slope aspects.
■ Cornice build-up.
■ Previous avalanche paths and debris.
■ Natural terrain traps.

Warning Signs: Weather
■ Heavy snowfall.
■ Wind loading on lee slopes.
■ Sudden rise in temperature; rain and warm
    winds soon after snowfall.
■ Prolonged periods of very warm and very cold
    weather.
■ Solar warming.
■ There can often be sudden and dramatic
    temperature changes throughout the winter
    period, so it is very important that you
    monitor the weather conditions before and
    during your trip.

Fact Finding
It is best to always base your avalanche-hazard
evaluation on solid facts, and never rely solely on
feelings, assumptions or guesses.

The first things that you should be thinking of
when faced with uncertainty are: is it safe or is it
unsafe? You must begin to fact-find and identify
meaningful information upon which you can
establish your evaluation. This is called the **fact-
find approach**:
■ Does a hazard exist?
■ Is the weather contributing to instability?
■ Can you recognise avalanche terrain?
■ Could the snow-pack slide?
■ What are the alternatives and any
    consequences?
Remember, you have lots of ways of gathering
information to form your hazard evaluation. For
instance, Met Office reports, local avalanche
forecasts and the ability to identify suspect slopes
all help to build the bigger picture.

The Fact-find Approach
WEATHER WARNING SIGNS
TERRAIN WARNING SIGNS
SNOW-PACK WARNING SIGNS
THE HUMAN FACTOR

■ Mountain Weather see pp10–14

Safe-travel Tips

BEFORE YOU GO

1 Always ensure that you are carrying essential safety equipment and prepare for the worst.
2 Spend some time with your companion, partner or clients discussing safe route travel options and procedures if caught in a avalanche.

PLANNING YOUR TRIP

1 Check the current weather and local avalanche forecasts.
2 Ensure that you have appropriate emergency equipment (see Gear Lists).
3 Check that all group members are capable of the proposed trip.
4 Consider alternative route options should conditions not be in your favour.
5 Leave information on your intended route, and time due back, with a responsible person.
6 Check that you have appropriate map and guide-book information.
7 Be aware of natural-terrain traps and known avalanche-producing slopes.
8 Never presume that the summer path will be safe in winter.
9 Be aware of the slope aspects in relation to the weather.

ON THE MOUNTAIN

1 Always consider where the stress point of a slope may be.
2 Be aware of travelling over cornices or underneath them.
3 When travelling through potential avalanche terrain, use natural islands of safety such as ridges and exposed high points.
4 Minimise your exposure time on a suspect slope.
5 Only allow one person to cross a suspect slope at any one time. Always consider the run out should someone be swept away.
6 It is an idea to favour one or other side of the slope, rather than the middle, as this will give you a better chance of escaping should an avalanche be triggered.
7 Always consider the slope angles, aspect and altitude.
8 Look out for stress points and fracture lines.

9 Stability tests should be carried out at relevant points along the route.
10 Never assume that others know better. Footprints ahead of you do not mean that the slope is necessarily safe to cross.

PREPARE FOR THE WORST

1 Choose your line of travel carefully.
2 Never stop in the middle or at the bottom of an avalanche-prone slope.
3 Ensure that clothing is fastened, gloves are on, hood up and goggles worn.
4 Remove ski-pole safety leashes from wrists, undo rucksack hip belts and loosen shoulder straps.
5 Protect with a rope if appropriate.
6 Think of the consequences if caught. Have a rescue plan and be prepared for the worst.

THE RUTSCHBLOCK TEST

This form of the Rutschblock test, or walking-shear test, has been developed by Avalex in Scotland, and is based on a Swiss-founded ski-shear test using a similar scale of stability. The following sequence will provide you with guidance as to the stability of the snow-pack.

The first step will be to select a safe test slope that is representative of the slope aspect and angle that your intended route will take. This site could be located down and to one side of the line you wish to take, perhaps under a small outcrop of rock or an island of safety.

Method

When preparing your test block, it is important not to disturb the snow-pack on the up-slope side of your test site. Mark out a 1m square on the snow. Using the axe pick and adze, carefully excavate the front and sides of your block, ensuring that the front face remains vertical. Excavate down to just past the first stable layer. Load the test block in the following sequence, noting which stage produces a failure, and identify what this means in the scale of instability.

Step 1
Fails while isolating the test block.
Category: Extremely Unstable

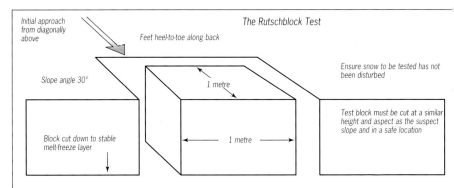

Initial approach from diagonally above

Feet heel-to-toe along back

The Rutschblock Test

Slope angle 30°

Ensure snow to be tested has not been disturbed

1 metre

Block cut down to stable melt-freeze layer

1 metre

Test block must be cut at a similar height and aspect as the suspect slope and in a safe location

Instability Scale

1 Fails while unloading block: *Extremely unstable*
2 Fails while approaching block: *Highly unstable*
3 Fails while rising from sitting position to standing on top of edge of block: *Very unstable*
4 Fails with downsink: *Unstable*
5 Fails with soft jump: *Potentially unstable*
6 Fails with hard jump: *Relatively stable*
7 No failure: *Stable*

TIP

If, when performing the Rutschblock test, a failure within the snow-pack occurs, identify the layer that has fractured and see if it matches any weak layers that you have observed. This information is a very useful way of learning more about snow-pack stability.
Remember: conditions and locations change, one test in a day is not enough. Combine shear tests with frequent hasty pits and on-going observations of the weather and terrain

Step 2

Fails while approaching the block from above. *Category: Highly Unstable*
In order to approach the block from above, it is an idea to first ascend the slope 3–4m clear of the test area, walk across the slope until above the test block, then walk directly down towards it. Should a companion be available, he can assist by observing any movement at the test block.

Step 3

Fails while shuffling feet heel-to-toe on the block and rising up. *Category: Very Unstable*
Before shuffling your feet heel-to-toe on to the top edge of the block, it is best to sit down above the block. This will ensure that the block is not shock-loaded with your body weight, which would then give a false result. It is important to maintain balance while standing. The stability result from a slide will be 'Very Unstable'.

Step 4

Block fails with a downsink. *Category: Unstable*
Maintain your feet in the heel-to-toe position to create the downsink effect. Simply bend your knees slightly, then straighten them, followed by relaxing your body weight back to the knees-bent position, all done in quick succession. Your feet should not leave the snow.

OBSERVATION

The Rutschblock test is a good method of evaluating the snow-pack, as it tests a large area and gives a feel for how sensitive that area of snow-pack is to body weight. However, the Rutschblock can be a rather time-consuming test to conduct. A more practical test is known as a 'hasty pit'. This could be described as a mini-Rutschblock but, as the name suggests, it takes only a fraction of the time to construct. Because of this, it is a very practical test to carry out at a number of points during the day.

Remember that conducting a single shear test in a day is not enough. As you travel around the mountains, the conditions underfoot can change rapidly. Therefore it is important to constantly evaluate the snow-pack and observe the weather and terrain clues.

Step 5

Fails with a soft jump.
Category: Potentially Unstable/Marginally Stable
Maintain your feet in the heel-to-toe position and jump softly on to the top edge of the block.

Step 6

Fails with a hard jump. *Category: Relatively Stable*

Step 7

No failure after several hard jumps.
Category: Stable

■ Mountain Weather see pp10–14

HASTY PITS

What is a hasty pit?
A hasty pit is a very quick and practical test to evaluate snow stability.

When and where is it used?
The hasty pit can be used at a number of places along your route, in order to evaluate the stability of the layers nearest the surface.

Method
- Use your axe to lightly mark out a 50cm-square test area. Be careful not to disturb the snow around the test site.
- Using the pick of the axe, cut around the sides and bottom of the square that you have marked out and remove the snow using the adze. Excavate down to the first stable layer.
- Cut along the top line of the square with the pick to the first suspect layer, ensuring that you do not disturb the central block, and carefully remove the snow from here, again with the adze. You should now have a free-standing block, separated from the snow-pack on all sides.
- Place both hands, with your fingers spread wide, a few inches down the slot at the back of the block, and pull down-slope with gently increasing pressure. If no sliding layers are detected, cut the back slot a little deeper, move your hands further down, and repeat the process. Continue until your hands are at the bottom of the slot, or until a failure has occurred.

Results
By applying progressive pressure to this column of snow at varying heights, unstable layers may shear off along a clean surface. If the test is incorrectly conducted by pulling hard at the bottom of the slot, weakly bonded layers further up the block may be missed.

1 If a layer slides as the block is being isolated from the up-slope side, or if a failure occurs when the snow is lightly touched with the hands, the result shows that the snow-pack within that area is extremely unstable, and a high avalanche hazard exists.

2 If the test reveals no obvious sliding layers,

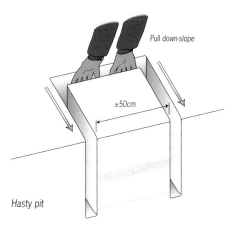

Pull down-slope

±50cm

Hasty pit

and sections of the block only break away in lumps after some effort, this indicates a stable and well-bonded snow-pack.

The ease with which a column of snow shears is rated as:

5 Very easy	Extremely Unstable
4 Easy	Highly Unstable
3 Moderate	Unstable
2 Hard	Relatively Stable
1 Very hard	Stable

SURVIVAL TIPS

If You Get Caught
- Shout out.
- Escape to the side.
- Discard gear, such as ice axe, ski poles etc.
- Attempt to stay on the surface by rolling or 'swimming'.
- As the avalanche stops, try to thrust your hand, foot, body to the surface, fighting with all your effort.
- Try to create a breathing space around your face as the avalanche slows.
- Once all movement has stopped, try to relax and conserve energy.

If Someone Else Is Caught
- Keep him in sight and note his last position.
- Check for further danger.
- If possible, attract the attention of other people to assist with a search.

Mountain Weather see pp10–14

- Appoint a look-out for further danger and decide on evasive action if necessary.
- If you have one, conduct a transceiver search.
- Mark where the victim was last seen.
- Search for surface clues.
- Probe likely burial areas with ice axe, etc, followed by a systematic probe line search.
- Only if numbers allow, send for help.
- Remember you are the victims only real chance of a live recovery – keep searching.

CHANCE OF SURVIVAL

In most cases people recovered from a burial within fifteen minutes will have a fair chance of survival. This is dependent upon them finishing with a sufficient air pocket around their face, as well as their final resting position within the snow-pack. Those that have sustained serious injuries as a consequence of the avalanche will have a lesser chance of survival.

Should their body be facing downhill, then there is a possibility that the snow will not have blocked their airway. If the victim is facing uphill, then snow may have got into the mouth and nose, and asphyxiation may result.

Up to one hour and beyond, the chance of survival is considerably reduced. However, victims have been known to survive burial for periods of up to 24 hours or more. KEEP SEARCHING.

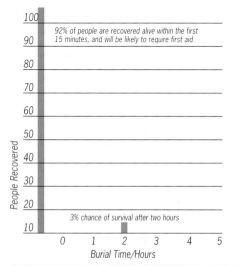

92% of people are recovered alive within the first 15 minutes, and will be likely to require first aid

3% chance of survival after two hours

People Recovered

Burial Time/Hours

WHAT TO DO

- Having assessed that there is little further immediate danger, the first to arrive at the scene of an avalanche should spread out across the debris and search the entire deposition zone. The aim of this initial search is to find any clues as to the possible whereabouts of a buried victim. You should spot-probe where clues are found, and in any obvious catchment areas.
- When you find clues, such as gloves, ski poles, ice axe, rucksack, etc, you should leave them in their exact position, as this will help to identify a pattern that may lead to a more defined search area. You should also conduct a transceiver search as the victim may have one with him, having first conducted a transceiver check while looking for clues.
- If the victim is not located after a very thorough initial search of the entire deposition zone, then begin a course probe in the obvious catchment area.
- Course probe: use either avalanche probes, ski sticks with baskets off or ice axes, spread out in a horizontal line with rescuers 2ft apart. Mark the two ends of the line with snow mounds or clothing to verify the start point, and continue to do so as the line progresses.

If using avalanche probes, this tactic has an approximate 70 per cent chance of finding your victim on the first pass.

COMMON PROBLEMS

- No leadership.
- No rescue plan.
- No rescue equipment.
- No probing in likely spots.
- Inadequate search patterns.
- Not searching the entire deposition zone.
- Not possessing, or knowing how to use, a transceiver beacon.

ELEMENTS OF A SUCCESSFUL RESCUE

- Self-reliance.
- Continuing to search until you have found the victim.

- Mountain Weather *see pp10–14*

- Having a plan.
- Speed with safety.
- Leadership.
- Efficient allocation of resources.
- Appropriate equipment (shovel, transceiver, probe).
- First aid.
- Evacuation.

OTHER CONSIDERATIONS

When searching, it must be thorough and fast for buried victims to have any chance of survival. In most circumstances you will not have the luxury of several extra people to assist you with the digging so you will need to shovel fast but carefully.

Once you have located the victim, immediately clear the snow from his head, airway and chest, observing whether his nose and mouth were blocked or not (this will have important implications for his treatment and evacuation), and continue first aid. It is also worth noting that when the victim is exposed to the weather elements his body will be cooling rapidly so you will need to react quickly and insulate him.

AVALANCHE TRANSCEIVERS

What is a transceiver?
It is a small compact electronic device that is designed to transmit and receive a signal to a distance of around 60–80m. The transceiver is battery powered, and has a chest strap attached.

How do you carry it?
Transceivers should be worn underneath your shell garment, switched on 'transmit' mode.

How do they work?
Working on an international frequency of 475khz, most transceivers emit a bleep sound when switched to search mode. The bleep is not directional; however the sound will get louder as you get closer to your target. An experienced searcher can usually find a buried transceiver in around 2 to 4 minutes. Some types of transceiver also incorporate a directional-arrow system.

OBSERVATIONS
1 Even when wearing transceivers, mountaineers have been killed in avalanches. Transceivers are simply victim locators, and offer a better chance of recovering a completely buried victim alive. However, they are no substitute for proper planning and preparation.
2 It is worth noting that should you be wearing a transceiver and do not know how to operate it, then there is not much point in wearing one in the first place.
3 When leaving your route information with someone responsible, remember to specify if transceivers are being worn.
4 Full information on transceiver usage, battery testing and search techniques is available from the manufacturers – practice is essential in order to be able to carry out a search in a proper and efficient manner. Remember that transceivers are of little practical use if shovels and avalanche probes are not carried as well. Most of all, remember: **transceivers are no substitute for safe-travel skills!**

AVALANCHE PROBES

Avalanche probes and line searches are usually the preserve of the professionally equipped rescue team, but it is interesting to understand how they are deployed. The notes below give an indication of this.

Line Searches
- When using a long avalanche probe, hold it vertically and lean it against your shoulder. Place the probe point directly in front of you with your feet either side of it, then push the probe into the snow as far as possible and retrieve it. Step forward approximately 30in and repeat the process. If at any time you detect something soft that could conceivably be a body, it should be investigated.
- Should you not have any success, the next option is a fine probe, First position your feet shoulder-width apart, angled slightly outwards. Begin to probe first at the toe of your left boot, then probe in between the feet, then probe at the toe of the right boot. Move one step forward and repeat the process.

OBSERVATION
In any line search there are a number of difficulties that can arise. The main one is maintaining a straight line. You should designate a leader who will organise the rescuers and give commands, eg: 'Probes in…probes out…probes forward… step forward…probes in' and so on.

Mountain Weather *see pp10–14*

PART TWO: WINTER

Snowcraft Skills

Snowcraft is the name given to the ability to progress
swiftly and safely over snow-covered terrain using axe,
crampon and boot skills.

Climber ascending the Fiacaill Couloir, Cairngorms, Scotland

The Ice Axe

No other piece of equipment, possibly throughout climbing in all its forms over both summer and winter seasons, is as essential as an ice axe. It is a tool with which to make progress, and, more importantly, it is the key to arresting a slip or fall on steep ground where, without its help, injury or death would certainly occur. Your ice axe should be chosen wisely.

AXE LENGTH

The question of axe length has for many years been accepted as being judged by one method – that when you stand with the axe head in your hand and your arm down by your side, the point of the axe should be approximately 2in off the ground. This method of selection is increasingly seen as being unhelpful. The days of an axe being used purely as a walking stick, with its secondary purpose being as a practical tool, have gone.

Axes have got shorter over a number of years, and they have now settled at a length of 50cm to 60cm – the choice is personal preference – measured from the tip of the spike to the top of the axe head. There is little difference in length between 'walking' axes and 'climbing' axes these days, the main noticeable contrast being the shape of the head section, notably the pick. Axes longer than 60cm are rather unwieldy, difficult to carry, lack precision and balance when swung, and are difficult to cut steps with; they may give little support on steep ground and make it awkward to perform an efficient self-arrest.

A short axe performs all of the above tasks with ease. The majority of our professional acquaintances never use anything more than 60cm, and, as an indicator that personal height is no longer a factor when choosing a tool, both authors use 50cm axes for all winter mountaineering: Stuart is 5ft 10in, Pete is 6ft 6in.

Why choose a shorter axe?

It may be necessary to explain exactly how a shorter axe is more efficient at self-arrest – this is rather tricky without demonstrating on snow, but the following simple test could help in understanding.

Stand upright, make a fist and bend your right arm to just below hip level by your right-hand side. Then get someone to push down on your arm as you push up and try to resist, and remember how it feels. Then bend your right arm to just above hip height and repeat the experiment. It should be felt that in the second position, you could resist far more effectively, as all the muscles in the upper arm were able to work together. This is the key to efficient self-arrest.

One hand holds the head of the axe, the other must completely cover the spike. If the axe is too long (1), the hand that covers the spike is almost completely ineffective, and it is extremely difficult to remain in control of the axe during a slide. With a shorter tool (2), both arms are able to work together, multiplying many times the efficiency of the arrest position.

1　　　　　　**2**

A GOOD AXE FOR GENERAL USE

There is a variety of considerations governing what makes a good axe. Most axes these days are made from composite materials that are extremely strong. Wooden axes, although warm to the touch, should be avoided as their strength is often in question. An axe intended for general walking and mountaineering use should not be of an ultra-light design, as it will have trouble

Self-arrest pp121–6 • Self Belay pp126–7 • Step Cutting pp131–4 • Stomper Belay pp142–3 • Boot-axe Belay pp143–4 • Buried-ice Anchors pp147–8 • Y-axe Anchor p149

TIP
When purchasing an axe, it is important how it feels in your hand. It is worth, from the very outset, getting right the way that the axe is carried. The axe should be picked up with the adze facing forwards, the pick pointing back. This is extremely important as far as self-arrest is concerned, and holding an axe in this way in the shop will tell you a lot about how it will feel on the hill.

Axes with a welded adze, and those with bolt arrangements at the head, can sometimes be uncomfortable. Remember to take a pair of winter gloves with you to the shop, as some material can be remarkably slippery on axe-shaft grips.

penetrating hard ground, especially with the adze when cutting steps. Apart from length, 50cm or 55cm, it should have a spike that is not too long. The longer the spike, the harder it is to hold on to in the event of a slip.

It is important that the spike is not too sharp either, as this will simply result in the ripping of expensive clothing. There should be some form

Classic   *Technical*

of grip, but this must not be too pronounced from the shaft as it will impede the axe when placed into snow. The head of the axe should be a one-piece construction, with a gentle curve to it. If the head is too flat, it will be very unstable when performing self-arrest and climbing techniques; if it is too steep a curve, then it will tend to snatch when placed in the snow and be wrenched out of the hand.

There should be a good-sized, slightly scooped adze, at an angle that continues the curve from the pick. A hole in line with the shaft through the head is important for the attachment of an axe safety loop. Do not be tempted to purchase an axe with the intention of using it for walking and general mountaineering if it has a reverse- curve shape to the pick, as such axes are designed for technical climbing.

Finally, the feel of the axe is all-important; if it is not a comfortable fit in the hand then there will be little incentive to have it ready to use.

Axe Loops and Leashes

There is a bewildering variety of ways of attaching your axe to yourself. It has been said that you should not use an axe leash of any sort, suggesting that to do so is in some way 'cheating'. Don't you believe it, get a wrist loop on! There may be an argument on lesser-angled ground for not using one, and certainly for self-arrest practice the loop should be left off, but for all other occasions one should be available.

One type of loop attaches the axe to the body by a long piece of cord or sling, either tied around the waist or clipped on to a rucksack shoulder strap. This is often used by winter climbers on steep technical ground. The advantage for the walker is that the hands are free when zigzagging up a slope, the main disadvantage being that in the event of a fall there is a high probability that the leash would wrap itself around the body, making axe recovery and self arrest almost impossible. Another method uses a sliding-ring system up the shaft of the axe. The main drawback here is that in very cold weather the shaft of the axe ices up and the ring is unable to slide.

The simplest and recommended way is to attach a plain purpose-made axe loop to the hole in the head of the axe, with a figure eight on the bight tied onto the sling, it being fixed onto the axe with a lark's-foot, ensuring that the knot ends up under but not too close to the adze (below). The length should be carefully measured so that your gloved hand can grip the end of the shaft covering the spike. The advantage of the lark's-foot connection is that it makes it very simple to remove and replace the sling quickly if necessary, without having to battle with frozen knots.

Self-arrest *pp121–6* • Self Belay *pp126–7* • Step Cutting *pp131–4* • Stomper Belay *pp142–3* • Boot-axe Belay *pp143–4* • Buried-ice Anchors *pp147–8* • Y-axe Anchor *p149*

When should I have an axe in my hand and not on my rucksack?

The correct time to get out an ice axe will always be early on, well before it is needed. This may be as early as leaving the car park, or at some point low along the trail. Standing in the middle of a snowfield, teetering in balance as you try to get off your rucksack to release your axe, is somewhat too late. As a general guide, the time to stop and get the axe ready is just before your foot hits a patch of snow, even a small dinner plate-sized patch on the flat. Always be prepared and think ahead.

Carrying the ice axe

There is a number of ways of conveniently carrying the ice axe so that it may be efficiently deployed.

- Firstly, to carry your axe on a rucksack (1), it is best to ignore the purpose-designed ice-axe carrying loops. Axes carried on the back of a rucksack can be a great hazard to others, particularly when walking in a group. You may indeed wish to cut off the loops to prevent the sack from snagging on awkward scrambles. The best position for the axe is to slide it down the compression straps which are found on the sides of most modern rucksacks. The axe should be arranged with the pick pointing backwards. Carried this way, the axe presents little opportunity for snagging, and is easy to lift out when required.

- A second method of carrying sees the axe positioned between the body and rucksack (2). Holding the head of the axe, lift it up behind you so that the point is placed between the shoulder straps, the shaft at a slight angle, with the pick pointing upwards. Slide it down between the straps, so that the spike emerges just above the shoulder-strap lower attachment point at your side. The head of the axe should be nestling comfortably on the top of the shoulder straps, and the shaft should at no point be digging into your spine. This method allows the axe to be ready in an instant, one hand able to push up on the spike while the other reaches back to hold the axe head. It is an ideal way to carry an axe when, for instance, navigating on a piece of flat terrain or when crossing snowfields intermittently.

- The third way of carrying the axe is the most important, as it ensures that the tool is ready to use in an instant for a self-arrest. The axe is picked up by the head, with the adze facing forward, the pick behind (3). Thumb and forefinger grip around the adze at the point nearest to the shaft, the middle finger runs down the line of the shaft, the last two fingers grip the pick near the shaft. This grip should be quite loose, as a tight grip will not allow the axe to be used effectively. Only by holding the axe in this manner can the correct arrest position be attained. Walking with the axe held as above should be practised until it becomes second nature.

TIP

Rubber spike and point protectors can be purchased to fit onto your axe, protecting others from its sharp point. These are an excellent idea for use when travelling on public transport, and indeed are a requirement in some countries. However, as soon as you set out for your day they can be safely removed and left behind.

Axes should not be stored at home with the protectors fitted, as they tend to trap moisture and can cause certain parts of the axe to corrode.

■ Self-arrest pp121–6

Self-arrest

Self-arrest, or ice-axe braking, is the basic discipline of winter mountaincraft. It is surprisingly easy to learn and is an essential skill when travelling in the hills and mountains under winter conditions. There are a variety of positions from which an arrest can be effected, and these should be practised until they become second nature. We have opted to write this section as if we were teaching an instructor, who would in turn be imparting the skills to his students. In this way, a logical progression can be gone through, and the skills learned in the best way possible.

SLOPE SELECTION

The area in which self-arrest is to be taught must be carefully selected. It should be a concave slope that allows a safe run-out if the arrest is not made, be steep enough to allow a slide to be made but not so steep as to be terrifying and difficult to negotiate for novices, and it should be free from boulders. Although a hard surface will be ideal for sliding, it may be painfully bumpy and deter the participant from using good style while practising. Conversely, a soft surface means that the knees will dig in and cause the arrest, rather than the axe. A deep trench will also soon be forged by sliding down the slope, and this will inhibit the amount of positions possible. An ideal surface will be a couple of centimetres of fresh snow on a base of older hard snow.

Also, pay attention to what is above you. The slope that you have selected may well be perfect on first inspection, but it may be below a large crag or buttress which could shed rocks and boulders as the temperature rises and the day's sun warms it. A further cause of accidents can be created by others, either by traversing or climbing above you and knocking down debris.

PREPARATION

There are a number of factors other than the practice-slope angle and condition. All participants should be wearing waterproof trousers and jacket, tucking the jacket into the trousers for the first part of the session if possible. An extra fleece underneath will not only help to keep you warm, but will also help to reduce the amount of bumping that you get while practising. Gloves should be worn, but there is a high probability that these will become very wet during practice so a spare pair should be available for breaks and the walk out. Helmets should be worn at all times, unless lunch is being taken in an area completely free from objective dangers.

It must be emphasised that crampons should **never** be worn when practising self-arrest. The consequences of catching the front points of a crampon when sliding down a slope are severe, with extreme upper- and lower-leg injury a high possibility. Rucksacks may be worn, but only after a good deal of practice without them. In bad visibility, ensure that the rucksacks are stored in an area easy to locate, otherwise you may have difficulty finding them again after a session. Place them near a prominent rock, or arrange ski poles in an X to help make their position more obvious.

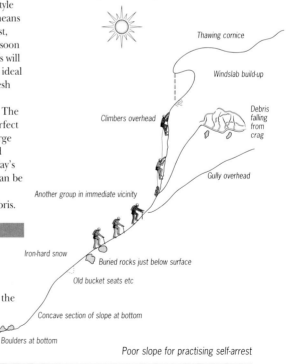

Thawing cornice

Windslab build-up

Debris falling from crag

Climbers overhead

Gully overhead

Another group in immediate vicinity

Iron-hard snow

Buried rocks just below surface

Old bucket seats etc

Concave section of slope at bottom

Lochan at bottom

Boulders at bottom

Poor slope for practising self-arrest

The Ice Axe *pp118–20* • Self Belay *pp126–7* ◼

1 Some of the starting positions of a few of the techniques are best practised by digging starting pits in the snow. Consider subsequent users of the slope, and fill in any holes at the end of the session.

2 For most novices, ice-axe braking *is* winter mountaineering; it is what they have heard most about and are the keenest to learn. Thus, there is a very real risk of your group members sliding into each other when starting to practise, caused partly by slipping on the slope, but mainly by enthusiasm. Keep a good eye on proceedings at the start of the session until all of the group have settled down and understand what is expected of them.

COACHING NOTE: Bi-lateral Transfer
There is now strong evidence in the coaching world that the early encouragement of students to practise techniques equally on either side of the body leads to a faster acquisition of skills. Thus, novices should be encouraged to practise self-arrest equally on both the left- and right-hand sides of their bodies.

TEACHING SELF-ARREST: PROGRESSION

The progression of arrest skills can be understood by the novice far more easily if a logical series of steps is taken. This also ensures that those imparting the information have less chance of neglecting to pass on to the participants something vital. In the following sequence, instructions are being given to someone who is holding the axe in his left hand, although it is essential to be equally proficient at arrest skills with both hands.

Step 1
The novice should be allowed to experience sliding on snow with no hindrance. Start the session by having him slide down from a short distance up the slope with no axe. This does two things:
■ Firstly, it lets him experience sliding, possibly for the first time, and allows him to see what it feels like. Permit him to slide on his back, side, front and headfirst.
■ Secondly, this allows you, as the person running the session, to assess how the slope is as regards slipperiness and speed, and to see how the participant's clothing works – some waterproof fabrics are extremely slippery, some need a steeper slope to get them sliding.

Step 2
This step allows you to talk and demonstrate the correct way to hold an ice axe when walking, with reference to using it to arrest a slide. It is also worthwhile demonstrating the incorrect method of holding it, so that the group can see how injury can occur, especially if the pick is fallen on to.

Ice axe carried in uphill hand. Climber walking on slope with body in upright position

Step 3
At this point, the group is shown the correct arrest position for the axe, still while standing at the bottom of the slope.

■ The left hand should be allowed to rotate on the head of the axe when bringing it up to the body from the walking ready position, so that the hand ends up pulling down on the axe head, the wrist ending up next to the attachment point of the head to the shaft.
■ The adze should slot into the recess immediately under the collar-bone at the front of the shoulder, with the shaft of the axe running across the chest at approximately 60 degrees to the opposite-side hip. The right hand covers the spike to ensure that it does not dig into the snow, and to stop it from puncturing you. Both elbows are tucked into the side of the body, and the user must look away from the head of the axe; in this case he will be looking to the right.

■ The Ice Axe *pp118–20* • Self Belay *pp126–7*

- It is important to look in the opposite direction to the axe head – if you look towards the axe head and it catches on a section of hard ice or a rock, facial injury is a real possibility.
- Once the position has been tried and understood, have your group members raise and lower their axes from the walking to arrest position a number of times, so that they may familiarise themselves with the process. It is important that they are equally proficient with either hand, and you must decide when to get them practising with both. People will naturally favour one hand or the other, and if they are quite able to swing up into the arrest position with their stronger hand, let them try with the other. Be careful, though, of making someone swap hands who is still struggling with his stronger side, as this will simply confuse him. Rather let him master one side, and introduce the other later in the day.

Step 4

Once the correct position for the axe has been demonstrated, this must now be combined with an effective body position. This should be practised while still on the flat.

- Get the group members to place their axes in the snow and lie on them face down. Each person's arms should hold the axe in the correct manner, one hand on the head, the other covering the spike. Start at the feet, getting them to raise them in the air. This is for two reasons – if crampons are being worn when a fall is made, it is imperative that the crampon points do not dig into the snow. But even if crampons are not worn, there is still a chance of the front of the boot digging into the snow. Either of these scenarios could cause injury or cart-wheeling.
- The knees must be apart, approximately one-and-a-half times shoulder width. This is to ensure stability when sliding in other than a straight line. The backside and stomach must be raised, and the chest and shoulders lowered. This allows the maximum amount of body weight to be transferred onto the axe shaft, imperative when sliding at speed. On very hard snow, it may be relevant to leave the stomach on the snow surface, in order to

avoid the knees being injured. The head should also be kept low, to help the weight transfer onto the shoulders.

Step 5

It is now relevant to introduce some motion to the session.

- With your group a short distance up the slope, have people position themselves correctly as regards axe and body, then get them to lift out the axe by arching the back and let them slide to the bottom, arresting every few feet. Slowly increase the height as their confidence builds, and increase the distance that they can slide before placing the axe in the snow. The pick should be placed positively and with firm pressure, never jabbed in, as the axe may be snatched from you in harder snow conditions.
- Be vigilant about correcting any wrong positions, as mistakes at this stage could be carried through to the rest of the session.

Step 6

When you are quite happy that all of the group can arrest in the 'normal' position, it is time to introduce a variation. Sliding down the slope in a sitting position is quite common, often the result of a slip while walking downhill facing out. This position is sometimes best practised on the flat at the bottom of the slope.

- Have someone sitting upright on the ground, legs out straight and together, axe held in the usual way, one hand on the head, the other on the spike. The important part of this arrest is to roll onto the chest, turning in a direction *towards* the head of the axe – for instance, if the axe head is held in the left hand, you would roll over to the left-hand side. Have the person roll over to the correct side, and assume the basic arrest position.

■ It is important to brief your group to keep their heads clear of the adze as the axe goes into the snow, as the tip of the pick contacts the snow surface before the body has finished rotating. Also, brief them to bend their knees as they rotate – this has the effect of keeping the feet away from the snow. Once all members of the group have practised the rolling on the flat ground, they can start to slide down the slope, starting from near the bottom and progressing slightly higher each time.

Step 7

Consideration must be given to the technique for arresting from a head-first downhill position; in this instance we will be starting face-down on the snow. The starting position of this technique is far easier to attain if a slot is cut across the fall line, for the boots to hook into while practising.

■ Start by lying face-down head-first on the slope, feet hooked into the slot to prevent a slide starting too early. The axe is held in exactly the same way as for all the other techniques, one hand on the head, the other on the spike. If the axe head is in the left hand, the axe pick is placed in the snow as far out to the left as is possible, in line with the shoulders, with the right arm now across in front of the face. You should be looking across at the axe, and not down the slope.

■ The manner in which the pick is placed into the snow is important – if it is plunged in, it may be snatched out of your hands; if it is not placed firmly enough then the arrest will not be performed efficiently. The best way will be to allow the pick to drag, firmly, at a slight

angle on the snow, and increase the downward pressure until you feel yourself starting to rotate.

■ Lift your feet from the slot, allow yourself to slide down the slope, place the axe in the correct manner and, with the pick placed in the snow on the left-hand side, your feet will swing round to the right. Keep the knees slightly bent during this manoeuvre, as it keeps the feet clear of the surface. When your feet reach approximately 90 degrees across the slope, lift your axe out and the momentum created should keep you rotating. Arch the back, place the axe into the shoulder and the normal braking posture is used.

■ It is extremely important to remove the axe from the snow and to keep this technique divided into two definite parts – the rotation and the arrest. If the axe is left in the snow for the whole time, it will be impossible to apply the correct amount of body weight to the axe, neither would it be possible to pull your body weight up slope onto it when sliding down.

■ Take great care when teaching this technique that your group keeps the initial axe placement as far out to the side as possible – the consequences of your body sliding over an adze at speed can be imagined.

Step 8

This arrest assumes that the walker or climber has tripped and ended up sliding down the slope head-first on his back.

■ To start this demonstration, enlarge the boot slot from the previous technique so that it turns into a ledge large enough to sit on. Sit

on it and run your feet round so that they are up-slope and you are lying on your back. It is a good idea to pull the hood of your jacket up and over your helmet before starting, as it may otherwise act as a brake or get damaged.

■ The axe is held, as ever, in the normal manner ready to arrest. If the axe is held in the left hand, it is placed out in the snow on the left-hand side in line with the hips, arm straight, with the right hand now over the left hip. This means that the pick will be placed into the snow approximately 20in from your body.

■ When the slide starts, the pick is placed in the snow in a similar manner to before, not too fast, not too slow, and at a slight angle from the vertical. This creates a pivot, and your legs will swing round to the right. As they swing round, you must rotate the down-slope hip, in this case the right one, up-slope. This is similar to performing a sit-up towards the head of the axe. Your feet should be together and knees bent; this facilitates the turn and helps to keep your boots clear of the snow surface. The object is to pivot your body through 180 degrees, both from down- to up-slope and from back to front. As your body rotates, the axe is taken out of the snow for the same reason as in Step 7 above, and an arrest is made in the normal manner.

■ Once again, it is imperative that the axe is removed between manoeuvres and the whole procedure is treated as two separate parts, the pivot and the arrest. One of the commonest mistakes is for the person arresting to end up rotating the wrong way when pivoting, and performing a log roll down the slope. This is extremely dangerous, as speed will soon be picked up and all control lost.

Step 9

This is the next logical progression once the above skills have been practised. The aim is to

perform an efficient arrest without the aid of an ice axe.

■ Part-way up the slope, have your group stand all of their axes in the snow to keep them out of the way. Lie on the snow, head up-slope and face down, arms out to the side. Lift your feet to allow the slide to start. The finishing position will be similar to that of a press-up, except with arms and legs wider.

■ As you slide, carefully place your feet on the

snow with the inside edges of the soles in contact, at the same time as pushing your upper-body weight up with your hands. These should be placed at just over shoulder-width apart, and ending up with arms straight.

■ There are a number of important factors with this type of arrest – the first is that it is a last-ditch effort to stop, and is not a replacement for an axe-assisted arrest. The second is to make sure that the edges of the boots are used, not the toes. If a toe is caught, injury may occur to the lower leg. Thirdly, it is not a suitable skill for use with crampons. Lastly, it can be seen that if the upper body is forced upright too quickly on a fast-moving slide, there is a chance that the person arresting will flick over backwards and end up in a somewhat worse predicament.

The Ice Axe pp118–20 • Self Belay pp126–7 ■

Self Belay

Step 10

This step is simply to let your group members spend time practising what they have just learnt. They may need to go through the full range of arrests, one at a time, or they may have one in particular that is causing them problems.

■ Get them to use the opposite hand to the one they have been using for the rest of the session – they are bound to have been favouring either their left or right hand. Demonstrate a method of disorientation – walk across the slope, place one boot toe behind the other's heel, trip, slide and perform an appropriate arrest. There is a method of performing a rolling arrest – two or three forward rolls followed by a stop – but this should be used with extreme caution owing to the chance of back injury caused by jarring on harder snow, hidden rocks etc.

■ Most importantly, let your group relax. A person who is holding on to his axe like grim death is unlikely to perform as efficient an arrest as someone who is slightly more laid back.

OBSERVATION

It is very easy, if dealing with a group of people, to lose track of what one person is doing when dealing with another, especially if abilities differ greatly. Keep to best practice as far as group control is concerned, and take into account the needs of the entire group. Be aware that someone sliding at speed into another person is likely to cause a great deal of damage, so be constantly alert to that danger. Specifying a side of the slope reserved for walking up will go some way to alleviating the problem.

COACHING NOTE

As your group progresses through the series of arrests, it is worth introducing the locating of the axe at each stage. This entails the group member holding the head of the axe, but not the spike, and pointing the axe shaft away from his body. He then slides down the snow, locating the axe shaft as he goes, and then performing the appropriate arrest technique. It should be noted that this locating technique should NOT be used for the head-first face-down arrest as there is a chance of the axe spike digging in the snow and being run over by a sliding body.

What is a self belay?

A self belay is the first line of defence when walking on snow-covered ground, and is designed to stop a slip from becoming a slide.

When do I use it?

You should be prepared to use the self-belay technique at any time when walking in the mountains.

Method

When walking up, down or across any slope, it is important that the axe is always carried on the uphill side of the body. This allows the axe to be positioned correctly for support, and also allows a self belay to be used to prevent a slide occurring.

■ For this description, we shall assume that you are travelling across a moderately steep slope from left to right, thus the axe is held in the left hand. The axe is also being presented to the slope so that it is vertical, the spike being placed firmly into the snow each time it is moved. The progression would be: kick step – kick step – place axe – kick step – kick step – place axe, etc.

■ The axe shaft needs to be placed vertically for maximum efficiency. If your feet slip, your right hand should move quickly to firmly grasp the axe shaft at the point where it meets the snow surface – keeping the hand as low as possible reduces leverage. Your left hand still holds the head of the axe, but it can be allowed to push the head uphill slightly to counter any chance of the axe shaft pulling out.

■ You will end up in a lying position suspended by the axe, and should not be sliding at all. You can now scuff a hole into the snow with your feet to help you back upright again. If for some reason the axe shaft pulls through the snow, you are in the correct position to perform self-arrest, remembering to slide your right hand down the shaft to cover the spike properly.

■ The Ice Axe pp118–20

Correct stance for the self belay

Correct hand position and ice-axe angle for a self belay

Incorrect stance for the self belay

Incorrect hand position and ice-axe angle for a self belay

The Boot as a Tool

REMEMBER THE WINTER PROGRESSION:
Walking on snow, kicking steps, cutting steps, crampons

Along with an ice axe, your boots are amongst the most important pieces of winter kit that you will use. To skimp on footwear because of cost is false economy, as your feet are your only contact with the ground and they should be looked after. They need to be comfortable, well supported, kept warm and provided with a base with which to walk without slipping. For the purposes of serious winter walking and mountaineering, boots of a fabric or similar construction should be avoided, with leather, plastic, kevlar and similar materials acceptable. The boots should be very stiff along the soles with little or no give, fully rigid boots being the best.

Boots whose soles can be bent more than 10 degrees at the toe sections are too bendy. (See the crampon section for an explanation of boot/crampon compatibility and flex, p135.) The soles should have a deep tread, with good square edges all round. There are a number of designs on the market with cut-away and stepped heels; these should be rejected as they are not suitable for use under winter conditions. Indeed, boots of this type should rarely be used in summer either, as the chances of a slip owing to reduced grip is extremely high.

PREPARATION

The self-arrest slope may also be used for step-kicking practice, or an altogether different area could be selected. Wherever is chosen, care should be taken to reduce risk from any objective dangers. Helmets should be worn while practising, as should gloves. If axes are carried, wrist loops should be left off. However, if the slope allows, it may be better to practise without having to carry axes, as novices will tend to find better balance and fluidity of movement without them.

The Slice Step
- This is the most basic and frequently used of all steps created by the boot. It relies on the sawing action of the edge of the sole to create

a platform, hence the need to ensure that your soles are in good order. We will assume here that you are going up vertically, facing to the right of the slope.

- From a ledge, or the flat ground at the bottom, stand with both feet facing across the slope, kick your left leg in and across the snow a few inches directly above your right foot, in order to create a ledge cut with the front outer section of the sole. Do not use your heel as part of the cutting tool, as it will jar. You are looking to form a ledge wide enough to place your foot on, thus it will be about half-a-boot width and nearly as long.
- Place your left foot on the ledge, move your right foot up to the place vacated by the left (opposite), and repeat the process. To help keep your feet from sliding off the ledges in harder snow, try to form the step so that it tilts slightly back into the hillside. Also, as with all steps, keep the knee a little further towards the snow than the ankle. This will

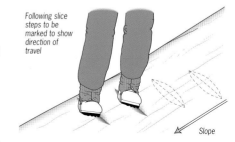

Following slice steps to be marked to show direction of travel

Slope

Crampons pp135–8 • Step Cutting pp131–5

present the sole of your boot to gravity and keep the placement more secure.

■ Safety is the prime consideration with step kicking; thus if you can create an adequate step with one kick then that is fine, but if you need five kicks to ensure security, then that is also fine. However, if you are on a surface that is requiring more than five kicks, it may be time to start thinking about cutting steps or using crampons.

■ Once you have travelled up-slope a little way, try to progress horizontally across. The steps created here will be staggered, that is, one forward and slightly above or below the other. After a few metres, make your way directly downwards, with the uphill foot being placed into the step left by the downhill foot.

■ The next logical direction is diagonally up, at an angle of about 45 degrees. Experiment a little to see how easy it is to kick steps by crossing your feet; it will come with practice.

■ When the time comes to change direction, first plunge the ice-axe shaft into the snow to give you extra balance and security. Use the toe of the outside foot to kick a good-sized ledge to step up into, known as a bucket step; step into it, swivel the axe shaft round in the snow so that the head is pointing in the correct direction, move your feet round and continue up.

Direction
of travel
pigeon
holes

Pigeon-hole Steps

This type of step is excellent for use on steeper terrain for progression up, down or across the slope. It is created by kicking in with the toe of the boot, swinging the leg from the knee down (below). Do not kick in with a full swing from the hips, as this is extremely tiring. Once a step has been formed, the heel is kept a little higher than the toe which helps to keep the step in one piece. The ice axe can be held either to one side or the other, or, on steeper ground, it can be held out in front away from your body in the arrest position, with the pick being used for stability.

Crampons *pp135–8* • Step Cutting *pp131–5* ■

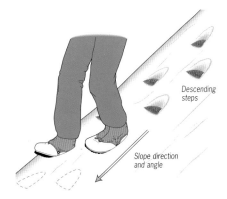

Descending steps

Slope direction and angle

Heel-plunge Steps

These are very effective for use in descent, but care must be taken that the snow is not too hard to allow the heel to dig in. Facing downhill, lock off your hip, knee and ankle, lifting the toes of your boots up slightly. The step is created by dropping your body weight down through your leg onto your heel, which punches a ledge into the snow. Do not swing your leg back into the slope; the movement needed is more akin to a hop than a step. A slight bend at the knee may reduce jarring in harder snow.

LEARNING STEP KICKING

The chart below shows a sequence and progression of learning for step kicking. It is purely for demonstration purposes, but clearly shows how a variety of steps can be linked together on one section of slope.

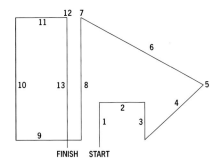

KEY

1 Slice steps up.
2 Slice steps across.
3 Slice steps down.
4 Slice steps diagonal.
5 Bucket step.
6 Slice step diagonal.
7 Bucket step (face into slope).
8 Pigeon-hole steps down.
9 Pigeon-hole steps – crab crawl.
10 Pigeon-hole steps up.
11 Pigeon-hole steps – crab crawl.
12 Bucket step (face out from slope).
13 Heel-plunge steps down.

■ Crampons *pp135–8* • Step Cutting *pp131–5*

Step Cutting

The art of step cutting has gone through something of a revival over the last twenty years. From being an essential skill in the pioneering days of mountaineering, its use faded somewhat as crampons took over the role of aiding progress on steep ground. These days, step cutting is back and firmly established as one of the most essential tools in a mountaineer's arsenal. Step cutting is extremely relevant to today's winter-mountain leader, as it is a method of speeding up and safeguarding the progress of your group on short sections of snow-covered terrain, where stopping to put on crampons, and the time involved in doing so, may be neither necessary or relevant. As with all things, practice makes perfect, and a little time spent trying out the various techniques will be a sound investment. ■

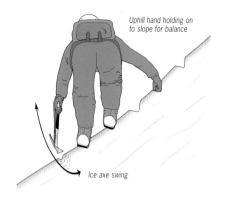

Uphill hand holding on to slope for balance

Ice axe swing

PREPARATION

Slope considerations are the same as those for self-arrest and step kicking. Helmets and gloves should be worn. Wrist loops should be used, as there is a chance of letting an ice axe slip from your grasp as it is being swung. An important consideration, and something which must be pointed out at the beginning to those whom you may be coaching, is what happens in case of a slip. It must be noted that when being used in the correct manner for cutting steps, the axe head will not be in the correct orientation for the adze to sit into the shoulder and an arrest to be performed. The axe head will have to be turned through 180 degrees for this to happen.

Slash Steps

The basic step is known as a slash step. These steps can be used in ascent or descent, with a variation being used for traversing. The best way to practise is to start by cutting steps in descent, as this allows you to understand the swing of the axe.

■ Make your way a short distance up the slope (by whatever means!) and turn to face to the right across it. Kick yourself a couple of slice steps, one above the other and approximately 6in apart. Stand upright, and, with your right hand holding the bottom of the axe shaft and the adze pointing behind you, start to swing the axe. This should be a pendulum motion, with the arm and axe in a straight line when

next to the down-slope leg, the axe at 90 degrees to the snow. Continue swinging in this arc, the top of which should be no more than shoulder height. Be extremely careful that there is no one behind or in front of you, as they could get badly injured if hit by the axe.

■ When you feel comfortable with the movement, start to bend both of your knees, axe still swinging, and lower your right shoulder until the adze is just scraping the ground about 6in directly down hill from you. Use six or eight cuts to form a step. This step should be longer than your boot sole, horizontal to the fall line, and angled very slightly into the slope to stop your foot from sliding off it. This angle is created by having your hand on the shaft very slightly up-slope of the adze.

■ Once this step is completed, stand up, put your right foot into it, move your left foot down to the step just used by your right, and repeat the process. This time, reduce the number of swings needed to make the step: maybe three or four slashes will do. If, after

some practice, you are managing to cut a step with one cut, then all well and good, but security is the prime consideration here, and if you need five swings, take five swings. Also consider your security as you step down; it may be necessary to place your axe in the slope above you for extra balance and security before you move. Continue cutting steps down until you reach safe ground.

■ A progression of this technique, after some practice, is to incorporate a slight swing from the wrist and elbow as the axe nears the snow, this allowing a little more force to be used for the cut. Start the swing with the axe slightly higher than the elbow, and ensure that arm and axe are in line when the snow is contacted. If the angle of the axe is too steep, the adze will dig into the snow and not follow through, so adjust the height accordingly so that all of the cut debris is carried away on the back-swing.

COACHING NOTE
When leading a party, it should be remembered that the size of the steps that you cut should be determined by the level of security required by the least-confident member of the group.

Slash Steps in Ascent
Slash steps may be created travelling either directly up the slope, or, more commonly, when zigzagging at an angle of between 45 and 60 degrees.

■ To practise travelling diagonally, face across the slope to the left, that is, your right shoulder closest to the snow. Your right foot should be no more than 6in higher up than the left, and it should be in advance of the left foot so that the toe of the left is in line with the heel of the right.

■ Lean your upper body forward, hold your axe in the uphill hand and, swinging from the shoulder as before, cut yourself a step on the up-slope side, the same distance up and in advance of your right foot as your left is behind it. The left foot is then moved up and into this step, crossing over the right, and the process repeated.

■ A couple of errors can occur when practising this method. Firstly, there is a tendency to

Important angles of slash steps

Uphill boot edges are used for balance

OBSERVATION
There is a tendency, when learning, for the novice to lift the down-slope foot off the snow surface before a step has been cut for it. This is often caused by him trying to cut too far away and over-reaching. Reduce the distance between steps, and the problem should stop.

reach too far away when cutting, which causes the step to be cut at an angle across the slope, instead of horizontally. Secondly,, care must be taken to ensure the axe swing is smooth and followed through, otherwise a chopping action will result which will cause a hole to be dug instead of a step. Cut a series of ten or twelve steps diagonally, then change direction. To accomplish this, cut yourself a larger step, place the axe in above it for security and support, step into it, turn the axe round, turn yourself round, change the axe loop onto the uphill hand, drop one leg down to the last step cut in the previous series, and continue up.

■ The Ice Axe pp118–20

Pigeon-hole Steps

These steps are the preserve of steeper ground, such as negotiating the steep side of a frozen stream gully. Once cut, they should appear as a ladder-type series of holds, and can be used for both hands and feet.

■ The easiest method in softer snow is simply to use the adze to fashion a series of holds, each being approximately 4in wide and flat-based. It may be found better to work two or three holds in advance. For instance, your foot would be on the third hold while you work on fashioning the sixth. If they are to be used for the hands as well as feet, a small lip can be created on the front edge to aid purchase.

■ In harder snow or ice, it will be necessary first to cut a shape in the surface to aid its removal. If you tried to cut the step simply using the adze, there would be a lot of resistance and energy would be wasted pulling off large chunks of snow or ice. To avoid this, make two cuts with the pick in a teepee shape, then chop out the centre with the adze.

Pigeon-hole steps using teepee cut

Cut down line 1 then 2 with axe pick, then remove A-B-C etc with the adze

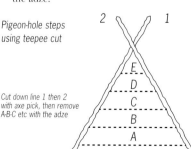

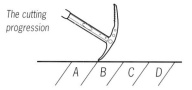

The cutting progression

CUTTING PROGRESSION FOR ALL STEPS AND EXCAVATIONS

The cutting of snow, for whatever reason, be it for letterbox steps or bucket seats, is much easier if a logical sequence is followed. In the diagram above, section A is cut first, then B, C and D. If you started cutting at D and proceeded forwards to A, there would be lot of resistance from continuously pulling up against the snow and a lot of effort would be needed.

Letterbox Steps

These are excellent for group use on short sections of steep ground.

■ Face across the slope to the right. Your left hand can be leaning on to the snow for balance, and the axe is held in the right hand. Present the head of the axe to the snow so that the shaft is at 90 degrees to the surface and just in front of your body at around thigh height.

■ Cut a slot in the snow with four or five swings using the usual cutting progression. The axe should not follow through, but should be chopping into the slope. It may be easier to work two slots ahead of yourself, so cut a second approximately 1ft above and about half a slot's length in advance of the first. Kick your boot into the bottom slot, then repeat the process.

■ The finished steps should look like their name, a series of letterboxes, and they provide good support for both hands and feet.

Master-blaster Steps

Apart from the slightly odd, but very descriptive, name, this style of step is very relevant for those leading groups over short sections of steep ground. The technique is rather more akin to open-cast mining than delicate step cutting, and as such is a favourite method of the authors!

The axe shaft is held in both hands, and the ground in front is pounded into submission with a number of blows from the adze. The object of the exercise is to create a large scooped step, big enough to make nervous party members feel secure when standing on it with either one or both feet. A series of these steps can be cut, and they do provide excellent security. As you can imagine, the process is quite tiring and, if a reasonable distance is to be covered, reverting to one of the more energy-efficient techniques such as slash steps may be more relevant.

Traversing Steps

These end up looking like slash steps, but are cut in a slightly different manner. If starting by facing left of the slope, have your right foot about 4in above and heel-to-toe distance in advance of your left foot. The axe will normally be held in the up-slope hand, but in practice it can be held in either.

Start by cutting the lower step, the one that your left foot will go into. The first cut with the adze should be in line with the toe of the uphill boot, and the cutting progression then followed. It is not possible to follow through with the axe swing; stop the adze after it has made its cut. It will take five or six swings to achieve a good step. Remember to ensure that it is longer than the sole of your boot, and that you have not left any bumps on the surface. The final swing of the axe can be used to drag the debris from the step to leave it tidy.

Repeat the process for the upper foot, starting the first cut in line with the toe end of the step that has just been prepared. You can now move your feet, first the left then the right, and cut the next two steps. The temptation may be to reach too far ahead. This is to be discouraged as it will cause the axe to tap on the surface without efficiently cutting it, and it will also cause you to become out of balance.

Crampons

COACHING NOTES

1 It is valuable for your group to practise step cutting on snow, and then to move them on to ice, as there is quite a difference in how the axe reacts when swung.

When practising any technique that requires the swinging of an axe, it should go without saying that you must ensure that there is a large gap between people. Keep your eyes open as the session progresses, as people will be moving at different speeds and may get rather close to each other.

Goggles may be a good idea when step cutting on ice, as shards are sent up at each cut.
2 Bear in mind that you are probably the most experienced in your group. Be aware all of the time that some members of your party may not be as happy as you on cut steps, and consideration must be given to stopping and fitting crampons. Remember that safety should always be paramount.

TIP

If leading a group who are finding the going a little tricky underfoot, it is quite possible that you could cut a series of steps for them, but not actually use the steps yourself. For instance, if traversing a slope, you might be completely happy walking along underneath the set of steps that you are cutting, which may allow an easier swing to be adopted.

This section will help you to understand a little more about crampons and their usage. It will talk a little about types, strapping systems and the learning and teaching progressions that are important if they are to be used effectively and safely.

CRAMPON TYPES: WHICH TO USE?

We do not intend to go into great detail about the many varieties that are available, as they all tend to fit conveniently into three categories: flexible, articulated and rigid. We do feel strongly, however, that great care must be put into creating a proper boot/crampon combination as, if this is wrong, your safety or the safety of those in your care will be compromised.

There are a variety of systems that compare crampon-and-boot compatibility; these are often difficult to understand and may even be invented by the manufacturers themselves. We suggest that you use the chart on p138 which has been designed with clarity in mind. It puts both crampons and boots into one of three possible categories: true mountain walking and climbing are deemed safe only with two types of either crampon or boot, while flexible boots and crampons are the preserve of the low-level walker. It should be emphasised that boots designed and suitable for winter use will be manufactured from leather, plastic, Kevlar or similar material, and boots with a fabric-based construction should be avoided.

Different crampon types

A *12-point articulated strap-on flexible crampon. Walking/general purpose*

B *12-point hybrid step-in with strap. Crampon semi-rigid. General mountaineering/ice climbing*

C *12-point hybrid or step-in. Fully rigid for ice climbing*

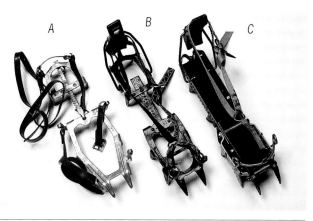

A   B   C

A Note on Boots

It is extremely important that you are happy with your boots and that they perform well. Having stiff boots is not, as may be thought, primarily to do with them being used with crampons, but is in fact to allow you to kick steps efficiently in hard snow before crampons are even put on.

The section on step kicking has a few more details about what makes a boot good for winter use but, when talking about boot/crampon compatibility, there is one golden rule: it is essential that your crampon flexes more than the sole of your boot. If it is the other way round, with your boot flexing more than the crampon, there is a very real danger of crampon breakage occurring, not an option when out walking or climbing in the mountains.

Strapping Systems

There are almost as many strapping systems as there are crampons. The most basic is a one- or two-piece neoprene strap with a buckle-fastening system; the next up is the so-called French-style O-ring strapping system. This has an O-ring linking the two straps from the toe section of the boot, this being threaded by a strap which goes back to a buckle. Step-in bindings are now very popular. These are divided into two main types: those with a bucket-type arrangement at the toe section and those with a curved-wire toe bail. The bucket arrangement is the more secure system, with the design enabling the front section of the crampon to withstand a fair amount of torsional twisting. The majority of the wire-bail designs have an extra strap linking the toe section to the safety strap around the ankle, greatly reducing the chance of a crampon being twisted or knocked off when on a route.

■ Crampon-and-Boot Compatibility Table *p138*

If you have a pair of step-in crampons that do not have a safety strap linking the front toe bail to the ankle strap, it is worth considering getting hold of or manufacturing one. They are sold in many shops and are easily and quickly fitted. The extra security that they give is well worth the small outlay involved.

OBSERVATIONS

1 It is very important, when choosing articulated crampons, that the crampon articulates at the same point as that at which your boot bends. If you choose a crampon which articulates 3in from the front points, and the boot to which it is to be fitted flexes slightly 2in further back, there is a good chance of the crampon breaking with extended use.

2 It is vital that the toe sections of crampons using the single- or double-strapping system are threaded correctly (see illustration). If this is not done, there is a chance that the crampon could be forced off to one side or the other of the boot toe when being used.

Front Points

There are many front-point arrangements available, each designed for a slightly different purpose. General-purpose points will have a gentle downward curve to them. Those with steeply angled straight points are excellent for buttress climbs, where they provide good support but minimal leverage. Vertically aligned front points are generally reserved for crampons designed for steep ice climbing, and they may tend to cut down through steep snow. A design using a single vertical front point is a specialist steep-ice tool, but they have been used with success on buttress routes where the ascent of thin cracks is the key to their success. Crampon designs that have no front points or 'lobster claws' at all are to be avoided.

There is no such thing as an ideal set of crampons. However, our recommendation for a pair of crampons that will deal with the majority of situations is as follows: twelve-point articulated with curved, not steeply inclined, front points, fitted with a French ring-strapping system and an uncomplicated adjustment mechanism. These crampons will perform well for both walking and climbing up to the middle grades, and should give many years of service.

Fitting

A well-fitting crampon will stick to the sole of the boot by the pressure of the side posts alone, with the exception of some step-in designs which do not rely on side posts. Adjustments should be made which allows the boot to be placed into the crampon, the straps left undone, and then lifted up sole-down with the crampon staying in place. Care must, however, be taken to ensure that the posts are not too tight. If the fit is such that the sole of the boot is not touching the full sole plate of the crampon, then it will be resting on two or more of the side posts. If the boot is then used in this manner, the posts will be progressively bent out with body weight and a stress fracture of the metal may occur.

Carrying Crampons

The majority of rucksacks designed for winter use come with crampon patches, designated reinforced carrying positions furnished with straps, often positioned on the top of the lid. If these are to be used, first place the crampons inside a purpose-made crampon bag made from a strong fabric. This stops the chance of you snagging yourself and other people on the points as they are carried. Better still, put the crampons in a bag and carry them inside the rucksack, well out of harm's way.

Putting on Crampons

This may seem simple, and indeed is, but there are a few points to remember. Crampons have a left and a right, with the buckles always being on the outside of the foot. Assuming strap-ons, lay the crampon on a firm piece of snow or an even-surfaced rock and move all of the straps and rings out of the way. Ensure that there is no snow adhering to the sole of the first foot to be placed in and, from a standing position (or kneeling in windy weather), put the foot into the crampon heel first, with the heel tight up against the rear posts. With a hand either side of the boot, pull up the front section of the crampon so that it fits correctly and snugly.

Now use the ground to enable you to put pressure on the foot, so that the crampon is forced into its final position. Do up the straps, starting with the heel, and make sure that they are snug. Tuck away the spare ends of the straps, then repeat the process for the other foot. After a few minutes of use, stop and check the straps again to make sure that they are still tight.

When fitting step-ins, run a crampon point along both the toe and the heel bail positions, if relevant, to dislodge any snow and ice that may have lodged there. Ensure that there is no snow sticking to the sole of the boot. Fit the toe section first, engaging the front bail, if one is used, into the correct position. Place the heel into the crampon, and clip up the rear arm. Care must be taken that this fits into the correct position on the heel welt, and that it does up with a healthy click. Finally, fit the ankle safety strap to the front bail strap and pull it tight.

It makes good sense to fit crampons on a flat area before reaching the slope to be climbed or descended. It is also a good idea to fit crampons after putting on anything else that may be needed, such as waterproof trousers or a harness.

1 Check that your crampons will fit correctly over any gaiter system that is to be used.
2 Any excess strap that is left when doing up the buckles can be cut off before going out on the hill, bearing in mind that you may be using gaiters, and that the crampons may be used for more than one pair of boots.
3 Crampon breakages, while rare, do sometimes occur. It is worth carrying a bit of spare kit with you to deal with the situation. This need be no more than an adjustment tool, such as a combination spanner and screwdriver, and a 2ft-long neoprene strap with a buckle at one end. This kit should always be carried if you are leading groups in the hills in winter.

Crampon-and-Boot Compatibility Table *p138* ■

TIPS

1 Crampons come ready with extremely sharp points which are, unless you intend to use them purely for hard-ice climbing, too sharp for general use. There is a big chance of catching crampons on skin and clothing, and sharp points will tear either with equal ease. Let your points dull down with use, or, indeed, take off the worst of the point with a file soon after purchase. It is extremely rare to need to sharpen your points.

Checking the points should be part of general maintenance, which will also include checking straps for wear and tear, and the adjustment mechanism for any give. The rubber point protectors which are commercially available for crampons should not be left on during storage, as they tend to trap moisture next to the metal and cause corrosion.

2 When purchasing crampons, ensure that you take your winter boots with you and that they are fitted correctly in the shop. Bear in mind all of the relevant information in this chapter, and you will avoid buying crampons unsuitable for your needs.

Crampon-and-Boot Compatibility Table

KEY TO TABLE

F denotes flexible crampons, those which flex along their entire length. These will often be of eight- or ten-point construction.

A denotes an articulated crampon, hinged at one point and consisting of ten or twelve points.

R denotes a fully rigid crampon with no flex built in. These will have from ten points up to around twenty on each foot, depending upon the purpose for which they were designed.

45 denotes a boot, the sole of which can easily be bent by hand to an angle of 45 degrees or more.

10 denotes a boot, the sole of which can only be bent to an angle of 10 degrees or less with some effort.

0 denotes a boot with a fully rigid sole.

TERRAIN	CRAMPON			BOOT		
MOORLAND	F			45		
LOW LEVEL						
MOUNTAINS		A			10	
SNOW GULLIES: GRADES 1 – 2						
SNOW GULLIES: GRADE 3 UP			R			0
BUTTRESS CLIMBING						
MIXED CLIMBING						
ICE-FALL CLIMBING						

It can be seen from the table that boots with a flex of 45 degrees or more would be entirely unsuitable for use with rigid crampons on steep ice routes, whereas articulated crampons could be used with 0-degree flex boots on buttress routes.

The Teaching of Crampon Techniques

The efficient teaching of crampon techniques is extremely difficult to do, and will only be possible with perseverance and experience. Below, we give a logical progression through the skills necessary and, if this is adhered to, progress may be quickly made. We are assuming that all group members have had their crampons fitted and checked, and that they are using a standard twelve-point crampon.

SLOPE SELECTION

It may well be that the same slope that has been used for self-arrest now doubles as the slope for practising cramponning. However, an ideal slope will be slightly different. Hard snow throughout, running from flat up to an angle of approximately 45 degrees would be perfect, still with few objective dangers, such as boulders at the bottom or crags overhead. This slope should not be too high, however, as there is the chance of a slip occurring. Areas such as the edge of moraine deposits make excellent crampon-practice sites.

PREPARATION

Firstly, ice axes should be put to one side and not used. Explain that the group members are now armed and dangerous, with twenty-four more ways to hurt themselves. Discuss the progression section that they are now in, the progression being: 'Walking on snow; kicking steps on snow; cutting steps on snow; crampons'.

Instil a realisation that if they catch a point on a gaiter or baggy clothing, they will be over in a split second, and get them to imagine a no-go area around each boot, that the other boot cannot get near. The image of a Star Trek-type impenetrable 6in shield around each boot usually gets a good understanding. Helmets should be worn, as should gloves.

Depending upon snow conditions, it may be necessary at this stage to introduce the problem of balling up, and its remedy. Balling up will often occur when the snow is sticky, such as when there is a slight thaw in progress. The snow then sticks between the points of the crampons and builds up into a lethal 'stilt'

which does not allow any of the crampon points to touch the snow, leading to loss of traction and a slip. The remedy is to use the axe and give the side of the boot a hard tap with the shaft. If these conditions are present, the axe will need to be carried for the session.

Step 1
Crampons on, walking on the flat. This is the basic movement and is useful as a confidence builder. Walk for a few metres in a straight line, lifting each foot and placing it with purpose in front of, and slightly to the side of, the other. The foot should be placed to the ground with the majority of the sole contacting at the same time, not with the heel touching and the boot rolling forward as we might do with normal walking. A turn is made by a series of small steps in a clockwise or anti-clockwise direction, stepping round on the spot, not crossing the feet at all.

Step 2
This time, use a gently angled slope and progress in the same manner as in Step 1. The only difference this time is that you must flex your ankles a little more and bend the knees slightly, and that when you come to turn round, do so by facing down-slope. Ensure that all ten downward-facing points on your crampons contact the snow at each step.

Step 3
Once a little height has been gained, step-turn so that you are facing down the slope. The descent is carried out using exactly the same technique, knees slightly bent, ankles flexed, almost a shallow squatting position adopted, sometimes called the 'wet nappy' position. Remember to place the crampon as squarely as possible on the snow, and to avoid rolling the foot down over the heel.

Step 4

Practise the two techniques together on the slope a number of times, zigzag up, turn to face downhill and walk down to the bottom. Make sure that your feet are not getting too close together as your confidence grows.

Step 5

It is now possible to progress on to walking uphill in a slightly more natural manner. Still zigzagging, walk up the slope but this time lift your feet high so that you may cross them over each other. Ensure that plenty of space is given between the crampon on one foot and the boot on the other, as there is a chance of catching a point if care is not taken. Pay attention to keeping the sole flat on the snow as you move. As the angle of the slope increases, you may find that the direction that you are facing changes to being up to 45 degrees across the slope, even though you are zigzagging at an angle of around 60 degrees. This is fine, but do not allow your feet to turn more than 45 degrees, as this then makes ascent very awkward and tiring. Let your ankles flex outwards to keep the presentation of the sole to the snow correct, ie flat.

Step 6

On slightly steeper slopes, we can introduce another way of using the crampons. This is called the American technique, and is a very logical method of ascent. One foot, for the sake of description we shall assume the right foot, is placed into the snow horizontally, using the front two, four or six crampon points for purchase. The left foot is placed in the flat-foot position, as we have been practising above. This foot could be turned out to the side at an angle of up to 45 degrees depending upon the gradient of the slope, but once again ensuring that all downward points are in contact.

Progress can be made in a line directly up the slope or at a slight angle to it. The front-pointing foot will be the easier of the two on which to balance body weight. Thus the stepping progression will be: the foot flat-footing moves up one step, the foot front-pointing moves up a half a step. When the leg that is front-pointing tires, you can swap

techniques for each foot and continue This method is only suitable for ascent, not descent, so after practice turn round, face downhill and flat-foot down.

Step 7

Steeper ground requires the use of front-pointing. This is a technique that uses the front two, four or six points of each crampon in turn. The crampon is presented horizontally to the slope, and it is important that the boot is kept at this angle once the points have been placed. If the heel is dropped, there is a chance that the front points will be levered out of the placement. If it is raised, the points may still be dislodged because of the toe of the boot pushing against the surface and, once again, causing them to be levered out. On steeper ground, front-point up a short way, then descend by the same technique. Pure front-

pointing is very tiring on the calf muscles, so, if travelling any distance, make the most of any irregularities on the surface of the snow or ice to give the crampon more purchase and the leg muscles a rest. Cutting a resting step at intervals is a good idea.

Step 8

Walking directly across the slope needs to be practised, and this can be done by either flat-footing or front-pointing.

On easier-angled terrain, face across the slope and flex the ankles so that all downward-facing points are in contact with the snow. The down-slope foot should be allowed to swing out and round the uphill leg, the uphill foot then being picked up high and brought through in front again, in order to avoid snagging a point.

On steeper ground, it may be necessary to crab-crawl. This is done simply by facing into the slope in the front-point position, and by stepping across the slope but *not* by crossing legs. For instance, if crossing a slope from left to right move the right leg first then bring the left across to meet it.

Step 9

As confidence builds, you can introduce one or two more learning methods when operating on an easy-angled patch of ice with little danger if a slip occurs. For instance, bunny hops, hopping down-slope, follow the leader and balance competitions can all be used as aids.

OBSERVATION

There are two important factors to consider when teaching novices the art of cramponning, both of which should be pointed out to students. First, it is not uncommon for a person to sit down on a snow or ice slope, in order to adjust their straps for example, only to find themselves suddenly sliding down the hill at a rapid rate of knots. A ledge, tilting back into the hillside, should be dug and an axe kept to hand if adjustments need to be made.

The second occurs at the end of any session, walk or climb when packing away kit. You are so used to placing your foot on the ground and it staying there that, when you finally take off your crampons, it takes a couple of minutes for your body to adjust to the difference underfoot. Be aware of this, and ensure that crampons are removed in a safe area where a slip will not be dangerous.

Step 10

Now it will be relevant to introduce the axe to the session. The carrying of the axe should make no difference to the way that the crampons are used. It may, however, be tempting to lean forwards onto it and alter the body weight over the feet; this must be avoided. Another common mistake is when the axe is used to aid progress over a small ice step. It is common to place the axe above the step and use it for support, forgetting about the angle of the sole of the boot. As the climber moves up, the crampons then have a real chance of ending up placed almost vertically to the ice, an angle of little purchase. It should also go without saying that the use of knees when surmounting a snow or ice bulge must never be contemplated.

Snow and Ice Anchors

This section is an introduction to the skills of belaying on snow and ice. There are many ways of achieving this successfully, but all of the methods shown rely on two major points: your assessment of the state of snow-pack and your choice of the most appropriate technique.

In winter, keeping your rope work tidy and simple is the key to success. Pay attention to detail, such as providing ledges for the rope to be coiled onto in order to prevent it from sliding down the hill. A rope draped down the slope not only has the chance of getting in the way of your second, but it also has a very real chance of snagging or freezing to the snow surface.

■

THE STOMPER BELAY

What is a stomper belay?

The stomper belay is an excellent way of safe-guarding progress on moderate ground, and ideal for lowering. It is also quick and simple to set up.

When and where do we use it?

The stomper is ideal for situations such as when speed is important in ascent or descent, for checking out a corniced descent gully, safeguarding a second over an awkward icy step, or even as an anchor at the finish of a simple route.

It must only be used from above, never to protect a leader, and the most important consideration is your own safety, as you are not anchored in any way if using the standard method. For this reason, it can only be recommended for use on terrain upon which you are entirely happy with your own safety, without the effect of external forces such as the wind, etc.

EQUIPMENT

One HMS screwgate, one ice axe.

Method

If not on level ground, either cut or stamp a ledge into the snow, inclined slightly back into the slope. This ledge will ideally be of a wedge shape, just wide enough for you to stand with your feet together. The depth of this ledge can be arranged so that you will have support from the snow at both the back of the legs from the up-slope side, and from the side walls.

Clip the rope into the krab, and do up the gate. Ensure that the rope is at the narrow end of the krab and emerging from the bottom side of it, and slide the krab up the shaft of the axe to rest just below the head. The axe is then driven into the ledge at an angle slightly back from vertical, with the head of the axe pointing across the slope.

The exact placement of the axe shaft can be ascertained by standing in position on the ledge, marking the snow with your heels, and placing the axe shaft in at just in front of the heel mark. Ensure that the axe head is flush with the snow surface, and that the rope can run smoothly. Place both feet close together on the head of the axe, one either side of the rope. The rope is taken in the left hand, passed behind the left shoulder and down the front over the right shoulder (reversed for left-handed belayers).

The rope is then managed as a shoulder belay, with sufficient friction being created by the system to remove the need for a twist around the dead-rope arm. (It is important that the rope is not taken up in front of the left shoulder, as any loading could cause the belayer to be pulled forwards at the waist.) When the climber arrives at the stance, it is important that he stops below the level of the axe so that he does not exert an upward pull on it, and so that, in the event of him slipping, he does not shock-load the system. It would be advantageous to have a ledge or bucket seat prepared for him just below the level of the ledge.

TIP
It is useful to have a ledge prepared for the rope to run into or out of, in order to avoid any chance of it running down the slope and snagging or getting in the way of your second.

It is very important to have the rope end secure, to stop any chance of it sliding through your hands and disappearing down the hill. Tying on round the waist or harness is the best and recommended way of ensuring this does not happen, although a large knot tied on to the end of the rope is acceptable. Also, consider the attachment of the person being lowered. As for the boot/axe method, if he is to be lowered down steep ground a simple waist tie may not be sufficient, and serious consideration should be given to using either a harness or Thompson knot for his safety and security.

COACHING NOTES
It is important to point out both the advantages and failings of this belay system. The main advantage over the boot–axe belay is the ability to take in the rope. The main failings are the fact that the belayer is unattached to the anchor, and that he may feel unstable in high winds. It should be made clear that the stomper and boot–axe belays are complementary methods, and skill is required in deciding when one is preferable to the other.

THE BOOT–AXE BELAY

What is a boot–axe belay?
The boot–axe belay, very much like the stomper, is a way of safeguarding descent on awkward ground, and is an excellent method of lowering.

When and where do we use use it?
On windy sections, for the security of another on awkward descents, and when speed is a factor. *It must only be used from above, never to protect a leader.* In windy conditions it may well be chosen over the stomper, as the body position of the belayer is low to the ground and thus more stable. The main drawback is the difficulty of bringing a climber up to the stance, and for this reason we recommend that this system is used in descent only.

OBSERVATION
There are alternative appropriate methods of controlling the rope with a stomper. Belaying directly from your harness is one option, though we feel that under load you get the sensation of your harness being slowly dragged down past your knees! It is also difficult to get a 'feel' of the rope with this method. The other way is to run the rope up and directly over your rucksack straps, to alleviate any load on your shoulders.

Our choice, though, is the shoulder-belay method given above, with the live rope being gripped snugly – if this is done, you are hardly aware of the load on your shoulder. Also, the method of arranging the krab mentioned above is better than the other option of clipping it through the eye of the axe head. This has the effect of twisting the rope, of loading the axe-head/shaft rivets incorrectly and of exerting a lot of leverage on the placement.

THE BOOT–AXE BELAY

EQUIPMENT
One ice axe.

Method
If not on level ground, either cut or stamp a ledge into the snow, inclined slightly back into the slope. This ledge should be large enough to easily accommodate a boot sideways. Place your right foot on the ledge, with the sole braced against a 2in lip fashioned on the down-slope side. A second ledge for the left foot can be cut a short distance below if required.

■ Place the axe shaft vertically into the snow next to your right boot, running in a line with the side of your shin and with the shaft inclined slightly uphill. The axe should be pushed into the snow as far as possible, leaving a boot-height between the surface and the head of the axe. The pick should be pointing behind you across the slope.

■ The rope is run from behind the belayer, between the legs, in front of the ankle of the right foot, around the head of the axe from the right-hand side (looking up-slope) and down to the climber. The belayer takes a stance allowing him to lean onto the axe with his right hand, his left hand gripping the rope between his legs and low down by the right ankle. When load is applied, the rope pulls the axe onto the boot, and the friction created is enough to hold a climber's weight. This friction can be varied by moving the left hand forwards or back as necessary.

■ The end of the rope needs to be secured in

OBSERVATION
In very hard snow where the shaft of the axe cannot be pushed far into the ground, this method can still be used. Care must be taken that the pick is braced securely behind the knee, and is securely gripped by the uphill hand. It is important that the controlling hand is low down next to the snow surface in order to minimise any leverage.

TIP
Like most things, preparation makes life a lot simpler. Run the rope through and make sure it ends up in the right place – in a neat pile at the back of the belayer. A shallow ledge can be dug to contain the rope and prevent it slipping off down the slope.

some way so that there is no danger of the end running through your hands – the safest method is to tie on to the rope before starting the lower. Consideration should also be given to the method used to secure the person being lowered – a simple waist tie may not be sufficient if a full-length lower is to be undertaken. Thought must be given to using a harness, Thompson knot, etc.

COACHING NOTES
When demonstrating the boot–axe belay, ensure that any loading on the system is below the level of the axe – if the loading is upwards on the axe, it has a high chance of failing in spectacular style. When running a session ensure that anyone trying out the system is aware of this.

Also ensure, if using this system for real, that you brief those being lowered before starting, so that they are in no doubt as to what to do when reaching the end of the pitch, such as digging in, cutting a ledge, untying, and so on.

■ The Ice Axe *pp118–20* • Knots *pp42–6*

THE BUCKET SEAT

What is a bucket seat?

The bucket seat is not only one of the simplest belays to construct, but also one of the most effective.

When and where do we use it?

The bucket seat can be used for most snow belay situations, such as climbing and lowering. Used in conjunction with a second anchor system, such as a buried axe, it forms one of the strongest snow anchors available.

EQUIPMENT

One ice axe.

TIP

Don't skimp on the depth or shape of the front wall. It is worth constructing a bucket seat and then testing it by having someone pull on the rope – if the seat is too shallow, you will pop out of it like a cork!

Method

The simplest way to construct a bucket seat is simply to dig a pit in the snow with either the axe, gloved hands, or a combination of both.

Scribe a semi-circle on the snow with your ice-axe, the straight edge on the downhill side, and excavate the snow inside. The pit needs to be large enough for you to sit in, usually while wearing a rucksack, and have sufficient room on either side of your body so that your arms can move freely.

The important details are to have the front face perpendicular to the angle of slope, and the depth of the seat sufficient so that when you sit in it your thighs are supported up to the knees. A ledge should be formed on the dead-rope side of the seat to prevent the rope sliding down-slope while belaying. When sat in the seat, kick your heels in for a little extra support.

OBSERVATIONS

1 A similar method has been taught for years, that of a saddle stance which looks like a horseshoe in design. This works well, but great care must be taken that the snow-pack, and the layers within it, are not weakened by the excavation process. There is a chance, in a varying snow-pack, of layers shearing off when loaded. This does not occur with the bucket seat, as it is a simple hole in the ground and the layers are disturbed very minimally during construction.

2 Although the bucket seat is primarily for use with a second system, such as a buried axe or dead-man anchor, it is possible to use the seat on its own, for instance when safeguarding group members over an awkward step, either in ascent or descent. This should only be attempted in solid snow conditions, and only for safeguarding a group member lower down the slope than yourself. An indirect belay should be adopted, as this will lessen the loading on you should the person ascending slip. As always, there should be no slack rope between you and him and, if in any doubt as to the properties of the snow, a second anchor should be used to ensure complete security.

3 Care must be taken to ensure the security of your group if using the bucket for negotiating an awkward step. There must be a safe place for them to stand or sit when arriving, and organising a group of four people, ascending one at a time over a short bulge.

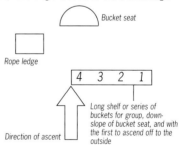

COACHING NOTES

This seat can be practically tested by having a person sit in the seat attached to the rope by his harness. It is not necessary for him to put on a waist belay. Test the bucket seat by pulling on the rope, but be careful not to shock-load the rope as back injury could occur. Start with a gentle pull and increase the pressure – it is quite possible to have two people pulling at once – and make sure that the belayer knows to say 'stop' if he starts to experience *any* back discomfort at all.

SNOW AND ICE BOLLARDS

Snow and Ice Anchors

These two anchors rely on the available material to work. They differ in size, but their shape remains essentially the same. They are beloved of winter-skills' courses and are rarely seen elsewhere. However, the snow bollard especially is very useful for retreat leaving no gear behind and is excellent for abseiling over a bergshrund. The ice bollard, or mushroom as it is often called, is very hard work to construct and relies upon the integrity of the ice. It may have its place on an epic descent when gear is at a premium, although many will choose to use an Abalakov thread in its place.

EQUIPMENT
One ice axe, with the addition of an 8ft or 16ft sling with screwgate for the ice bollard.

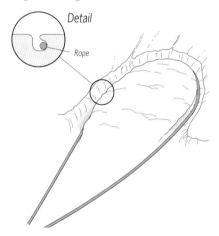

Detail

Rope

Snow Bollard
The size of the bollard is dependent upon the quality of the snow, about 2m across will be average. Cut a horsehoe shape with the pick of the axe, taking care not to disturb the snow in the body of the bollard. When the outline is formed, cut around the outside of the line with the adze. The depth of the trench created will vary with the snow-pack, but should be no less than 6in. The bollard is finished off, as its name would imply, by running either the adze or a gloved hand around under the rim to create a lip for the rope to seat into.

Constructing an ice bollard is extremely hard work and very wearing on the wrists. It is possible to use icicles as threads, but, as they are often not physically connected to the rest of the ice, you must be extremely careful about their strength.

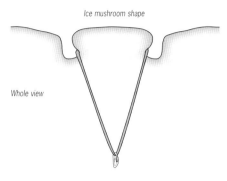

Ice mushroom shape

Whole view

Ice Bollard
The ice bollard will only be as strong as the material it is made from – careful selection of solid ice is important. The size will be about 40cm across, with the lip being about 10cm deep.

A rough outline can be scraped onto the ice and the pick then used to chisel out a rough shape. This can be refined using a combination of both pick and adze and great care must be taken not to chip off too large a lump of the bollard, compromising its strength. The finished article should be able to confortably take an 8ft sling, which should sit well under the lip.

COACHING NOTE
To scribe out a symmetrical shape for a bollard in good-quality snow, rest your elbow gently at the centre of the snow and mark out the shape with the pick of the axe in a semi-circle. Make it clear that the snow should be disturbed as little as possible in the processs. It is often a good idea to arrange a simple abseil demonstration from the bollard, even on a moderate slope, to show the strength of the snow.

TIP

Although the snow bollard is often constructed on open slopes, it is quite possible to make use of the gap between a gully wall and the shrinking snow to help make one. In this case, you often end up with something more akin to a spike belay, but still very strong.

■ Winter Considerations p60 • The Abalakov Thread pp152–3

BURIED-AXE ANCHORS

What is a buried-axe anchor?

The buried-axe anchor is the basic belay on snow, and is taught almost from the outset on many a winter-skills' course. There are a variety of ways of organising either one or two axes into a solid anchor; here we will concentrate on the buried axe and the reinforced buried axe. Other systems such as the T-axe and vertical axe are worth experimenting with, but we have found that the system below deals with the majority of situations perfectly.

When and where do we use it?

This anchor can be used for most belaying, climbing and lowering situations, on both moderate and steep snow slopes.

EQUIPMENT

One or two ice axes, an 8ft sling and a screwgate.

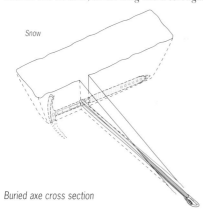

Snow

Buried axe cross section

Method

Select a relevant area of undisturbed snow and try, while constructing the anchor, not to disturb the snow-pack on the down-slope side any more than is necessary. Cut across the slope at right angles to the fall line with the pick of the axe, with the pick vertical, to a length slightly longer than the axe shaft. About 6in above this, cut another line parallel to it. Using the adze, remove the snow between the two lines, taking care to avoid disturbing the down-slope internal face. The depth of this slot is dependent on the snow type, but will be

between 12–18in for the majority. Care must be taken to ensure that the full length of the axe shaft is flush with the down-slope face of the slot. This face should be either vertical or slightly undercut which can be achieved by running the adze along the bottom of the slot.

A second slot then needs to be cut running down-slope from approximately two-thirds of the way along. This should be only wide enough to allow the sling to run along it (start with the pick and make it sling-width by using the shaft of the axe to clear it out; the adze of the axe is too wide and may compromise the strength of the snow), starting at the same depth as the main slot, and reaching the surface about 5ft below. If a bucket seat is being used, this vertical slot should emerge from the wall, approximately halfway down its height. A clove hitch is tied in the sling and placed around the axe shaft at the central point of the surface area, which is normally nearer the head at about two-thirds distance up the shaft. The clove hitch needs to be inverted onto the up-slope side of the axe by taking one loop of the sling around the axe shaft. The axe is then placed in the slot with the pick facing vertically down, and bedded in

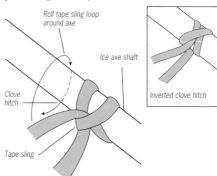

Roll tape sling loop around axe

Ice axe shaft

Clove hitch

Inverted clove hitch

Tape sling

Inverting clove

Knots *pp142–6* • Winter Considerations *p60* ■

firmly. The sling is run down the narrow slot, taking care that no debris has fallen into it, and the rope is clipped into the krab. A downward pull on the sling will ensure that the axe has embedded itself into the correct position. The stance should be taken at least 2m below the axe, with a bucket seat being the most secure.

To improve the holding power of the system, insert another ice tool vertically through the sling at the top of the vertical slot, making sure that you do not disturb the horizontal axe. Push the second ice tool down into the snow as far as it will go, with the pick and adze running horizontally across the fall line.

Once the axe/s have been placed and you are happy with the set-up, the slot can be filled in with snow. This should be firmed down by foot, with care being taken to not disturb the axe placement or the downslope face of the slot.

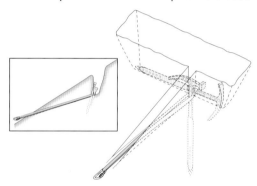

COACHING NOTES

1 It may be worth demonstrating the strength of the anchor by having a couple of people pull on a rope attached to the sling; novices are often surprised by its holding power. You should be holding tight to the end of a 4m rope tail, just up-slope of the anchor, in case it does fail.
2 When showing the axe anchor together with the bucket seat, explain how important is the correct alignment of the rope, from the climber, through the belayer, to the anchor. A simple demonstration can be made by having someone wearing a harness sitting just down-slope of the seat using a classic waist belay with the live rope on the side opposite to the anchor. The twisting motion can be created by pulling *gently* on the rope – the effect is remarkable!

Indirect Belay *pp60–1*

OBSERVATION

When using a waist belay, which should always be adopted when dealing with any snow or ice anchor, and you are wearing front point attachment harness, it is essential that the rope from the anchor runs under the same arm that is dealing with the live rope to the climber. For instance, if you are right handed, you may well have the live rope on your left-hand side – the rope to the anchor should be arranged on this side of the body as well. If the ropes enter and exit on different sides of your body, a dangerous twisting motion will be exerted on you in the event of a falling climber loading the system, which could result in loss of control of the rope, and in spinal injury for the belayer.

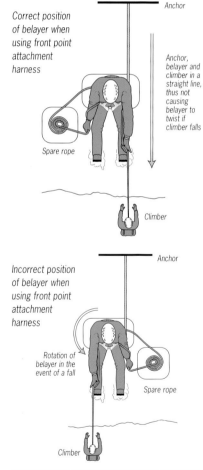

Correct position of belayer when using front point attachment harness

Anchor

Anchor, belayer and climber in a straight line, thus not causing belayer to twist if climber falls

Spare rope

Climber

Incorrect position of belayer when using front point attachment harness

Anchor

Rotation of belayer in the event of a fall

Spare rope

Climber

TIP

Dig your bucket seat before burying your axe!

Y-AXE ANCHOR

What is a Y-axe anchor?
This is the linking of two axes together to provide an anchor.

When and where do we use it?
This method of belaying is normally reserved for use in situations where the more conventional buried- and reinforced buried-axe systems will not work, such as on ground with shallow but good-quality snow cover.

EQUIPMENT
Two ice tools, two 8ft slings, one screwgate karabiner.

Method
Slots are prepared as for the standard buried-axe system, except that in this case they are angled across the slope. This angle is quite critical – both axes must be at 45 degrees to the slope, with the axe heads at the up-slope side of the slots. The heads of the axes should be 50cm from each other, and the entire arrangement should be symmetrical. Each axe has an 8ft sling attached in the normal way, a reversed clove hitch at the balance point of the shaft. The slings are run in prepared slots at 90 degrees to the axe shafts, so that both slings meet at an angle of approximately 90 degrees, and are then joined with a screwgate. A stance, preferably a bucket seat, is then taken a minimum of 1.5m below this point.

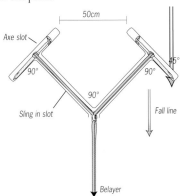

Angles and distances for Y-axes

THE DEADMAN ANCHOR

What is a deadman anchor?
A flat metal plate with a 2m wire attached, the deadman anchor is a very efficient way of belaying on snow. It has one main advantage over other methods in that you do not use your axe as part of the system, so you still have it to hand for your own security.

When and where do we use it?
This anchor can be used in most belaying, climbing and lowering situations, on flat, moderate and reasonably steep slopes.

EQUIPMENT
Deadman, one screwgate, ice axe and hammer.

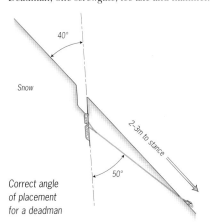

Correct angle of placement for a deadman

Method
It is essential that the deadman is placed at the correct angle to the slope – 40 degrees on the uphill side. Place your ice axe into the snow at 90 degrees to the slope, using the sides of the deadman as a square to check the angle. Ensuring that you are working across the fall-line, place the point of the deadman on the snow level with but a little distance from the axe. Look along the line from the side and bisect the angle between the axe and the slope – that will give you 45 degrees. Set the deadman back a few degrees from there to give you 40 degrees, and push it into the snow a little way.

Remove your axe, and, using the deadman as a guide, cut a narrow slot with the pick to the side of the deadman and at exactly the same angle. This slot will be used to guide it in at the correct angle, so be careful not to disturb the down-slope face or snow-pack. Remove snow from the uphill side of this line creating a shallow trough and remove any debris. Again using the pick, now create a narrow 2m slot running down-slope and at exactly 90 degrees to the slot for the wire to run through. Place the deadman flush against the horizontal slot you have cut and, while holding it in place by keeping the wire in tension, hammer it down to below the surface, ensuring that it follows your guide slot and ends up at 40 degrees as required. The wire must run in a straight line from its attachment point on the deadman down the slot towards the stance; be careful to ensure that no debris has fallen in and clogged it.

Use the shaft of the axe or hammer through the loop of the wire to give it a tug, in line with the snow surface, which helps the plate bed in. Keep tugging the wire until there is no more creepage of the plate. It should then be well seated in the snow pack. The climbing rope is connected to the wire with a screwgate, and the stance is taken a further 1m below, with a bucket seat being recommended.

OBSERVATION

Many mountaineers never use the deadman, as they feel it is too awkward to place, and that it is a piece of equipment that only does one job. Great care must be taken to avoid placing it against snow layers of a different hardness, which could cause pivoting. The critical angle of the placement is not, in fact, the 40-degree angle viewed on the surface of the snow, but the 50 degrees that is created between the wire and the plate on the underneath of the down-slope side, with this angle being dictated by the position of the belayer and his distance from the placement.

TIP

Notoriously awkward to carry, the deadman is best clipped on to your rucksack loops well away from the front of your body. Care and time should be taken to ensure that the wire remains firmly wrapped around the deadman, clipped into the carrying krab to help prevent it from unwrapping.

COACHING NOTES

It is worth discussing the relative merits of buried axes against the deadman; would a lot of steep snow be encountered, in which case burying the axe may not be satisfactory?

Alternatively, would there be little steep snow, making the carrying of a deadman unnecessary? It is important to put across both points, with the final yardstick being the safety of the climbing party in any given situation. For the novice, carrying a deadman would be a very sensible thing to do; he could then make his own choice after climbing a number of routes.

Snow

Snow

Although the placement angle is correct, pulling on the wire will cause the plate to slide out

Incorrect angles of placement for a deadman

What are ice screws and drive-ins?

Modern ice screws have evolved a long way in the last few years. They have progressed from requiring both hands to place, one to turn and the other to hammer, to a single-handed operation with the screw turning in with great ease. Drive-ins come as three basic types: the warthog, which is solid in section, a tubular drive-in, and an ice-axe-pick-shaped drive-in.

When and where do we use them?

It used to be that drive-ins were placed on the lead for speed, with screws being reserved for stances, but the position is now often reversed. Modern screws are ideal for ice, and warthogs are excellent for turf placements on mixed routes.

EQUIPMENT

Ice screw, warthog, hammer as required.

Ice Screw

Ice-screw placements will only be as good as the ice in which they are placed, so select the area carefully. The correct angle for a screw placement is at 100 degrees to the slope, so it is necessary to first prepare the ice surface to allow the eye of the screw to rotate when fully screwed home. The screw should be presented at 90 degrees to the ice, then cast back slightly to give an angle of 100 degrees. It may be that you need to make a small hole with the pick of your axe to start the teeth cutting, after that the screw is simply wound in by hand.

If the ice starts to go opaque or 'dinner plate', cut away the bad ice and continue the placement. The eye should end up lying flush with the surface and facing downhill. To remove, tap down with an ice tool on to the head of the screw, to break the bonds between itself and the ice, and unscrew. Never hit the shaft of a screw sideways, as damage will occur to the thread, and the shaft itself may bend rendering the screw useless for future use.

1 Dinner-plating is the process by which ice shatters from around a screw or warthog placement, often in large pieces. If placing screws on the lead, ensure that any sections of ice from dinner-plating placements do not drop and endanger your second.

2 Ice screws should not be used in isolation as a main belay anchor, they should always be placed in pairs. The correct position for the second screw will be 2ft to the side and 2ft above the first placement, making them a metre diagonally apart. This helps to ensure that the strength of the ice is not compromised, and that any internal lines of stress within it will have a minimal chance of running into each other.

When using two ice screws as part of an anchor system, great care should be taken to ensure that the loading on each is the same. Bringing the two down to one point using a sling is the most practical way of achieving this.

Two screws equalised using a sling with overhand knot

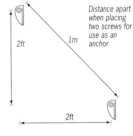

Distance apart when placing two screws for use as an anchor

2ft   1m   2ft

3 It is important to remove the core of ice from the ice screw before it can be used again. The larger-bore screws are the ideal size to permit a standard warthog to fit inside, so check that you have a compatible screw/hog set-up. Some screws and hogs are manufactured with a cleaning slot along one side, which allows for ice removal with an axe.

4 The third type is the modern drive-in shaped like a reverse-curve axe pick. These can be placed into axe marks on steep ice, or driven into iced-up cracks on mixed routes.

1. If a screw cannot be placed to its full depth, and it is not of the floating-eye type, it needs to be tied off to reduce leverage. Leave the eye facing uppermost, and either clove hitch a tape around the tube next to the ice, or use an extender and slip it over the eye ring and down to the surface.

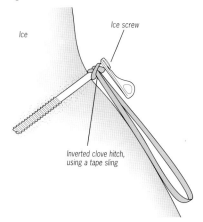

Ice

Ice screw

Inverted clove hitch, using a tape sling

2 When buying an ice screw, it is worth purchasing the more modern designs, which will have a large diameter tube, and you should choose ones with no less than four or more than six cutting teeth. Some screws have a floating-eye bracket, which helps to reduce leverage in shallow placements.

3 When clipping ice screws on the lead, it is worth using extenders, as a single krab tends to exert a lot of leverage on the eye and shaft. There is also a danger of the krab levering the screw to the extent that it unscrews it slightly from its original position.

Drive-ins

As for the ice screw, the ideal warthog placement will be made with the stem at 100 degrees to the ice. Hold the eye at about four o'clock, as the threads of the hog will cause it to rotate as it is driven. Drive the hog fully in so that the eye is flush with the ice and pointing downhill. Solid-section hogs tend to shatter the ice and 'dinner-plating' is quite common. You will need to cut away the shattered ice to continue the placement.

Hollow-section drive-ins tend to shatter the ice less. Solid-section warthogs are, however, ideal for frozen-turf placements, and are almost exclusively used in this manner these days. It is important to consider removal and to ensure that you do not place the eye too close to rock which will stop the hog turning when being retrieved.

■ Knots pp42–6

THE ABALAKOV THREAD

What is an Abalakov thread?

The Abalakov thread, sometimes called the ice-screw thread, is exactly as it sounds – a length of cord or tape threaded through the ice. It appears to be one of those tricks that people show you but never gets used. However, a well-constructed Abalakov is extremely strong, leaves no gear behind except for a length of cord or tape and is quick to construct.

When and where do we use it?

The thread is useful when ice screws are becoming scarce, or if you do not wish to leave any gear behind, such as on an abseil. They are made from the available ice, so are a very real and reasonable alternative to a bollard.

EQUIPMENT

One long ice screw, a length of strong accessory cord or tape.

Method

The ice is the weakest point of this structure, so ensure that the thread will not be compromising the strength of the area in which you wish to

The Abalakov thread

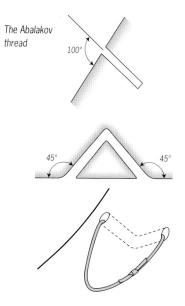

100°

45°   45°

Snow Shelters

The most important factor is the strength of the ice, and the accuracy and size of the hole. Some manufacturers make screws that are designed to help construct Abalakov threads – their main advantage being the eye which tilts back at 45 degrees. Difficulty can be found in threading the tape or cord through the hole. There are special hooks on the market for solving this problem, or you can fashion one from a wire coat hanger. But unless you are intending to use them a lot, it is better to practise bending the tip of the cord at a slight angle before beginning to thread it – patience often pays off!

If multiple threads are required, repeat the process approximately 2ft above the first hole, and use a longer piece of tape, cord or sling to help equalise it. Sometimes, natural ice threads will be seen, such as where an icicle reaches and bonds with the ground. These features may be threaded, but great care must be exercised when assessing their strength – they will generally be weaker than a thread constructed from solid ice.

work. The ice screw is placed into the ice at 45 degrees to the surface and back at an angle of 100 degrees, in as far as the eye of the screw will allow. Withdraw it and repeat the process in the opposite direction a sufficient distance away, just enough so that the teeth of the screw emerge into the bottom of the previously drilled hole. When completed, the two holes should meet under the ice at a 90-degree angle. The accessory cord or tape is manoeuvred through the two holes and a thread created, with the threaded material being tied off with a suitable knot.

COACHING NOTES
Testing the thread by pulling on it with the rope and a couple of people helps to show its strength. Obviously, ensure that anyone doing the pulling is in no danger of injury if the ice should fail – this includes factors such as ensuring they are not wearing crampons, and that there is no danger of them slipping and hitting boulders if the ice should fail.

The following pages show a variety of snow shelters. The majority of these are emergency bivouacs, and are reserved for when there is simply no alternative but to dig in. There is also a snow hole, which is designed for a planned night out, the construction of which is quite lengthy but can provide comfy accommodation for a number of people.

■

EMERGENCY SNOW SHELTERS

What is an emergency snow shelter?
This is exactly as it sounds – only for use in an extreme emergency. The decision to spend the night out in the mountains under winter conditions must not be taken lightly. It will be seen that the construction of a snow shelter is a very tiring task, expensive on both time and energy, both of which may be better utilised making your way down if possible.

When and where do we use it?
We could only recommend the use of a shelter in the case of injury, benightment in foul weather, lost in poor visibility on dangerous terrain, and so on, when all other options have been exhausted.

EQUIPMENT
Anything to hand, such as an ice axe, deadman, plate, lunchbox, helmet, bivi bag, ski poles. It is greatly simplified in a leadership situation if a shovel and snow-saw are carried.

Lean-to Sitting Bivi
This is the most practical of all the bivis shown, and meets the basic requirement of seeking shelter from the wind. It is the recommended method of sheltering from the weather during an enforced stopover.

A wedge-shaped slot slightly over shoulder-width is cut into the snow bank, with the depth sufficient to ensure the head is below snow level. A seat can be fashioned at the back of the slot from debris, and insulated with spare kit and rope. The slot needs to be roofed over in some fashion. This can be done by weighing down a bivi bag or group shelter with snow blocks around the edge, supported across the roof of the slot by ski poles if possible.

Lean-to Sitting Bivi (continued)

In the right snow conditions, it should be possible to cut a series of snow blocks, slightly longer than the width of the bivi, which can be placed over the shelter to provide a roof. This, of course, will take a little more time and energy, but will be not only more substantial, but also thermally more efficient. The narrower the width of the shelter, the easier it will be to cut blocks to fit. As with any emergency shelter, it is important to mark your position somehow, by weighing down a bivi bag for instance, or by placing your ice axe or ski poles in the snow above your shelter.

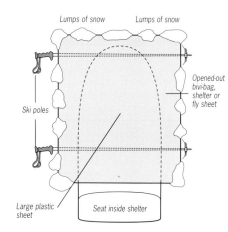

Lumps of snow   Lumps of snow

Opened-out bivi-bag, shelter or fly sheet

Ski poles

Large plastic sheet

Seat inside shelter

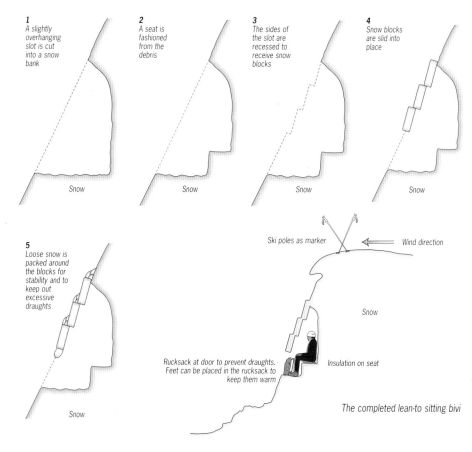

1
A slightly overhanging slot is cut into a snow bank

Snow

2
A seat is fashioned from the debris

Snow

3
The sides of the slot are recessed to receive snow blocks

Snow

4
Snow blocks are slid into place

Snow

5
Loose snow is packed around the blocks for stability and to keep out excessive draughts

Snow

Ski poles as marker   ⟵ Wind direction

Snow

Rucksack at door to prevent draughts. Feet can be placed in the rucksack to keep them warm

Insulation on seat

The completed lean-to sitting bivi

■ Gear Lists *p159*

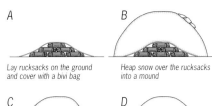

A — Lay rucksacks on the ground and cover with a bivi bag

B — Heap snow over the rucksacks into a mound

Sitting Bivi

This bivi requires a steep bank of snow for construction, the steeper the better, such as that found at the edge of burns and re-entrants. Start by tunnelling in and slightly up-slope, before turning and digging straight up. The distance in is dictated by the snow-pack angle and strength – in a vertical drift and good snow this may be as little as 6in.

Imagine yourself sitting on a chair – this is the internal shape that you are looking for; a small seat can be fashioned out of debris from the vertical section. Allow room enough to enable you to sit up straight, with a couple of inches clearance above your head. Smooth across the roof of the sitting area to help prevent drips. You may wish to fashion a ventilation hole in the wall in front of your face by using the shaft of your axe. Although when completed this may appear to be the same as the lean-to bivi, it is in fact much more awkward to construct as you end up in a position of having to dig upwards and excavating above your head – a sure way to get covered in snow with the knock-on effect of damp and heat loss.

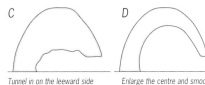

C — Tunnel in on the leeward side and remove the rucksacks and bivi bag

D — Enlarge the centre and smooth off the ceiling to prevent drips

Mousehole bivi

dig in a small entrance on the leeward side. Remove the bivi-bag and rucksacks, and sculpt the inside to shape. Smooth the roof to prevent dripping.

Snow Grave

Intended for use on flat terrain, the snow grave is the least practical of the methods shown here. However, it does have its place and has been used in the high mountains, hence its inclusion. It is reliant upon the snow having a layer of hard slab or thick crust. Using the axe pick, cut out an outline of approximately 2ft x 4ft on the ground. Divide this into 1ft x 2ft slabs, and carefully lift them out. Scoop out the snow underneath, hollowing out an undercut section for the feet. Ensure that you leave a lip for the slabs to rest on when they are replaced. Carefully put back two of the slabs, climb underneath, and lower the final slabs down on top. Ensure that there is sufficient ventilation. Use all available kit to help minimise body contact with the snow.

TIPS

1 Excellent lightweight shovels are available which split into two to carry. These are handy when out on a trip, and absolutely essential when leading a group. Those with a curved blade tend to be more efficient at digging and snow removal than the straighter design.

2 It is important to mark your location, whichever type of shelter you use. Ski poles are ideal, and if you can tear a strip from an orange bivi bag and attach it to the end, it would assist location immensely.

Mousehole Bivi

The mousehole bivi, or 'shovel-up', is a reasonable option for a relatively flat area, as long as the wind will not cause the snow to blow away during construction. Place all of the groups' rucksacks on the ground and cover them with a bivi-bag. Pile as much snow as possible on top of the sacks to create an igloo-shaped structure. The effect of moving the snow from one place to another helps the consolidation process. Lightly firm the snow down with shovels, hands etc if necessary, and

Snow

Insulation: Rucksack, rope etc

Snow grave side view

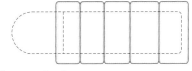

Snow grave top view

Gear Lists *p159* ■

OBSERVATION

1 There are a whole variety of possibilities for biviing out, often using a hybrid of the methods given above. Large boulders often have soft drifts behind them, these can be scooped out relatively easily and shelter found there. Below the tree line, the lower branches of trees can often support snow but leave a sheltered area underneath.

2 The important things to remember are: get out of the wind; insulate yourself from the snow; ensure adequate ventilation; mark your position; keep up your morale.

3 The most important factor in any bivi situation is to minimise the amount of your body touching the snow, otherwise heat is wicked away at an alarming speed. Masses of insulation would be needed to prevent this from happening if you were in the prone position, such as in the snow grave; for that reason the lean-to sitting bivi would always be our first choice. Insulation can be provided by sitting on your rucksack, rope, etc, and the sitting position is far comfier than any other for an extended period of time.

COACHING NOTES

It is an extremely valuable experience for people to try digging a shelter. Allow about fifteen minutes for the exercise, and get them to sit/lie in it after completion. It is also worthwhile spending time with a map, helping people identify areas that may be suitable as bivi sites. It should be made clear that life is far easier if a shovel is available, and a group's kit should always include one. An avalanche probe, which should also be part of the group's kit, is useful in determining the depth of a bivi site before construction starts.

TIP

If at all possible, urinate before going into your shelter. This is for two reasons. Firstly, once you are in your shelter you should not come out any more than is necessary – this will lose you a lot of body heat, and there is a chance that you may not locate your shelter again in bad visibility. If you need the toilet while you are inside, do it where you are.

Secondly, if you have been missed in the valley and a search is in progress, not only does dehydration-coloured urine stand out in the snow as a locator, but it gives a search dog a large scent target to head for.

SNOW-HOLE CONSTRUCTION

What is a snow hole?

A snow hole, as opposed to a snow shelter, is a well-constructed place for a pre-planned stay of one or more nights. They can range in size from the most basic, which will sleep two people, up to those sleeping twelve or more.

When and where do we use it?

The snow hole is a pre-planned activity, thus it can be used almost anywhere the snow build-up is sufficient as a base for climbing, walking or, for many people, as an experience in its own right.

EQUIPMENT

Ice axe, shovel, snow saw; an avalanche probe is useful but not essential.

Method

The hole site needs to selected carefully, not only from a safety point of view, but also for ease of digging. Lee slopes in a variety of forms will hold sufficient snow, and the steeper the snow the better, re-entrants and the lee of moraine deposits are ideal. There are a number of ways to construct the hole. The following is the one that we find to be most efficient in time and effort in the majority of cases.

Mark out a shape on the steep slope in front of you, approximately 2ft wide and 4ft high. This will be your entrance passageway, the size of it can always be reduced at a later stage. For now, it makes life easier having room to work. Tunnel in and slightly up. The distance in will be dictated by the strength of the snow, the angle of the slope and the size the finished hole needs to be. The thickness of the wall may well be around 2–3ft on steep ground, but much thicker if the slope is at an angle.

The inside of the hole can then be constructed, which is done by digging out an area large enough for you to lie down in. This will normally be at 90 degrees to the entrance tunnel, and the floor of the sleeping area needs to be fashioned so that it is higher than the access level. Building it this way allows for warm air to be trapped in the living space, and allows easy removal of debris while digging. This inner

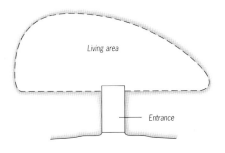

Snow hole: cross-section from front

area can be wedge shaped, and care should be taken to ensure that the floor ends up with a smooth and level surface. The walls and ceiling should also be smoothed over, using either a gloved hand or the back of the shovel, sometimes both, to reduce the likelihood of drips when the temperature within the hole rises.

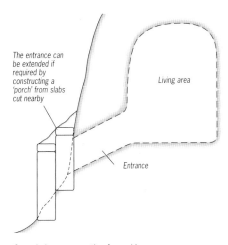

The entrance can be extended if required by constructing a 'porch' from slabs cut nearby

Living area

Entrance

Snow hole: cross-section from side

1 The slopes which are ideal as snow-hole sites are also those that will be holding a large weight of snow, thus possibly avalanche prone. More than one person has been carried off by an avalanche while looking for a suitable place to stay, so be aware of your surroundings, the nature of the terrain and the state of the snow-pack. Test for the stability of the slope if in any doubt.

2 A well-organised snow hole will generally be a comfy one, so there are a couple of things that you can do at the construction stage that will make life more pleasant later on. The storage of gear is important, so a couple of long shelves can be fashioned by digging into the walls. It would be a good idea if the kit stored here was not left loose, as it would tend to attract moisture from the atmosphere when the interior temperature warms up from body heat or cooking. Kit placed into plastic bags or boxes will stay dry.

Consideration should be given to the area in which cooking will take place. This is not only a very time-consuming process, but also can be a little messy if care is not taken. It therefore makes sense not to have the stove in the centre of the hole in case of any spillage. The best location for it will be near the entrance tunnel – this not only keeps it out of the way, but also allows poisonous vapours created by the cooking process to sink to the outside and not be trapped in the hole itself.

Lighting is also another essential, and the effect of having a candle will lift not only the amount of light, but also the temperature. A single candle will appear very bright, as the light will be reflected off the snow. The best position for this is in a triangular slot near the cooking area, the back of the recess shaped to reflect light.

Snow Shelters

3 When dug into a lee slope, care must be taken that the entrance to the snow hole does not drift over during the night. If winds are forecast, it may be necessary to get up as often as every hour to dig out the front of the hole to ensure that ventilation is maintained. Cooking becomes an extremely hazardous operation when there is no ventilation, as poisonous fumes are given off, and cooking should not be undertaken if there is no fresh air. This is particularly important in the morning, when the temptation is to light the stove and roll over back to sleep while it heats up – any ventilation may have disappeared during the night.

4 Leaving the snow hole for any reason must be thought through, especially if needing to answer the call of nature during the night. You may be tempted to go outside for a couple of minutes, but in windy or misty weather the snow-hole entrance can be impossible to relocate once left and the chances are that all of your warm clothing will still be inside. On a clear still night, the glow of a candle from inside the hole can be seen from some distance, but in bad weather great care must be taken. A climbing rope can be used to link a number of hole entrances, so that location is made easier, and it can be tied around any person needing to venture outside, and used like a lifeline. The rule here is that if you do not have to venture outside in bad weather, don't. If you have to, ensure that you have a torch and warm clothing on, and avoid the temptation to 'nip out' lightly clad.

5 Snow holes and snow-hole sites must be left spotlessly clean. Any debris left behind will not only be distasteful for any subsequent occupiers, but will also be left when the snow melts. Matches and candle stubs are but a small example.

Consideration must be made to carrying out human waste. If left, this is not only extremely unpleasant and unsightly, but also presents a large problem with the pollution of waterways and local habitat. Crapping into a plastic bag, then placing this in a stout screwtop plastic container for later disposal at a lower level is the best remedy, and is to be encouraged.

TIPS

1 Digging a snow hole is extremely damp work, and if nothing more than your gloves get wet you are doing well. It is worth wearing waterproofs with a minimum of clothing underneath to save perspiring too much, with your spare clothing packed away but easily to hand for when the digging stops. Gloves will get sodden, so having an old pair to use for the digging is a good idea, keeping your better pairs dry for the rest of the trip.

2 A handy way to remove debris is to lay a plastic bivi bag on the floor of the hole beneath where you are digging. The debris will fall onto this, and it can then be easily dragged out.

3 Following the actual construction of a snow hole, cooking is the next longest process. Make things comfortable for yourself by ensuring that all the required food and utensils are to hand. You can then get into your sleeping bag and operate from there. Avoid the temptation to carve out large pieces of your snow hole to melt for water, have a pile of snow ready cut into chunks. Start with a little and, once there is some water in your pan, add pieces slowly. Placing the stove on a flat piece of rock or small piece of plywood carried for the purpose will stop it melting itself into the floor of the snow hole quite as fast as otherwise it might – care should be taken with boiling liquids for this very reason.

Gear Lists

Recommended Lead Rack: Summer

The following list of equipment gives a good idea of what a lead rack should consist of. It allows for most single- and multi-pitch applications, where best-practice and personal safety are prime considerations. The use of any particular manufac-turer's product name is not designed to promote a particular brand, but denotes the type, shape and quality of the piece of equipment desired.

Helmet
Harness
Rock boots
Rope

On harness

Belay device on HMS karabiner.
2 or 3 spare HMS screwgates.
1 x D-shape screwgate with 2 prussik loops, made from 6mm kernmantle, 30cm long when tied with a double fisherman's knot.
1 x D-shape karabiner with a 15cm extender, for abseiling.
For longer routes: penknife on small snapgate or screwgate karabiner.
For working with groups: selection of elastic bands or hair ties to hand out if required.

On rack

Wires, ie rocks, sizes 1 to 9, doubled up.
Hexentrics, sizes 6,7,8,9, tied with 9mm kernmantle. The 6 hex takes over in size from where the 9 rock leaves off, making a logical size progression.
Extenders x 6. Not too long, pre-sewn approx 15cm long.
Spring-loaded Camming Devices (SLCDs), set of four, flexible stem, sizes 1/2,1,2,3.
Nut key, with pullers for releasing jammed camming devices.
23 snap karabiners, straight gates, to use with all the above.
1 x 16ft sling with HMS screwgate.
2 x 8ft slings with 1 HMS screwgate each.
For longer routes: 1 extra 16ft sling and HMS krab, 2 x 4ft slings with two D-shape screwgates on each.

Recommended Lead Rack: Winter

A winter lead rack is very hard to design, due to the vast variation in route types, climbing styles, weather conditions etc. For instance, a rack for climbing icefalls on Ben Nevis will vary somewhat from a rack for climbing buttress routes in the Cairngorms. The rack below is therefore a very personal view, and is seen by the authors as the sort of rack they would take out on a 'let's go and see what's in nick' sort of day. Much of what is listed may be chosen to be left at home. Huge variations are possible, apart from the more practical aspect of having to carry it all!

Helmet
Harness
Rope
Axes to suit
Crampons to suit

On harness

As for summer kit.
Penknife.

On rack

4 extenders.
Wires 1-9, doubled up.
Hexs 6,7,8,9 on 9mm kernmantle.
SLCDs, size 2 & 3.
3 drive-in warthogs, useful for frozen turf.
3 ice screws, various lengths.
Rock pegs. A selection of knife blades, angles and kingpins will be found useful, about eight in total.
22 x snap karabiners with straight gates, to use with the above.
4 x 4ft slings, each with 2 karabiners on (may be snap gates).
2 x 8ft slings, each with an HMS screwgate.
1 x 16ft sling with HMS screwgate.
2 x 3m lengths of tape, to be used for abseil retreat, can live in rucksack.
2 x 1.5m lengths 8mm kernmantle, used for rigging Abalakov threads, can live in rucksack.

Summer-walking Rucksack Contents

The list below is a recommended selection of kit for the summer recreational walker. It is assumed that some high terrain will be covered, and that the walker will not be responsible for the safety of others in his charge. Personal choice will dictate the final selection of contents, but the following should be carefully considered.

Rucksack, of around 30–40 litres, with hip belt.
Waterproof trousers.
Waterproof jacket.
Spare fleece (in addition to one being worn).
Woollen or fleece hat and spare.
Gloves x 2 pairs.
Survival bag or bivi shelter.
First-aid kit.
Food.
Hot or cold drink.
Any personal medicines.
Headtorch with spare bulb and battery.
Map, covered with plastic. Taking a second as a spare is a sensible precaution if walking alone.
OHP pen, useful for making notes on a map.
Compass.
Whistle.
Sun hat.
Sun cream.
Small amount of high-energy emergency food.
Coins for 'phone box.
Mobile telephone. This item, if carried, should be switched off, padded and left at the bottom of the rucksack for emergency use only. Owing to unreliable coverage, a mobile phone cannot be relied upon to receive a signal all the time.

Winter-walking Rucksack Contents

All of the 'Summer-walking Rucksack Contents', plus:

Ice axe.
Crampons.
Long neoprene strap with buckle to effect crampon repair.
Ski goggles with anti-mist lenses.
Balaclava from fleece or similar material.
Extra fleece or down duvet.
Thick gloves or mitts.
Hot drink.

Summer-leader's Rucksack Contents

The rucksack of a summer mountain leader should contain adequate kit for not only himself, but a few extra essentials for group use. It cannot be expected that a leader carries enough kit for all of the group, and a lot of emphasis must be put into briefings prior to departure from base to ensure that participants are properly equipped. A final check of their rucksack contents should be made just before departure, making sure that clothing that you have specified as needing to be waterproof is not just 'showerproof'.

It is quite acceptable that one or two of the group items are carried by the group members themselves, as long as it is not hindering their own pace. All equipment listed for 'Summer-walking Rucksack Contents', plus:

2 extra pairs of gloves for group use.
30–40m 9mm kernmantle rope.
16ft sling and HMS karabiner.
Group shelter, large enough to accommodate all group members.
Large first-aid kit.
Group vacuum flask containing hot juice rather than tea.
Duplicates of group members' personal medicines.
List of contact names and addresses.
Spare map.
Spare compass.

Winter-leader's Rucksack Contents

The extra kit needed for winter group walking can also be shared out amongst the group.
All of the 'Summer-leader's Rucksack Contents', plus:

Ice axe.
Crampons.
Crampon spares kit, containing 2 long straps with buckles and a combination crampon spanner/screwdriver.
Helmet, depending on terrain and objectives.
Spare fleece or down duvet.
Snow shovel.
Avalanche probe.

Index